## PRAISE FOR *UNTIL I COULD BE SURE*

"This book is the compelling, personal, and highly evocative story of a man who finds himself confronting a long-held belief—that the death penalty was a necessary part of the criminal justice system—and finding that belief shattered by the facts. Ryan's transforma-tion from death penalty supporter to death penalty opponent is fascinating, instructive, and, ultimately, inspiring."—**Andrea D. Lyon**, professor emeritus, Valparaiso University Law School; principal at Lyon Law

"This book is not only about the death penalty. It is a chronicle that teaches us about integrity, leadership, growth, and the struggle to do the right thing. Those who care to listen will be touched by the lessons from George H. Ryan Sr.'s journey for decades to come. He leads us on."—**Michael L. Radelet**, University of Colorado

"Illinois put innocence on the map and that is still the most influential issue for many people when it comes to the death penalty."—**Richard Dieter**, former executive director, Death Penalty Information Center

"Under Ryan's leadership, Illinois consolidated the forces that diminished the death pen-alty's use, emboldening the abolition of the death penalty in other states, other governors' moratoria on executions, and prosecutors' decisions across the country to stop using the punishment."—**James Liebman**, professor, Columbia Law School; author of *The Wrong Carlos: Anatomy of a Wrongful Execution*

"Ryan had a great impact during the time between declaring the moratorium and announc-ing the commutations and pardons. The fact that he was a Republican and former support-er of the death penalty and that his mind was changed by seeing that many people sentenced to death were innocent made it impossible to dismiss him. The impact that he had on the media, officials, and the public was substantial. I assign students in my class each year to read his statement, 'I Must Act,' announcing the commutations and pardons. It was a truly historic moment in the history of the death penalty in the United States."—**Stephen Bright,** director, Southern Center for Human Rights 1982–2005, president 2006–2017; lecturer, Yale Law School

"Lost faith in our justice system? Cynical about politicians who only purse their self-interest? Read this inspiring book. It's a gripping story about the events that led to the end of the death penalty in Illinois. But it's about more than society's ultimate punishment. It's also a remarkable tale about how lawyers, investigators, journalists, and even journal-ism students came together to free innocents on death row, and at the center of it all, a career politician who found his moral compass and acted boldly on it. The book reads like a novel yet has the virtue of being true."—**David Protess**, (ret.), Chicago Innocence Project

"Although I am a liberal Democratic feminist and Ryan is a Republican, we became friends based on his principles and values and his willingness to do what was right despite the consequences. The elimination of the death penalty was not popular in downstate Illinois, where he comes from. It also was not popular with his Republican colleagues. But despite the political ramifications, Governor Ryan did what was right once he understood the issues and saw the miscarriage of justice in so many cases. This book is an intimate view of the rationale behind his decision and into the character of the man who made that critically important decision."—**Hedy Ratner**, founder, co-president emerita consultant, Women's Business Development Center, Chicago

"*Until I Could Be Sure* is a powerful memoir of how Illinois governor Ryan declared a moratorium on the death penalty, emptied the state's death row, and endorsed 'innocence' reforms to fix a broken system. These landmark decisions by a conservative Republican at the beginning of the twenty-first century, when opposition to the death penalty was seen as a political third rail, were from the heart, based on the merits, and acts of moral courage. Ryan's journey on these issues was one I hope more twenty-first-century politi-cians emulate."—**Barry Scheck**, co-founder of the Innocence Project

"A fascinating and impressively informative read from beginning to end, [*Until I Could be Sure*] is unreservedly recommended for both community and col-lege/university library Criminology collections and supplemental curriculum studies lists."—**Midwest Book Review**

"Ryan's decision to commute the sentences of all Illinois death row inmates will go down in history as an act that shifted the momentum of the death pen-alty debate in the United States. Ryan presents us with a rare glimpse inside his journey from being an ardent supporter of the death penalty to becoming one its most powerful critics."—**Lawrence C. Marshall**, Stanford Law School

# UNTIL I COULD BE SURE

# UNTIL I COULD BE SURE

## *How I Stopped the Death Penalty in Illinois*

George H. Ryan Sr.

With Maurice Possley

ROWMAN & LITTLEFIELD

Lanham • Boulder • New York • London

Published by Rowman & Littlefield
An imprint of The Rowman & Littlefield Publishing Group, Inc.
4501 Forbes Boulevard, Suite 200, Lanham, Maryland 20706
www.rowman.com

86-90 Paul Street, London EC2A 4NE, United Kingdom



British Library Cataloguing in Publication Information Available

**Library of Congress Cataloging-in-Publication Data**

Names: Ryan, George H., author. | Possley, Maurice, author.
Title: Until I could be sure : how I stopped the death penalty in Illinois / by George H. Ryan Sr., with Maurice Possley.
Description: Lanham : Rowman & Littlefield, [2020] | Includes index.
Identifiers: LCCN 2019057377 (print) | LCCN 2019057378 (ebook) | ISBN 9781538134542 (cloth) | ISBN 9781538134559 (epub) | ISBN 9781538171714 (paperback)
Subjects: LCSH: Capital punishment—Illinois. | Criminal justice, Administration of—Illinois. | Ryan, George H.
Classification: LCC HV8699.U6 I378 2020 (print) | LCC HV8699.U6 (ebook) | DDC 364.6609773—dc23
LC record available at https://lccn.loc.gov/2019057377
LC ebook record available at https://lccn.loc.gov/2019057378

∞™ The paper used in this publication meets the minimum requirements of American National Standard for Information Sciences—Permanence of Paper for Printed Library Materials, ANSI/NISO Z39.48-1992.

I dedicate this book to Lura Lynn. And to my solid family, who have surrounded me with love and affection: My father and mother, Thomas and Jeanette; my brother, Tom, Jr., and his wife Stella; my sister, Kathleen, and her husband, Duane; and my sister, Nancy, and her husband, Bob. Heroes all. I was the youngest, and they all took special care of me. Lura Lynn and I met as freshman in high school—1948—it was love at first sight. Ours was a marriage made in heaven, a strong, loving companionship that lasted for sixty-three years and produced five daughters and a son: Nancy (husband John Coghlan), Lynda (husband Mike Fairman), Julie (husband Jeff Koehl), Joanne Barrow, Jeanette (husband Jim Schneider), George, Jr. (wife Amy). This prolific group produced seventeen grandchildren and fourteen great grandchildren). Lura Lynn and I were blessed to have them all, as they are a loving bunch.

I was heartsick when Lura Lynn died on June 27, 2011 and like many widowers my age (I turned 86 this year), life can be very lonely. Despite the continued love and support of my family, I was in that dark place until I was fortunate enough to meet another wonderful woman, a widow of seventeen years herself, Alice "Kitty" Kelly. We had a great relationship for six years that made my life a joy. Then, tragically, Kitty died in June of 2019. I inherited her family and they inherited me: Kitty's son, John, his wife, Julie, and their two daughters; and her daughter, Colleen, and her husband, Rob Cassidy, and their two daughters. I am now blessed with an even bigger loving family that keeps me busy. Thanks to you all!

To University of Illinois law professor Francis Boyle, who nominated e for the Nobel Peace Prize six times, thank you for your continuing ipport and for honoring my work.

To my agent Regina Ryan, thank you for our newfound friendship and our support in getting me published.

To Maurice Possley, thank you for your wonderful insights and putng the right words in the right places to make this book a success.

And finally, I am grateful for the title of Uncle George from my nieces nd nephews from the Dean Family, the Ryan Family, and the Ferguson amily. All my life they have been a steady source of love and support. hank you all!

# CONTENTS

# ACKNOWLEDGMENTS

I spent thirty-five years in service to the people of Illinois. I be chairman of the Kankakee County Board and ended as the go During that time, I was fortunate to have the support, help, dedi loyalty, and professionalism of many people. The list is long, but give special recognition to the people that were the core of my w the death penalty. They are: Roger Bickel, Matthew Bettenhausen Duchossois, Vicki Easley, Dianne Ford, Phil Gonet, John Kell Ladd, Bridgett Lamont, Tony Leone, Al Lerner, Jennifer Linzer, A Lyon, Larry Marshall, Pam McDonough, Bob Newtson, Sam Pan vich, Rich Parrillo, Pete Peters, George (Homer) Ryan Jr., Mike Jim Thompson, David Urbanek, Frank Vala, Rob Warden, Larr Cindy Warner, and Dan Webb. I thank one and all for their hard w will always treasure what each provided to the mission.

I want to give special thanks to the people of Kankakee, my l town. I am forever grateful to so many of you for your suppor friendship.

I am thankful for the people at Winston and Strawn, especiall Thompson, who taught me how to be governor, and Dan Webb, with his staff, for the excellent defense they provided on my behalf.

To my friend Andrea Lyon, thank you for your counsel, patienc friendship.

To Dave Urbanek, thank you for your continued support, advic search for this book, and your loyal friendship.

# FOREWORD

The first time I met George Ryan was in 1999 at a small dinner party at the home of mutual friends. He was already governor of Illinois, but when the meal was over, he got up to clear his plate. That, my friends would tell me later, is George. Down to earth. Plainspoken. A straightforward person who would forever see himself as a family pharmacist from Kankakee.

I also learned that night that he possessed one of the most important assets of a successful politician—an absolute charmer of a wife. The late Lura Lynn, who I was lucky enough to frequently spend time within the coming years, was smart, frank, and slyly funny. Her death was, I am sure, a terrible blow to Governor Ryan; a loss made even more painful due to the fact that George Ryan was in the federal penitentiary when she passed.

Governor Ryan and Maurice Possley—who I knew as a top courthouse reporter during my eight years as a federal prosecutor—have told Governor Ryan's remarkable story in the following pages, focusing on his dramatic journey confronting the death penalty. They have written a wonderfully lucid and compelling book. I was a close witness to some of the events they describe, but because the governor tells the story so well, I will let him speak for himself.

I do have a few personal comments to add. Governor Ryan's bona fides on capital punishment were subject to frequent attack because by the time he declared a moratorium on executions in 2000, it was well-known publicly that he was under investigation by the US attorney's office. A reckless truck driver, who killed six children in a fiery highway collision in Wisconsin, turned out to have bribed someone in the Illinois secretary of state's office, the agency which handles vehicle licensing in Illinois, to get his driver's license without having to go through the testing procedures. George Ryan had been the secretary of state at the time of the accident and the prosecutors kept turning stones until they were at his door after he was elected governor. I represented several witnesses in that grand jury investigation, including Ryan's deputy governor, and from that limited vantage I couldn't understand what the prosecutors were thinking. There was not a shred of evidence connecting George Ryan to that horrible, fatal accident. But because of my client's interests, I kept close track of the trial evidence and attended a number of court sessions. To get the unpleasantries out of the way, despite my affection for Governor Ryan, I believe the evidence supported his conviction on corruption charges not related to the accident. That said, I also thought the manipulations that occurred with the jury during its deliberations, a plain effort to avoid repeating a months-long trial, violated the Constitution and deprived the governor of a fair trial. He should have gotten a new trial, in my view. But I would be lying if I said I expected a different outcome the second time around.

Importantly to me, however, what George Ryan was convicted of had nothing to do with his years in the governor's mansion. The case was about what had happened years before in the secretary of state's office. One thing you learn in a career practicing criminal law is that good and bad often sit side by side in people's souls. And George Ryan did an enormous amount of good in his years of public service. He probably will turn out to be, in the judgment of history, the pivotal figure in the evolution of Americans' attitudes toward capital punishment. But his career was far larger than one issue.

George Ryan's four years as governor of Illinois was in my view the best gubernatorial term since I returned to Illinois in 1978. A long-time veteran of the Illinois General Assembly, the governor knew Springfield inside and out. He had strong relationships of many years standing with all legislative leaders, and in Illinois most major legislation passed as a result of deal-making between the so-called Four Tops, the speaker and minority leader in the Illinois House and their counterparts in the Illinois Senate. Watching the years of legislative stalemate that followed George Ryan's time as governor, one can only marvel at how deft he was in getting things done. One reason he succeeded was because he was intensely nonideological. He held the line on taxes but dramatically increased Illinois's spending on infrastructure, especially roads, while also significantly enhancing the state's annual contribution to public education. He called himself a conservative, with good reason, but he refused to get caught up in the absolute positions of either the Left or Right. Pro-life, he nonetheless vetoed a bill to prohibit Medicaid payments for abortion because the bill's sponsors insisted that poor women with serious health issues would have to go without. Governor Ryan didn't want taxpayers to have to pay for abortion on demand. Yet it was just cruel, in his view, to tell women with no options that they would have to sacrifice their health and carry a child to full term. In another significant action, he traveled to Cuba, notwithstanding the long time US embargo on Cuban goods, in the hope of drumming up business for Illinois enterprises. Even communists' money is green, I am sure George Ryan would tell you. And on the issue on which I dealt with him most frequently—capital punishment—I found him courageous and entirely earnest.

By 2000, thirteen men who had been convicted and sentenced to death had been exonerated, that is, found legally blameless for the murders for which they once had sat on death row. Facing mounting evidence that the Illinois capital system was grotesquely prone to error—thirteen exonerations with 171 people sitting on death row—Governor Ryan declared a moratorium on executions. With his political gifts, George Ryan understood the one point of consensus between the overwhelming majority of death penalty supporters and opponents: capital punishment could not mean putting innocent people to death.

To ensure that did not happen, Governor Ryan appointed a fourteen-member commission made up of people who had diverse experiences with capital punishment, whether as prosecutors or defense lawyers or ordinary citizens. The job of the Commission on Capital Punishment, as the governor described it, was to figure out "what reforms, if any, would ensure that the Illinois capital punishment system is fair, just and accurate." I was one of the fourteen persons the governor asked to serve on the commission because I'd had some experience as a pro bono lawyer representing people who'd been sentenced to death. One of those thirteen Illinois men previously exonerated had been my client, the victim of ugly behavior by prosecutors who spent a decade fighting the fact—ultimately corroborated by DNA—that another man had committed the murder for which my client once sat on death row. After he was freed, due to the work of more than a dozen committed defense attorneys over thirteen years, I took on another death row case, critically different because, this time, I realized that my client had committed the crime. But in many ways that case showed even deeper and more abiding problems with capital punishment: I could see from the start that there were countless mitigating factors in that case, and that my client would never have been sentenced to death if he had more diligent and better-funded public defenders. Fortunately, my colleagues and I at Dentons, our firm, eventually convinced the courts of that point, and our client was resentenced to spend fifty years in prison if he met the terms for parole late in his life.

Thus, when I was appointed to the Commission on Capital Punishment, I had witnessed firsthand the system's many problems that could lead the innocent or undeserving to be sentenced to death. Even so, after my years as a prosecutor, I still wasn't completely sure that there weren't cases when the death penalty was appropriate. My own doubts led me to have great sympathy for Governor Ryan's own journey and the sincerity with which he made it.

The twenty-four months I spent on the commission were among the most involved and worthwhile of my legal career. And they allowed me to sort out my conflicted feelings about the death penalty. All in all, I realized that capital punishment was a bad idea, not because there weren't cases where death was arguably a fit punishment, but because we would never design a legal system able to identify only the right cases for execution. Capital punishment, no matter how carefully practiced, would inevitably mean occasionally putting to death the innocent or the undeserving.

My own struggle to think systematically about capital punishment mirrored that of my fellow commission members who were remarkably diligent in embracing the assignment we had from Governor Ryan. As a group, we started out with diverse points of view about capital punishment and that was true at the end. But we were unanimous in believing the system in Illinois required extensive reform. Overall, we made eighty-five recommendations for specific measures that needed to be adopted; everything from how interrogations of suspects should be conducted to avoid the phenomenon of false confession to the requirements for funding capital defense.

The Illinois General Assembly enacted none of those measures, leaving George Ryan in an impossible position as he approached the end of his term. What was the right response to a system that public study had shown to be riddled with inequities and haunted by error? How could he be faithful to the commitment he'd made when imposing the moratorium, that executions would resume only when the fairness and accuracy of the capital punishment system could be guaranteed?

Here I need to say that I have never comprehended the arguments of people who think George Ryan's response to the problems of capital punishment was driven by ulterior motives. Some seem to believe that Ryan was somehow preparing for his subsequent indictment and trial. But no one has ever made a coherent argument to me on that point. For one thing, I doubt Governor Ryan ever really expected to be indicted. More important, the death penalty for years had been one of those third-rail issues, damaging to political careers. That, frankly, was why the General Assembly had done nothing, because inaction, despite the massive problems, was the safest course politically. If George Ryan supposedly had an eye on the jury he might face, it made no sense for him to take any action that risked antagonizing so many voters who would make up the pool of potential jurors.

As I watched the governor wrestle with the question of what to do in the waning days of his term, I saw a person of deep faith and good conscience trying to sort out an impossibly complicated issue. As he was pondering his choices, I advised him to take a moderate course. I was afraid that any dramatic action, like clearing death row, would inspire an intense public backlash that would set back any hope of reforming the capital system.

But George Ryan wasn't interested in playing a political guessing game. More moderate measures would not have solved the fundamental problem that the capital system didn't function fairly. Instead, just before he left office, Governor Ryan pardoned four more people who were demonstrably innocent and commuted to life in prison without parole the death sentences of 163 men and four women on death row. His actions provoked howls of outrage from prosecutors and police. But to the surprise of many, including me, Illinoisans were surprisingly understanding of the fact that George Ryan had been left with no choice: a system with documented failures that the legislature had refused to correct. Polling in the aftermath showed that roughly half of Illinois voters agreed with the governor's action.

That response inspired a young Illinois senator, a guy I'd known for years and called "Barack" in those days, to spearhead an effort to pass a number of legislative reforms based on the commission's findings. I worked with him occasionally, more or less representing the commission's point of view, and Senator Obama succeeded in shepherding his bill to passage. It was a brave thing for him to do, since he was frank about his ambition to run for higher office. Although I never heard then-Senator Obama say this, it might well have been the case that he felt inspired by George Ryan's example and his willingness to do the right thing, even at the risk of making his conviction in his forthcoming trial more likely.

George Ryan's successor, the Democrat Rod Blagojevich (who, yes, spent years in the federal penitentiary) facing the mixed public response to George Ryan's commutations, found it most practical to keep the moratorium in place. But the long period without executions, which had begun with George Ryan, slowly convinced Illinoisans that nobody particularly missed the death penalty, especially after the Great Recession when the state had much greater needs for its limited funds. On March 9, 2011, Governor Pat Quinn, who had taken office when Rod Blagojevich was impeached following his federal arrest, signed the legislation abolishing the death penalty in Illinois. It was a remarkable change on an essential policy issue, one where the public had been willing to learn from experience and to adhere to the widely held moral consensus that whatever the value of the death penalty, it wasn't worth executing innocent persons. And in making that change, in moving an entire state, and perhaps a nation, no one was more important than George Ryan.

—Scott Turow
author of *The Last Trial* (Grand Central, 2020)

# I

# THE BEGINNING

Topping out at 361 feet, the Illinois State Capitol in Springfield is the tallest of the nonskyscraper-style state capitol buildings in the United States. By law, it is the tallest building in Springfield. No other structure is allowed to exceed its height. One of its grander features is the unobstructed view one gets from the center of the first floor all the way up to the stained glass replica of the state seal in the oculus of the 91-foot tall dome.

That view can be daunting for anyone, let alone a newly-elected state representative. As I stood there at the end of my very first day in office in 1972, I felt much like a college freshman far away from the security of home.

I was lost in thought for a bit, thinking back to about a decade earlier. If you had asked me then to predict my future, my answer would have been easy: I was going to be a pharmacist and run the pharmacy that my father, Thomas Ryan Sr., had started in 1949 in Kankakee, Illinois. My father's father was a railroad worker. My mother, Jeanette Bowman, came from a cattle ranching family. I was born February 24, 1934, in Maquoketa, Iowa, and was just a toddler when my father took a job as a pharmacist at a Walgreens drugstore on the South Side of Chicago. Not long after, he was offered a job as an assistant manager of a pharmacy in Kankakee, situated sixty miles south of Chicago on the banks of the Kankakee River. Kankakee would be my lifetime home and where I expected to spend my life as a pharmacist.

But years later here I was, standing at the vortex of this law-making, deal-cutting, and legend-creating building that had been completed in 1888 at a cost of $4.5 million. This was the home of the Illinois General Assembly, and my new "office" was in the House of Representatives, overseen by the stern visage of Stephen Douglas, one of the state's most renowned representatives of the nineteenth century. Across the way was the Illinois Senate chamber where a portrait of Abraham Lincoln, the state's most prominent Republican figure of all time, kept silent watch.

"Hey, Ryan!"

I was jolted out of my reverie by the booming voice of Emil Jones, a Chicago Democrat, who, like me, was a freshman legislator.

"Ryan," he declared. "What are you doing tonight?"

"I don't know," I said, somewhat sheepishly, figuring I should have something important to do.

"Let's go play some pool," Jones said and flashed a grin. He clapped a hand on my shoulder. "What do you say?"

"Well, why not?" I replied.

Two hours later, I had lost twenty dollars. I thought I had gained a friend and for years we were. But some friends don't last forever. Such are the fortunes of living a political life.

In 1952, I graduated from Kankakee High School where I played linebacker on the football team and fell in love with a girl in my English class named Lura Lynn Lowe. Two years later, while I was attending Butler University in Indianapolis, Indiana, I was drafted into the US Army. I served from 1954 to 1956. While stationed in South Korea for thirteen months, I was detailed to a military pharmacy. Lura Lynn and I married in 1956. In 1957, after our daughter, Nancy, was born, I went back to school. In 1961, I graduated from Ferris State University College of Pharmacy in Big Rapids, Michigan, with a bachelor's degree in pharmacy. Our second daughter, Lynda, was born that same year.

By 1962, there were two pharmacies in the family, and I was part owner with my family. I loved it. Working fourteen-hour days, it seemed as if I were in contact with just about everyone in Kankakee. I helped young mothers who were concerned about the health of their babies. I consulted daily with the elderly about their medications. This was small-town America and on a daily basis I spoke with and listened to people from all walks of life about their worries and fears. These were plainspoken folks. They said what was on their minds and weren't afraid to say what they liked and didn't like.

It was, in a powerful way, the beginning of my political education.

And so, in 1962, when Edward McBroom, a Kankakee farmer and businessman, who owned a car dealership and a travel agency, decided to run for the state legislature and asked me to be his campaign manager, I thought why not? That was my first taste of politics. And I found that I liked it as much as I enjoyed being a pharmacist. In 1966, when a vacancy opened on the Kankakee County Board of Supervisors, I accepted an appointment to fill the slot. By then, our family had grown. Triplet daughters, Julie, Joanne, and Jeanette were born in 1963 and my son, George, was born in 1964. When my county board seat came up for reelection in 1968, I decided to run and I was successful. Two years later, in 1970, I was elected County Board president. Then, in 1972, the Kankakee County Republican chairman asked me to run for a position in the Illinois House of Representatives. I was honored to be asked and I said I would run. And I was elected.

Five years later, I was standing at my desk in the House of Representatives for what I thought would be an easy vote—the restoration of capital punishment. I was aware that in 1972, during my first year as a state representative, the US Supreme Court, in the case *Furman v. Georgia*, struck down capital punishment. The state death penalty laws, the justices declared, were "haphazard" and "racially discriminatory." As a result of that ruling, all death row inmates in death penalty states, such as Illinois, were automatically spared execution. Most were resentenced to life in prison.

Almost immediately after the decision, state legislatures scrambled to create new death penalty laws that would pass constitutional muster, essentially following a blueprint of sorts laid out by the Supreme Court ruling. Illinois had been no exception and in November 1973, the Illinois General Assembly passed, and Governor Dan Walker signed, a new death penalty law. Its chief feature was the creation of three-judge "sentencing panels" for all capital cases. The accused would be tried before a single judge with guilt decided by either a jury or the judge, as is the case in criminal trials. But after conviction, defendants would go before a sentencing panel that would decide whether or not to impose a death sentence. In theory, this structure was designed to prevent any miscarriage of justice. But that law was barely on the books when, in 1975, the Illinois

Supreme Court struck it down, concluding that the legislature lacked the constitutional authority to create three-judge sentencing panels.

And so, on March 10, 1977, my time to confront the issue of capital punishment finally arrived when House Bill 10 came before the Illinois House of Representatives. This second attempt to reinstate capital punishment separated the guilt phase from the punishment phase. A defendant would first have a trial which, if it culminated in a guilty verdict, would then proceed to a sentencing hearing before a judge or a jury. The choice would be up to the defendant. The sentencing hearing would be conducted in two stages. The first stage determined whether the defendant was eligible for a death sentence. The second, if eligibility was found, would be to determine whether death was the appropriate punishment.

There was more than a hint of spring in the air that day. The sun shone brightly and the temperature topped seventy degrees. It was that time of year when cautious optimism begins to bubble after the cold and snow and bluster of winter.

Representative Roman Kosinski, one of the cosponsors of the bill, spoke first. "House Bill 10 is the work product of many people over a period of a year and a half," he began. "The work product of staff, Legislator attorneys, prosecutors, experts we flew into Springfield from Chicago, and the public. This legislation is needed. It is needed because of escalating murder rates. It is needed because of its implied deterrent effects. It is needed because of the demands of the people of Illinois.

"It is needed as a swing of the pendulum back to the realities of law and order—law and order which is much needed to ensure an orderly society," Kosinski said. After a quick description of the legalities of the law, he wrapped up. "I have said before that in an educated, cultivated and organized society, it is unfortunate the death penalty is needed, but Illinois laws are so lenient presently they almost condone murder. I offer House Bill 10 for your consideration."

More speeches were made. Some representatives were for the bill. Some were opposed to it. Some were more passionate than others.

Don Duester, a Republican from Mundelein, a suburb north of Chicago, was adamantly in favor of it. "I think that if we enact this law and just one person, just one person who is on the verge of committing murder hesitates and stops because of the fear of death to himself, we've saved one life. And by putting this statute on the books, if we can save one life, we have shown that this is a civilized society that holds life to be sacred and dear. And I think the death penalty is a real reflection of a society that does believe that life is sacred and anyone who takes a life ought to be dealt with seriously."

On the other side was Bob Mann, a Chicago Democrat who predicted that the poor and minorities would populate death row. "I tell you that capital punishment is a lethal lottery and the poor and the black are the losers," Mann declared. "This is an awesome responsibility we have. It's a moral dilemma. Remember, you can't justify killing by the state unless you really feel that killing by one justifies killing by another."

His next words were chilling.

"I say to you here today that if you vote for this bill, you might as well be there to push the switch that kills the next man who dies in Illinois. And the more sober among you will wonder: Has a mistake been made? There is no way of turning it around—it is an irreversible mistake.

"How many of you would stand down there and pull that switch?" Mann asked. "That's not our job. Our job is to make sure that everyone, regardless of economic status or race be protected against killing. And killing is not our business—preserving human life is our business." He implored us to "take cognizance of the fact that our courts are not perfect, will take cognizance of the fact that there is a rich man's justice and a poor man's justice. Please, ladies and gentlemen, I ask you—do not pass this bill."

Years later, I am still struck by the memory of how stirring the debate was on both sides of the aisle as Republicans and Democrats alike favored and opposed the issue. At that time, the death penalty wasn't a wedge issue that split the chamber down party lines. It wasn't a predictable "Republican issue" or a "Democrat issue." While there were more Republicans for the death penalty than Democrats, there also was bipartisan support. This was a true public policy debate, not a political debate.

On both sides of the House chamber were large tote boards that showed how each legislator was voting. Each board contained the names of all 177 representatives. Next to each name was a horizontal row of three light bulbs: one green bulb, signifying a yes vote; a red bulb, signifying a no vote; and a yellow bulb, signifying a vote of "present," essentially an abstention. On each of our desks were three switches that corresponded to the bulbs—a green switch, a red switch, and a yellow switch. I had already voted "green" as the debate continued when Elroy

C. Sandquist Jr., a Chicago Republican, stood up, perhaps emboldened by Bob Mann's comments.

"Most of us when we came down here probably had our minds made up as to how we feel about this. It is an emotional issue," Sandquist said. "But I think what we really must do is be leaders of our people too. If something is wrong, just because they are clamoring for it, we should not bet on that bandwagon and join it. We should really look at it closely to see if it is going to solve the problem that the people are concerned about, which is safety in the street; freedom from crime. And I really don't think this death penalty is going to do that.

"I spent four years in the State's Attorney's Office in Cook County when we had the death penalty on the book," Sandquist said. "Was it carried out? No, it was not carried out. Because people are afraid of that last step—of pushing the button to execute a person. So, I ask each and every one of when you push your switch to vote: Would you also push your switch to turn on the electricity to take someone's life?"

Sandquist paused ever so briefly. For a moment, the chamber was hushed.

"Because that is what you're doing when you pull that switch for a yes vote," he concluded. "I honestly ask you to vote no."

I believed the law was necessary. And so, I pressed green to vote yes.

The bill passed by a vote of 118 to 41.

The debate in the Illinois Senate mirrored the House debate and on June 2, 1977, the Senate passed the bill with a vote of 40 to 13. Nineteen days later, Illinois governor James Thompson, a former federal prosecutor, signed the bill into law.

And while I went on about my business as a state legislator—my responsibilities were expanding because I had been elected the House minority leader and would soon become Speaker of the House—that debate ever remained clear. The words of Bob Mann and Elroy Sandquist had, for a moment, given me pause. I remember saying to myself, "Yes, this law is necessary, but I don't want to be the guy who throws the switch."

Little did I know that twenty-two years later, my hand would be on that very switch.

# 2

# MACHINERY OF DEATH

On July 2, 1976, the US Supreme Court, in the decision *Gregg v. Georgia*, ruled that the newly enacted death penalty statutes of Florida, Georgia, and Texas were constitutional. The court also held that the death penalty itself was constitutional. That decision essentially cleared the way for other states, such as Illinois, to move ahead with statutes that would withstand Supreme Court scrutiny. Six months later, on January 17, 1977, the first execution in this new era was carried out in Utah.

Gary Gilmore, who was convicted of committing two murders in Utah in 1976, gave up his appeals and demanded to be put to death by firing squad. He was strapped to a chair in front of a wall of sandbags while five police officers from the county of his crime stood twenty feet away behind a curtain with holes cut out for the barrels of their rifles. The protocol called for four rifles to have live ammunition and one to have a blank so that the officers would not know for sure whose bullet was the fatal shot. Gilmore earned national and international fame when, after being asked if he had any final words, said, "Let's do it." Family members later said they found five bullet holes in Gilmore's shirt.

Illinois had a moment in the death penalty spotlight in 1980 when John Wayne Gacy, then the most prolific serial killer in the history of the United States, was sentenced to death in Cook County for the murders of thirty-three young men and boys. If anyone deserved the death penalty, it was Gacy as far as I was concerned.

Over the next decade, the only real attention that I paid to the death penalty was to vote in favor of expanding it, typically by adding additional "aggravating factors," which expanded the pool of murders that were eligible for it. The version of the death penalty that I voted for in 1977 contained eight of these factors. Over time, Illinois would enact more than twenty of these categories, essentially turning virtually all murders into death penalty crimes. I voted for them whenever I was given the opportunity because I believed that there was a place in the system for the death penalty. I assumed the system was working fairly and accurately to determine who should live and who should die. I was a typical legislator, I believe, in that the death penalty did not occupy much of my attention and I really didn't bother or feel the need to examine how the system worked.

In 1983, I left the General Assembly when I was elected Illinois lieutenant governor. I served in this capacity for two terms under Governor James Thompson. In 1991, I ran for and was elected Illinois secretary of state.

By that time, Illinois had exonerated two men and executed one. The exonerations actually came before anyone was put to death. In 1987, Perry Cobb and Darby Tillis were acquitted at a retrial in Cook County. They had been sentenced to death for a 1977 murder of a hot dog stand owner and one of his employees in Chicago. They were arrested after a witness, Phyllis Santini, told police they committed the crime. Although Cobb and Tillis said they were innocent, they were charged after police found a watch in Cobb's room that belonged to one of the victims. Cobb claimed he bought it for ten dollars from Santini's boyfriend. Their first two trials resulted in mistrials when the jurors could not reach unanimous agreement. At their third trial, when a purported eyewitness who was unable to identify them at the first two trials suddenly positively identified them, Cobb and Tillis were convicted and sentenced to death. They were granted a new trial due to judicial error. After the reversal, Rob Warden, a veteran Chicago journalist, published an account of the evidence in *Chicago Lawyer* magazine. Michael Falconer, a recent graduate of DePaul University College of Law, read the article and remembered that prior to law school, he worked for a summer in a factory where Santini also worked. Falconer contacted the lawyers for Cobb and Tillis and reported that Santini had admitted to him that she and her boyfriend, the same man Cobb said sold him the incriminating watch, had robbed a restaurant and shot someone. Falconer's testimony at the retrial was critical to their acquittal.

The first execution carried out in Illinois under the new death penalty law occurred in September 1990, when Charles Walker abandoned his appeals, saying he preferred death rather than remaining in prison during a lengthy court battle. He had been convicted of robbing a young couple who were fishing in a creek near Mascoutah, Illinois, tying them to a tree, and shooting them to death in 1983. Walker was the 139th person executed in the United States since the return of the death penalty in what was by now referred to as the "modern day" death penalty system. With that execution, Illinois became the sixteenth state to resume executions.

The death penalty scene was quiet in Illinois for the next several years, although the number of executions nationally was beginning to increase. Fourteen inmates were executed in 1991, thirty-one in 1992, and thirty-eight in 1993.

However, there was a notable exoneration. In Maryland, Kirk Bloodsworth became the first person who had been sentenced to death to be exonerated by DNA testing. Bloodsworth had been convicted of a 1984 murder of a nine-year-old girl and sentenced to death. His conviction was overturned, and he was reconvicted at a second trial and sentenced to life in prison. In the spring of 2003, a forensic biologist studying the evidence found stains on a sheet that had been used to wrap the victim that had not been analyzed. DNA testing was performed, and the subsequent DNA profile was submitted to the FBI'S national DNA database. The DNA profile linked to Kimberly Shay Ruffner, who had been convicted of a separate crime and actually had been housed in the same prison with Bloodsworth, just one floor above his cell. Although the Bloodsworth exoneration did really not register with me at the time, I would come to understand that it provided a spark to the antideath penalty movement nationally because there was no doubt that he had been wrongly convicted.

In February 1994, US Supreme Court justice Harry A. Blackmun, in a seven thousand-word dissent, declared that he had concluded that "the death penalty experiment has failed." He said that the idea that capital punishment was constitutional was a "delusion."

"From this day forward, I no longer shall tinker with the machinery of death," Justice Blackmun wrote in a case involving a Texas man whose appeal the majority of the justices had refused to hear. Blackmun said he had concluded "that no sentence of death may be constitutionally imposed under our death penalty scheme."

Justice Blackmun's words would ever be cited by the antideath penalty movement in the United States, but like many pronouncements in dissents, it was good rhetoric. Little, if anything, changed.

Three months later, in May 1994, serial killer John Wayne Gacy was executed in Illinois. As far as I was concerned, no one deserved the death penalty more.

In September of that year, Joseph Burrows became the third person to be exonerated from death row in Illinois. Burrows had been sentenced to death for the 1988 murder of eighty-eight-year-old William Dulin, a retired farmer whose body had been found in his home in Sheldon, Illinois, about forty miles south of my home in Kankakee. According to the prosecution, a few hours after the murder, Chuck Gullion attempted to cash a $4,050 check in Dulin's name at the Iroquois Farmer's State Bank. Word of Dulin's murder had already reached the bank. Police were called and arrested Gullion in a car with thirty-two-year-old Gayle Potter. Potter admitted forging the check and taking part in the crime and then implicated Ralph Frye, a man with an IQ of seventy-five and Frye's friend, Burrows. Potter claimed the thirty-two-year-old Burrows pulled the trigger. The facts seemed to belie Potter's version. Her blood was found at the scene and the murder weapon was hers. Four witnesses said they saw Burrows sixty miles away at the time of the crime. However, following an interrogation by police, Frye gave a statement that aligned with Potter's account. Frye and Potter pled guilty and testified for the prosecution against Burrows. Gullion was never charged.

Burrows was tried twice. The first trial ended in a mistrial when the jury could not agree on a verdict. But at a second trial, he was convicted and sentenced to death. The Illinois Supreme Court upheld the conviction and death sentence in 1992. However, Frye subsequently recanted his testimony. Peter Rooney, a reporter for the Champaign-Urbana *News-Gazette*, published Frye's recantation, prompting Kathleen Zellner and Michael Hemstreet, lawyers for Burrows, to dig deeper into the case. They found a letter Potter had written to a friend asking him to falsely claim he saw her in a blue truck that she claimed Burrows drove to and from Dulin's home. Potter then admitted that her account was false, and that Burrows and Frye were not involved. She admitted that she had been alone with Dulin and that she killed him to try to get money to buy drugs.

Burrows was granted a new trial and on September 8, 1994, the prosecution dismissed the case and he was freed. Even though the case had unfolded almost in my backyard, it barely registered with me. But by now, there had been one execution and three exonerations.

The machinery of death moved along briskly in 1995. On March 22, the state carried out its first double execution in forty-three years. Hernando Williams was executed for a 1978 abduction, rape, and murder of a childbirth instructor in Chicago named Linda Goldstone. James Free was executed for an attack in 1978 in a Chicago suburb that left one woman, Bonnie Serpico, dead and another woman wounded.

Witnesses quoted Free as giving a three-minute speech denouncing the death penalty and those who imposed it. "Taking my life will not bring back the victims," Free was quoted as saying. "Capital punishment is not the answer."

Williams had no last words.

On May 17, Girvies Davis was executed for the 1978 murder of Charles Biebel, who was fatally shot in his mobile home in Belleville, Illinois. The crime had gone unsolved for nearly a year until police arrested Davis for a robbery and claimed that he confessed to the murder. Police said he also confessed to about twenty other crimes, most of which turned out to be false; prosecutors admitted as much in court. That didn't stop them from using his confession to Biebel's murder, even though there was no physical or forensic evidence connecting him to the crime. Davis said that police had taken him out of the jail, which the jail logs confirmed, and out into the country where they removed his handcuffs, drew their guns, and told him to sign the confessions. If he refused, they threatened to kill him and report that he was shot trying to escape. Girvies's lawyers found a parole officer and a teacher who signed affidavits saying he was illiterate and could not have understood what he was signing. Girvies was executed after then-Governor Jim Edgar rejected his clemency petition.

Four months later, on September 30, 1995, Charles Albanese was executed for the murders of his father, his mother-in-law, and his wife's grandmother. Prosecutors said he fed them food laced with arsenic so he could get an inheritance and take over the family's business.

The last two months of the year were marked by another execution and two more exonerations. On November 3, Rolando Cruz, who had been sentenced to death for the 1983 abduction, rape, and murder of ten-year-old Jeanine Nicarico, was acquitted at his third trial after a DuPage County Sheriff's lieutenant admitted that he had testified falsely. The Cruz case had a tortured history. He had been indicted in 1984 with two others—Stephen Buckley and Alejandro Hernandez. They were tried jointly in 1985. Cruz and Hernandez were convicted and sentenced to death. The jury could not reach a unanimous verdict on Buckley and a mistrial was declared. The charges against him were dismissed. In 1989, the Illinois Supreme Court reversed the convictions and death sentences of Cruz and Hernandez because of prejudicial errors by the trial judge and the prosecutors. By that time, a serial killer named Brian Dugan had confessed that he, acting alone, had abducted, raped, and murdered Janine. However, the prosecution refused to believe Dugan acted alone and was instead acting in concert with Cruz and Hernandez.

Cruz and Hernandez came to trial again in separate courtrooms and were convicted again, primarily because much of the evidence of Dugan's involvement was kept out of the trial. Cruz again was sentenced to death and Hernandez was sentenced to eighty years in prison.

While Hernandez's appeal was pending, the Illinois Supreme Court reversed Cruz's conviction a second time. In 1995, while preparing for a third trial, a police lieutenant testified at a pretrial hearing that he took a telephone call from two detectives who reported that Cruz had made statements revealing knowledge that only the killer should have known. At the third trial, the lieutenant testified he had discovered that he was on vacation in Florida on the day that he had said he took the call. He admitted he could not have taken any call—an admission that undercut the credibility of the claim that Cruz had made admissions of involvement. The admission was a critical factor in the judge acquitting Cruz after the prosecution finished presenting evidence and before the defense began presenting its evidence. Shortly thereafter, Hernandez's conviction was vacated, and the charge was dismissed.

The execution of forty-seven-year-old George Del Vecchio on November 22 closed the books on the death penalty in Illinois in 1995. Del Vecchio was executed for the murder of a six-year-old boy and the rape of the boy's mother in Chicago. At the time of the crime, Del Vecchio was on parole for taking part in a murder in 1965 when he was sixteen years old.

Del Vecchio was the seventh person executed in Illinois and was among fifty-six prisoners executed nationwide that year. Burrows, Cruz, and Hernandez were the third, fourth, and fifth inmates to leave death row in Illinois.

In 1996, four more men were exonerated from death row—Verneal Jimerson, Dennis Williams, Carl Lawson, and Gary Gauger.

In the summer of 1996, DNA testing exonerated Williams and Jimerson of a double murder in Ford Heights, Illinois. Two codefendants who had not been sentenced to death, Kenneth Adams and Willie Rainge, also were exonerated by DNA testing. The real killers were identified as a result.

In October 1996, Gauger's conviction and death sentence were vacated when the Illinois Appellate Court held that police lacked probable cause to arrest him for the murders of his parents. Police claimed Gauger confessed to the crime, an assertion he denied. It would later be discovered by the Ffederal Bureau of Alcohol, Tobacco, and Firearms that the real killers were from a motorcycle gang in Wisconsin.

On December 12, 1996, Lawson became the state's ninth exonerated death row prisoner when forensic testing discredited the state's claim that Lawson left his shoeprints at the scene of the fatal stabbing of an eight-year-old boy in East St. Louis, Illinois.

Executions continued.

In September 1996, Raymond Stewart was executed. He was convicted after admitting he killed six people in Rockford, Illinois, and Beloit, Wisconsin.

Thirteen months later, in October 1997, Larry Marshall, a law professor at Northwestern University School of Law, who had represented Gauger and Cruz, testified before a subcommittee in the Illinois Legislature where Coy Pugh, a Democratic representative from Chicago, had introduced a bill asking the Illinois Supreme Court to establish a commission to examine the death penalty system.

Invoking the names of the exonerated, Marshall said, "These men are free because of some fortuitous event, some serendipity, that led to their exoneration; they weren't cleared because the system worked."

He added, "If those who want to expedite capital punishment had their way, many of these men would have been long dead by the time their exoneration came down the road." Marshall was joined by lawyers, the clergy, human rights groups, and former death row inmates, including Cruz, Gauger, and Cobb.

Marshall declared, "There is absolutely no basis for taking false comfort in some naive assumption that we have already ferreted out all the innocent people from death row, that these nine men are all there is and there is no more. It's a criminal act to rely on luck and serendipity when innocent lives are at stake."

A month later, as Illinois prepared for a second double execution, a small, but growing group of voices called on Governor Jim Edgar to halt executions due to the rising number of exonerations. The *Chicago Tribune* published an editorial urging Edgar to halt the executions, noting that the previous February the American Bar Association had concluded that "fundamental due process is now systematically lacking in capital cases."

That plea was rejected.

On November 19, 1997, Durlynn Eddmonds and Walter Stewart were put to death. Eddmonds, a schizophrenic whose own lawyers called a sociopath, was executed for the rape and murder of a nine-year-old boy in Chicago. Stewart was put to death for gunning down the owner and an employee of a jewelry store in Berwyn, Illinois. He would have killed another employee, but he ran out of ammunition.

In January 1998, Lloyd Hampton was executed for the murder of a sixty-nine-year-old man in Troy, Illinois.

So, the tally read this way: since the reinstatement of the death penalty in Illinois in 1977, eleven men had been executed and nine men had exonerated. The antideath penalty movement, always a minority, was beginning to gather data and more supporters as the number of exonerations in Illinois and across the nation began to pile up.

The Death Penalty Information Center, a national nonprofit dedicated to tracking the death penalty, reported that since 1973, a total of seventy-two condemned inmates—seventy-one men and one woman—had been exonerated.

Meanwhile, executions nationally were steadily rising. After forty-five executions in 1996, a total of seventy-four condemned inmates were executed in 1997, the highest yearly total at that time in the modern-day death penalty era. The total death row population in the United States had swelled to more than 3,300.

Nonetheless, in 1998, a group of lawyers, religious leaders, and ordinary citizens quietly began planning for an event that would breathe new life in the antideath penalty movement.

At the same time, my arc was bending away from the death penalty. I was about to complete my second term as Illinois secretary of state when Governor Edgar, who had succeeded James Thompson in 1991 and served two terms, announced that he would not run for reelection.

After talking it over with my family, I decided to run for governor, a decision that would change my life forever.

# 3

# THE FACE OF DEATH ROW

During my campaign, I supported the death penalty, as did my opponent, Glenn Poshard, a conservative Democrat who was a five-time member of the US House of Representatives.

Question asked.

Question answered.

Although most Democrats opposed capital punishment, I believed Poshard did not want to get tagged as a "soft-on-crime" candidate. That's what had happened four years earlier in 1994 when Jim Edgar, the Republican incumbent governor ran against Dawn Clark Netsch, a Chicago Democrat. Netsch was a long-time vocal opponent of the death penalty and Edgar hammered her for it.

My campaign against Poshard was different. I didn't talk about it. And neither did Poshard.

Of course, there were always questions about the death penalty on written questionnaires submitted by the media and special interest groups, but the future of prisoners on death row was nowhere close to being an important subject. It was a box to check off. My belief that capital punishment was needed to help prevent crime was just as strong as it was in 1977 when I pressed the green button to support its reinstatement.

The big issue in that election was gun control. More than 70 percent of the voters favored some form of gun control and these folks were solidly behind me. And on November 3, 1998, I was elected with 52 percent of the vote.

Ten days later, on November 13, 1998, at the Northwestern University School of Law, Lawrence Marshall, a law professor who would soon cofound the law school's Center on Wrongful Convictions, convened the first ever National Conference on Wrongful Convictions and the Death Penalty. Marshall had played a role in five of the nine Illinois death row exonerations. The three-day conference drew a crowd estimated to be from 1,000 to 1,200 and included defense lawyers, journalists, professors and, most importantly, thirty-one of the men and women who had been exonerated from death rows across the nation.

I did not attend but watched with interest as the television news aired the highlight of the conference. Each exoneree crossed the stage to announce their name and recite: "The state of [whichever state that exoneree was from] tried to kill me for a crime I did not commit. If the state had its way, I'd be dead today."

The power was undeniable.

The conference was a tipping point for many journalists, the majority of whom were longtime skeptics and believers that death row exonerations were anomalies. It also breathed new life into what had been largely a quiet antideath penalty movement.

On January 11, 1999, I was sworn in as the 39th governor of the State of Illinois along with other constitutional officers. That afternoon, Lura Lynn and I along with my lieutenant governor Corinne Wood and her husband, Paul, held an open house at the Executive Mansion. The inaugural ball was held at the Prairie Capital Convention Center just a few blocks from the capital. It was a grand affair.

My true education about the death penalty began early in the day, before I had uttered the oath of office. That very morning, the *Chicago Tribune* published the first part of a five-part series on prosecutorial misconduct, titled "Trial & Error—The Verdict: Dishonor."

The series, written by reporters Ken Armstrong and Maurice Possley, described how prosecutors, acting with "impunity," had committed misconduct in a vast array of cases including "defendants who came within hours of being executed, only to be exonerated." The first article said that they had identified nearly four hundred homicide convictions across the nation beginning in 1963—a twenty-five-year period—that had been reversed (and many of them subsequently dismissed) because prosecutors had either failed to disclose evidence of a defendant's innocence or knowingly used false evidence.

"The U.S. Supreme Court has declared such misconduct by prosecutors to be so reprehensible that it warrants criminal charges and disbarment," the article said. "But not one of those prosecutors was convicted of a crime. Not one was barred from practicing law. Instead, many saw their careers advance, becoming judges or district attorneys. One became a congressman."

A total of sixty-seven of these defendants had been sentenced to death and ultimately thirty of them were freed.

Illinois had the second most—forty-six—of these erroneous convictions. Only New York had more, partly because the state had a rule that lessened restrictions on reversals.

The newspaper also documented 326 convictions in all manner of cases—not just homicides—that had been reversed in the state of Illinois, including 207 in Illinois since December 31, 1977. Nearly half of the Illinois reversals were homicide cases. The numbers were startling to me. One statement was particularly jarring: "As a result, about once a month, on average, for the past two decades, a conviction has been set aside in Cook County because of a judicial finding of improper conduct by prosecutors." The newspaper said that discipline for the misconduct was rarely imposed.

But death penalty news wasn't just happening in Chicago. On January 27, 1999, Pope John Paul II was in St. Louis, Missouri, a state that strongly embraced the death penalty. During his homily at the Papal Mass, the pope declared, "I renew the appeal I made most recently at Christmas for a consensus to end the death penalty, which is both cruel and unnecessary."

And later that day, at a prayer service at the St. Louis Cathedral, the pope walked over to Missouri governor Mel Carnahan, a Southern Baptist and staunch supporter of the death penalty. The pope asked Carnahan to "show mercy" to Darrell Mease, who was scheduled to be executed by the State of Missouri on February 10 for a triple murder committed in 1988. Carnahan, who had signed off on twenty-six prior executions since taking office in 1993, listened to the pope's request and commuted Mease's sentence to life in prison without parole.

Neither of these events, however prepared me for what happened on February 5, 1999. That night, I was stunned to my core.

Lura Lynn and I were in the Executive Mansion and turned on the six o'clock evening Chicago news. I watched in amazement as Anthony Porter, an Illinois death row inmate, walked out of Cook County Jail and into the embrace of David Protess, a professor at Northwestern University's Medill School of Journalism. Arrested in 1982 and convicted and sentenced to death in 1983 for a double murder on Chicago's South Side, Porter was freed following an investigation by Protess's journalism students. During their investigation, a man named Alstory Simon confessed on videotape that he committed the crime. Simon said that he shot eighteen-year-old Jerry Hillard in self-defense and didn't mean to kill nineteen-year-old Marilyn Green.

Journalism students! WOW!

I listened in stunned silence as the report continued. Porter was said to have an IQ of fifty-one and had been two days away from being executed in September 1998—while I was still on the campaign trail—when his lawyer, Daniel Sanders, persuaded the Illinois Supreme Court to issue a stay of the execution so that Porter could have a mental competency hearing. That delay gave the students and private investigator Paul Ciolino time to finish their investigative work and to get the confession from Simon that he committed the crime. Porter had been so close to execution that his family had picked out the suit to bury him in, he had been measured for his state-issued coffin, and he had filled out the menu for his last meal.

"How does this happen in America?" I said aloud. "What is going on that journalism students—not the courts, not a jury, not a prosecutor—got to the bottom of this? What is wrong with a system that allows somebody to get sentenced to death and spend sixteen years on death row and then someone finds out that they are innocent?"

The next day, I called Protess's home number and left a message with his son, Ben. That night, when Protess called me back at the mansion, he joked that at first, he thought his son was playing a prank until Ben assured him that he recognized my voice.

"How can I help you?" Protess asked me.

"I want to help Anthony Porter," I told him. "What can I do to help that poor guy?"

I explained that I had been watching the news on television when I saw the report about Porter being freed and that I wanted to know if there was anything I could do.

Protess explained that if I granted Porter a gubernatorial pardon, it would speed up the process for Porter to obtain state compensation for his years in prison. I told him that I would do whatever it took to get it done as soon as possible within the bureaucracy that existed. (Porter later was awarded $145,875 in compensation as a result of the pardon.)

As I talked with Protess, I admitted that I had been a lifelong supporter of the death penalty, but watching Porter's release and learning how close he had come to being executed had caused something inside me to shift.

"I have to think about this," I told Protess. "I am horrified to think that Porter had almost been executed on my watch. I am going to have to start rethinking my view on the death penalty. And I would like to keep talking to you."

Protess said he would talk whenever and wherever I wanted.

"I want to meet him," I said. "Can you bring him to my office at the State of Illinois building in Chicago?"

Protess said he would work with my staff to arrange a meeting.

The next day, I set about learning the details of the Porter case and the state of the death penalty in Illinois. I discovered that since reinstatement in 1977, eleven men had been executed and ten men had been exonerated. This was even more unsettling.

Porter's release provided more ammunition for death penalty opponents. The call for a moratorium, which had begun bubbling after the Northwestern conference in November, became more full-throated. For several days, my official position was to defend the system. It was working, I said.

"The process did work," David Urbanek, my chief spokesman, told the media. "Sure, it took seventeen years, but it also took seventeen years for that journalism professor to sic his kids on that case." He added, "We're not even sure any problems do exist."

Chicago mayor Richard Daley's spokesperson said something similar—that "if anything, this case demonstrates that the system does work."

*Chicago Tribune* columnist Clarence Page fired back, asking, "Is it the fault of Protess's journalism students that Porter sat so long on Death Row for a double murder it now appears he did not commit?"

And the *Tribune* published an editorial calling for a state moratorium. "What saved Anthony Porter was not 'the system,' as apologists have said piously, but a spit-and-chewing-gum network of volunteers, enterprising Northwestern University journalism students—and an eleventh-hour mental competency hearing, which provided enough of a delay for his supporters to dig up new evidence," the newspaper declared. "That's not a 'system,' but happenstance: the charity of concerned strangers and sheer luck."

In response, Mayor Richard Daley took a step back and said that although he supported the death penalty, he would support a moratorium on executions.

I was not ready to support a moratorium, but I did say, "I think there's got to be some kind of another check put into place. I'm just not sure yet what it is."

The pressure to impose a moratorium reached the state's highest court. On Thursday, February 11, Illinois Supreme Court Justice Charles Freeman announced that the court did not have the authority to halt executions. The court's spokesman, Joseph Tybor, said Freeman felt that "for the court to impose a moratorium would be an improper exercise of judicial authority."

That meant the ball was in my court.

In response, I issued a new statement saying that I felt there were some problems at the trial court level. "We're open to looking at any solutions. We've had a situation where everyone is running around saying we need a summit. Everything I've seen has just been a bunch of half-baked ideas."

Among the proposals that surfaced in the week following Porter's release were legislative initiatives to place moratoriums on executions in order to study the cases of all 179 inmates on death row. The Illinois attorney general proposed an increase in the budget of a criminal litigation division that helps inmates prove their innocence and called for a new clemency review board to handle capital punishment cases.

Justice Freeman, along with fellow Supreme Court Justice Moses Harrison II, a vocal opponent of the death penalty, chimed in, saying that I could use my executive power to grant temporary stays of execution as a way to impose a blanket moratorium while the issue was studied. "The present crisis in Illinois death penalty law presents just the sort of situation where a reprieve would be appropriate," Harrison declared. "With the next execution scheduled for March, there is no time for delay."

I did not like the concept of a moratorium. I felt that if I were going to do anything, it would be to look at each individual case and make an appropriate judgment at the appropriate time.

It turned out I only had about a month to figure out my first one.

# 4

# A HUMAN FACE

For nearly seventeen years, Anthony Porter's protestations of his innocence were largely ignored. After the Illinois Supreme Court's decision by a vote of four to three to uphold his conviction in 1986, each subsequent decision against him had been unanimous or near unanimous; almost pro forma. To police, to prosecutors, the media, and the general public, Porter was just another criminal in line to receive the state's justice for a double murder.

Of course, he said he didn't do it—doesn't almost every criminal on death row say the same thing? Police and prosecutors had done their jobs, a jury had agreed and that was the end of it. No need to double-check the facts. No need to revisit the case beyond the finite number of appeals called for by state and federal law. If his lawyer had not obtained the stay of execution when he did, Porter's proverbial fifteen minutes of fame would have been the news stories about his execution.

But now, Anthony Porter was a household name. And it was going to be for a lot longer than fifteen minutes. And not just in Illinois. The antideath penalty movement was latching onto what was going on in Illinois to make broader arguments about abolishing the death penalty. Illinois was "Exhibit A" of the movement. What could be a more compelling narrative than the story of a man wrongly convicted by the state getting released from prison right before the state could execute him? Executing an innocent man was the worst nightmare imaginable for those who supported the death penalty too. Police and prosecutors were going into overdrive trying to put a good face on Porter's release. The system had worked, they said. An innocent man was not executed.

On February 19, 1999, another death row inmate was exonerated. The Illinois Supreme Court vacated the conviction and death sentence of Steven Smith, who had been convicted of killing an off-duty state correctional officer. With Smith's release, the tally stood dead even—eleven men executed and eleven men exonerated.

The court noted that the ruling did not find Smith innocent, but rather that the state had failed to prove his guilt. The court declared,

> While there are those who may criticize courts for turning criminals loose, courts have a duty to ensure that all citizens receive those rights which are applicable equally to every citizen who may find himself charged with a crime, whatever the crime and whatever the circumstances. When the state cannot meet its burden of proof, the defendant must go free. . . . It is no help to speculate that the defendant may have killed the victim. No citizen would be safe from prosecution under such a standard.

On March 11, 1999, following Alstory Simon's confession of guilt, the prosecution dismissed the double murder charges against Porter. He was officially a free man. Every television report from then on seemed to always feature Porter's jubilant release and his embrace with Protess. I saw it and the public saw it again and again and again in Illinois and across the country. The case had done what previously had seemed almost impossible to the antideath penalty movement—it had thrust the death penalty debate not only into the media's consciousness, but also into the homes of average Americans who never before doubted or even debated capital punishment. This time the debate was different. This was not about whether it was morally right for the state to kill. This was about whether the system could be trusted to kill only the guilty .

I soon met Rob Warden and Lawrence Marshall. These two men not only were highly influential in the criminal justice community in Chicago, but also would each play a critical role in my education about the flaws of the death penalty system in Illinois.

Warden had founded the Chicago *Lawyer* magazine and had exposed numerous unjust convictions and steadily crusaded for death penalty reforms during the 1980s and 1990s. Marshall, a Northwestern University law professor, had organized the death penalty conference that had injected new life into the antideath penalty movement and had just formed Northwestern University Law School's Center on Wrongful Convictions.

Rob and Larry introduced me to a number of people who understood firsthand the problems with the capital punishment system, and even those who had suffered personally at the hands of the system.

Larry introduced me to Gary Gauger, who was sentenced to death for the 1993 murder of his parents, Morris and Ruth, on their farm and motorcycle shop in Richmond, Illinois, a small town just south of the Wisconsin border. I took an interest in the case because not only had Gauger been exonerated and released from death row, but also because the case was a prime example of how difficult it was to convince prosecutors and police that they had gotten it wrong.

One morning, Gauger woke up and his parents were not in the home where all three lived on a dairy farm in McHenry County, Illinois. In addition to the dairy business, his parents operated a motorcycle shop on the property. When a customer came looking to buy a motorcycle part, Gauger opened up the shop and found his father's body in a pool of blood with his throat slit. He called the police who searched the property and found his mother's body in a trailer from which the couple had sold imported rugs. She had suffered the same fate. The police interrogated Gauger aggressively and harangued him. They put him through the wringer and kept asking him, "Well if you didn't do it, how do you think it happened?"

They asked him if he had been drinking and committed the murders during an alcohol-induced blackout, robbing him of any memory of killing his parents. His interrogation lasted eighteen hours during which detectives lied to him. They claimed they found bloody clothes in his bedroom. After Gauger took a polygraph, they told him he had failed when in fact the results were inconclusive. Finally, when he was asked to describe how he might have killed his parents while blacked out, detectives said he provided details that indicated he had killed them. The interrogation was not recorded and Gauger had not signed a confession. Nonetheless, he was convicted based on the testimony of the detectives about his statements and by the testimony of a jailhouse snitch who claimed Gauger admitted to the crime while in jail before the trial.

After Gauger was sentenced to death in December 1994, Marshall agreed to handle Gauger's appeal. In the fall of 1995, the truth was discovered. Mark Quinn, a member of the Outlaws motorcycle gang in

Wisconsin, had become an informant for the Bureau of Alcohol, Tobacco, and Firearms (ATF). Quinn told the ATF that Outlaws members Randall Miller and James Schneider had admitted they were the killers and were laughing about Gauger being sent to death row. Within a year of Gauger's conviction, a judge commuted the sentence to life in prison when Marshall sought to intervene to challenge Gauger's death sentence.

In March 1996, the Illinois Appellate Court delivered a unanimous ruling that Gauger's so-called confession should not have been admitted into evidence because it was the product of an illegal arrest without probable cause. Although the ATF had passed the information about Miller and Schneider to McHenry County law enforcement in 1995, Gauger remained in custody until October 4, 1996. That's when he was released after State's Attorney Gary Pack dismissed the charges, although Pack continued to maintain that Gauger was involved in the murders.

In June 1997, a federal grand jury indicted Schneider and Miller on thirty-four counts of racketeering, including the murders of Morris and Ruth Gauger. Schneider pled guilty to acts relating to the murders in 1998 and was sentenced to forty-five years in prison. Miller was convicted in June 2000. At Miller's trial, prosecutors played a recording of a conversation made by Quinn in which Miller said that the authorities could not link him to the Gauger murders because he had been careful not to leave physical evidence. Miller was sentenced to two consecutive life sentences.

Anthony Porter had put a human face on the issue of wrongfully convicted death row inmates and gave me a new perspective. To me, he seemed to be just a poor little soul who was happy to be out of prison and really wasn't all that sure how it happened. I felt badly for him having spent all those years in prison. I felt badly that it took that long to get the right kind of help to get freed instead of getting it at the outset when it could have prevented him from being thrown into prison for a crime he didn't commit. I began to see Anthony Porter as just a victim—an absolute victim. I kept saying afterward to members of my staff: "What if we had executed this guy? What if we had executed an innocent guy?"

The meeting with Gauger gave me more perspective. I could hear the pain in his voice when he talked about being under a continuing cloud because of the refusal of McHenry County officials to acknowledge his innocence.

I had begun to adopt US Supreme Court Justice Harry Blackmun's term—"the machinery of death"—when I referred to the death penalty system. I could see that the process was clinical and antiseptic so as to almost disguise the fact that it was about killing someone. I supposed it was designed that way to help people deal with their responsibilities after the deed was done. But it really was a machine, and I was realizing that there had not been enough emphasis on whether the machine ran correctly.

I realized that some people accepted the idea that there's collateral damage in a lot of areas of the law. And if you're going to have the death penalty, undoubtedly there will be mistakes and there are going to be some innocent people that are going to be killed. The more I thought about it, I began to think that was just not right and that if you're going to have a death penalty, it better be perfect or you better not have it; especially since there is a good alternative—life without parole.

I was really dumbfounded by it all. The cases of Anthony Porter, Steven Smith, and Gary Gauger not only inspired the antideath penalty advocates, they prompted me to begin a thoughtful investigation to determine whether the death penalty system should be—or could be—changed. I didn't know how bad our system really was. I couldn't believe the system that I had trusted in could come that close to executing an innocent man—within two days of killing Anthony Porter for a crime he didn't commit.

But first, I had to confront that moment I had pondered that day in 1977 when I voted to reinstate the death penalty. Now it was my turn to have my finger on the throttle of the machinery of death.

There was a man scheduled to die in the execution chamber. It would be my job to decide whether to go ahead. The man poised to die was Andrew Kokoraleis, one of the most despicable criminals in Illinois history.

# 5

# EXECUTION ON DECK

I never saw combat when I was in Korea with the US Army, so I never had to pull the trigger with someone at the other end of the barrel of my rifle. That must be a tough thing to do. For men who have fought in combat, I imagine that most of the time, the act of shooting is a split-second decision. It's a matter of kill or be killed. This is my conjecture. Most of the men I know who were in combat and pointed a rifle in fear or anger prefer not to talk about it.

I learned that being the last person to decide whether someone is executed is a more drawn out process. It's not a split-second decision about someone living or dying. There's more time to think when you're faced with that decision; more time to question yourself and the reasons you're doing what you're doing. From a cynical perspective, it's a matter of a file on my desk and little more. And that would have been the easy way to approach it, since, as governor, I was removed from the actual event, both physically and, for the most part, emotionally. But that's not the way I did it.

And so, the case of Andrew Kokoraleis was tough for me.

Kokoraleis was convicted, along with his brother and two friends, for a series of sadistic murders in Chicago and its suburbs. Young women, total strangers to them, were abducted off the street, tortured, raped, mutilated, and eventually killed in an imagined satanic ritual. Their crimes were characterized in the media as the "Chicago Ripper" killings. The convicted killers were known as the "Ripper Crew."

Although the Anthony Porter exoneration was troubling me, and I was still at a bit of a loss about what I could—or should—do about the death penalty, I had to set that to the side to focus on Kokoraleis, who was scheduled to be executed shortly after midnight on March 17—St. Patrick's Day.

Kokoraleis had spent much of his adult life confined in the Pontiac Correctional Center, a grim place snug against a pleasant Central Illinois community of the same name that prefers to be known for its antique shops along the fabled Route 66. The prison opened in 1871 and now housed all death row prisoners.

As I began to study the case, I painstakingly read the detailed descriptions of the crimes. The decomposed body of the first victim, twenty-six-year-old Linda Sutton, a prostitute, was discovered in June of 1981 along a stream bank in Villa Park, a small bedroom community in Chicago's western suburbs. Sutton, a mother of two from the West Side of Chicago had been abducted on May 23, 1981, as she walked near Wrigley Field. She had been assaulted and raped. Investigators were puzzled at first because the body was in such an advanced state of decomposition. The ultimate answer to this puzzle became the source for the nickname applied to this murder as well as the subsequent killings: a legion of parasites had invaded her body through two huge wounds in her chest, causing the rapid decay. Both of Sutton's breasts had been sliced off.

"Ripper"—as in Jack—was the appropriate adjective.

On May 15, 1982, twenty-one-year-old Lorraine Borowski was abducted as she arrived to open the realtor's office where she worked in Elmhurst, a Chicago suburb. Her body would not be found until five months later. On May 28, 1982, thirty-year-old Shui Mak was abducted from suburban Hanover Park. Like Borowski, her body would remain undiscovered for several months.

On June 13, 1982, police thought they had a break in the case when twenty-three-year-old Angel York reported that she had been abducted by a gang of men in a red van. They had beaten and raped her, then forced her to cut her own breasts with a knife. She had been dumped from the van on a road and left for dead. Although she had survived, police were unable to capitalize on her description of the vehicle and her attackers.

Two months later, in August, eighteen-year-old Sandra Delaware was raped and strangled in Chicago. Her body was found on the banks of the Chicago River. Her left breast had been cut off.

On September 8, thirty-year-old Rose Beck Davis, who lived in suburban Broadview, was found beaten to death behind the wooden stairs of an apartment on Lake Shore Drive in Chicago.

On September 30, a truck driver spotted a body in a field near the suburb of South Barrington, about a mile from where Shui Mak was last seen. Her family identified her body, which had a fractured skull.

On October 6, a twenty-year-old prostitute named Beverly Washington was abducted, beaten, raped, mutilated, and left for dead. An elderly man collecting aluminum cans had found her alive, but unconscious, and summoned police. Like York, she survived and gave a detailed description of the van she got into and where the attack occurred.

Four days later, on October 10, a young man stumbled across the skeletal remains of Lorraine Borowski. Her body was in an unused area of Clarendon Hills Cemetery near suburban Westmont.

On October 20, Chicago police officers stopped a reddish-orange van that matched a description given by Beverly Washington. The van was being driven by twenty-one-year-old Edward Spreitzer and belonged to Robin Gecht, a twenty-eight-year-old married contractor from Chicago. Three knives were found in the back of the van. The inside handle on the back door was missing and could only be opened by inserting a tool where the lock should have been. A sedative was found in the van that Washington identified as being similar to the one she was forced to take. Police showed Washington a photographic array and she identified Gecht as her attacker.

Spreitzer and Gecht were arrested and on the evening of November 7, 1982, Spreitzer led police officers to the suburban Villa Park home of nineteen-year-old Andrew Kokoraleis. The officers took Kokoraleis to a detective station where they questioned him that night and for the next two days. During the interrogation, Kokoraleis said, "I know you talked to Robin (Gecht). Did he tell you about all of them? All eighteen murders?"

Three days later, police arrested Thomas Kokoraleis. During questioning, he was shown a photograph of Lorraine Borowski and asked if he knew who it was. "That is the girl that Eddie Spreitzer and I killed in the cemetery," he replied.

During their interrogations, the Kokoraleis brothers and Spreitzer all told the same story—a story that seemed almost too incredible to be true: Gecht had a powerful psychological grip on them and had planned and led the murder spree in a ritualistic fashion to honor Satan and to satisfy a perverse sexual gratification.

Ultimately, Gecht would be convicted only of the attack on Beverly Washington. In 1983, at Gecht's trial in Cook County Circuit Court, Washington described how Gecht drugged, raped, and then forced her to cut her own breasts. She said he then cut a hole in one of her breasts and stuck his penis in it. One of her breasts had been completely cut off and the other was severely slashed. Gecht was convicted and sentenced to 120 years in prison.

In 1984, Thomas Kokoraleis was convicted in DuPage County Circuit Court of the murder of Lorraine Borowski and was sentenced to seventy years in prison. In 1985, Andrew Kokoraleis also was convicted of the Borowski murder. The prosecution also presented evidence that he had participated in the murders of Linda Sutton in 1981 and the murder of Shui Mak in 1982. Andrew Kokoraleis was sentenced to death.

A year later, in March 1986, Spreitzer was convicted in DuPage County Circuit Court of the murder of Sutton—the first victim in the gruesome spree. By the time of his trial, he had already pled guilty to the murders of Shui Mak; eighteen-year-old Sandra Delaware in August 1982; thirty-year-old Rose Beck Davis in September 1982; and the random murder of twenty-eight-year-old Raphael Torado, gunned down on a street in Chicago's North Side in October 1982. Spreitzer also confessed to, but was not charged with, participating in the Borowski murder. Like Andrew Kokoraleis, Spreitzer also was sentenced to death.

By March 1999, fifteen years after his conviction and following more than a dozen failed court appeals, Andrew Kokoraleis was running out of legal challenges. His lawyers tried every avenue available to him to try to delay or prevent his execution. None of them worked. He had confessed to the crimes and although he had recanted, those statements were not believed.

I threw myself into all the grizzly details of the "Chicago Ripper" murders. It was disgusting and horrifying. I personally reviewed the case file and talked to experts on both sides of the capital punishment debate as well as the prosecutors who had convicted him. I checked and double-checked and triple-checked the facts. It became obvious throughout my office that I was deeply unsettled and unsure about a case that, to many people, was open-and-shut.

Meanwhile, I was inundated by people urging me to commute Kokoraleis's sentence. Letters were arriving daily from all over the world—Norway, Denmark, and Australia, to name a few—asking me, imploring me, to stop the execution. The letters, nearly five hundred, came handwritten in French, Japanese, German, and an array of other languages, apparently the result of the urgings of antideath penalty advocates such as the National Coalition to Abolish the Death Penalty and Amnesty International. Since January, I had received 492 letters on the death penalty—480 asking me to consider a moratorium on executions. Just twelve letters opposed a moratorium.

But no matter how hard I tried to focus just on Kokoraleis's case, I kept thinking over and over how Anthony Porter, a mentally-challenged man, came within two days of execution, and if not for those journalism students, would have been dead and buried—an innocent man. I had been jolted into reexamining everything I believed in.

Although Kokoraleis had been convicted of committing horrible crimes against women and I was the father of five daughters, I kept thinking about the mistakes the system had made with Porter. The more time I devoted to the case, the more unsure I became about what to do.

I agonized and felt unmoored.

# 6

# DEBATING DEATH

"This is not the case to make a point with. There are no doubts about this guy's guilt. In some ways, these guys were worse than Gacy."

Surrounded by aides, I stared at the speakerphone in the center of the conference table. Disembodied voices of staff members in Springfield were urging me to get on with it—sign off on Kokoraleis's death warrant. This wasn't the first time Kokoraleis was being compared to John Wayne Gacy, one of the worst serial killers in the nation's history.

We were sitting in my office on the sixteenth floor of the James R. Thompson State of Illinois Building in downtown Chicago. The building had opened in 1985 and was renamed after James R. Thompson in 1993, the governor who signed the Illinois death penalty legislation into law in 1977.

Early in March, Kokoraleis's execution had been temporarily halted on the order of Illinois Supreme Court Justice Moses Harrison II, an outspoken opponent of capital punishment. Harrison granted the delay so Kokoraleis's defense attorneys could take one last chance to ask the US Supreme Court to review an appeal.

We were now a week away from the execution, which was scheduled for March 17. Kokoraleis's defense attorneys had asked the US Supreme Court to halt the execution to review another appeal. Although there had been no ruling yet from the Supreme Court, the smart money was on a decision to let the execution go forward—which meant it would be irrevocably in my hands.

Lawyers for Kokoraleis also submitted a clemency petition to my office. His lawyers said there was reason to believe that Kokoraleis was innocent of the murder of Lorraine Borowski—although they did concede he was guilty of other killings. They noted that the only evidence that linked him to the murder was the confession he had recanted by the time he went to trial. Three of the eleven men who were exonerated from death row were said to have confessed—Gary Gauger, Rolando Cruz, and Alejandro Hernandez. The lawyers argued that Kokoraleis's confession didn't match the facts of the crime and that the results of a polygraph showed Kokoraleis was truthful when he said police beat him before he confessed.

Meanwhile, police, prosecutors, and victims' rights advocates were calling loudly for Kokoraleis to be put to death. And at the same time, I was getting a lot of pressure from the religious community to stop the execution, mostly led by Reverend Demetrios Kantzavelos, a Greek Orthodox priest (and later a bishop), who was the chancellor of the Greek Orthodox Diocese of Chicago.

Reverend Kantzavelos had become Kokoraleis's spiritual advisor and taken up Kokoraleis's cause after Kokoraleis reembraced his Greek Orthodox faith in prison. Reverend Kantzavelos had been joined by Cardinal Francis George, the head of the Archdiocese of Chicago. Reverend Kantzavelos was loudly urging that I delay the execution to allow a comprehensive study of the death penalty system.

I also had been reading studies. Lots of them. Pete Peters, who at the time was one of my oldest friends and a trusted advisor, was responsible for a growing mound of independent evidence on my desk aimed at convincing me that I ought to commute Kokoraleis's sentence and place a moratorium on the entire death penalty in Illinois.

In June of 1998, for example, the Death Penalty Information Center in Washington, DC, released a report entitled, *The Death Penalty in Black and White: Who Lives, Who Dies, Who Decides*. The study synthesized the research of three legal scholars and showed that evidence of racism against African Americans in the administration of the death penalty was less myth than reality and could be quantified with statistics. The report cited research of capital cases in Philadelphia, Pennsylvania, and found that the odds of receiving a death sentence were four times higher for African Americans than for white defendants after they were convicted of similar crimes. The center's report also pointed to a study that found that across the country, 98 percent of the chief prosecutors at the county level—state's attorneys, district attorneys, and similar positions—were white.

"The decisions about who lives and who dies are being made along racial lines by a nearly all-white group of prosecutors," the report concluded.

Peters stressed over and over that all I had to do was take a close look at the list of the eleven men who had served time while locked up on death row for crimes they did not commit—lifetimes wasted because of the errors of others. That list, he insisted, was proof enough that something was wrong with the death penalty in Illinois.

I instructed one of my aides to prepare a document that would grant Kokoraleis a ninety-day stay of execution. I wanted it ready should that be my decision. I had been saying that I was giving some thought to the idea of not signing the death warrant for Kokoraleis. I said several times, "I can't put someone to death."

This was causing a great stir among my assistants and staff. More than one person responded by saying, "You're not putting anyone to death, the legal system has determined his fate. You just have to get out of the way."

Among my staff, Peters led the opposition to Kokoraleis's execution. Pete was a former state legislator from Chicago and we had been allies on many issues and in many debates over the years. Pete was urging me to use the Kokoraleis case to send a larger message to the world about the injustice of capital punishment. The crimes committed by Kokoraleis were secondary, he maintained.

Among those leading the charge for execution was my chief counsel, Diane Ford. As deputy counsel when my predecessor, Jim Edgar, was governor, she had advised him on death penalty issues. Ten of the eleven executions since Illinois reinstated the death penalty had occurred under Edgar's watch—all conducted after he signed their death warrants and stood back as the executions were carried out. Ford, who had followed the Kokoraleis case as it wound its way through the complicated appeals system, had the support of Dave Urbanek, my press secretary and a former newspaper reporter, who as a journalist had written several news stories about the appellate challenges brought by Gecht, Spreitzer, and the Kokoraleis brothers. In their opinion, Kokoraleis *had earned* the death penalty.

Mediating the debate, as always in my office, was my chief of staff, Robert Newtson. Bob had been with me in various positions for more than twenty years, dating back to my days in the House of Representatives. Bob had always been a rock for me. He always told me what I needed to hear, whether I wanted to hear it or not. Bob told me he believed Kokoraleis was a very bad guy. But he also encouraged the discussion and debate to help me sort through things.

I have always liked to hear others talk about the issues, whether it was something facing the state or matters that affected my administration. Throughout my life, I probably spent most of every working day talking with people, either in person or on the telephone. The debate over Kokoraleis was no different. There had been weeks of give-and-take.

And now, it was coming to a head during this conference call. There was concern about how I would position myself if I signed the death warrant in light of all the exonerations of death row prisoners. Everyone there knew I was conflicted about what to do. And everyone had their own ideas about what to do. So, I let them talk.

"This is a chance to take a stand here that no other governor in this country has the guts to take—and you would be right," Peters declared. "No one will blame you if you call this off. You'll look like a hero."

"He can still be that hero," Newtson said. "Just not with this case. He can call a moratorium on all the other death sentences after this one if that's what he wants to do. But if he allows this to go ahead, then he'll have a certain amount of cover against the backlash from victims' rights groups and everybody in the Republican Party who will call him a coward and wonder what happened to a guy who ran as a tough-on-crime candidate."

"To hell with the Republican Party," Peters said. "I'm telling you that the good will and support he'll get from the clergy and from other quarters will more than make up for those guys. Half of them run the other way when they see their own shadow. I'm talking about taking the lead on a national issue."

"But Pete, you've got to take the crime into account," Newtson declared. "We have showed the case to some of the legislators in the House who are the biggest supporters of a death penalty moratorium. They don't want to touch this one. They don't care. This guy is not their poster boy! They're not going to go after George if Kokoraleis dies."

The call ended without resolution.

# 7

# THE EXECUTION

On March 11—six days before the scheduled execution—Reverend Kantzavelos testified at a clemency hearing for Kokoraleis before the Illinois Prisoner Review Board asking for mercy as did Kokoraleis's lawyers. Opposing clemency were the prosecutor who obtained the conviction and Lorraine Borowski's parents.

It was an emotional affair.

"It has been just short of seventeen years that our daughter, Lorry Ann, walked the face of the earth for the last time because Andrew and his satanic crew decided to make sure of it," Raymond Borowski declared. "And now it's his turn to take that final walk, a more humane one than that which was afforded Lorry. We have suffered enough. All the years of pain, depression, and anger should end. We are anticipating some relief from the tremendous pressure we have encountered during these trying years."

Borowski's mother, also named Lorraine, said, "Thanks to Andrew Kokoraleis, our daughter's voice cannot be heard today. Lorry cannot tell of the agony she endured, the pain she felt, the fear and trembling she sustained at the hands of this monster."

DuPage County First Assistant State's Attorney John Kinsella urged the board to reject Kokoraleis's request for clemency. "Stephen King could not dream up crimes like this," Kinsella said. He added that even John Wayne Gacy's thirty-three murders paled before the "indescribably evil" torture and mutilations of the Ripper Crew.

Kathy Kelly, one of Kokoraleis's lawyers, said that "just because he committed some of the murders does not mean he committed this one. That's against our whole system of justice. You don't execute someone for a crime they didn't commit because they committed another crime."

That argument had been rejected a day earlier by DuPage County Circuit Court judge Ann Jorgensen as well as Illinois Attorney General Jim Ryan.

Joining Reverend Kantzavelos in opposing the execution were Cardinal Francis George of the Catholic Archdiocese of Chicago and Joseph Tobias of the American Jewish Congress. They cited their opposition to the death penalty and Tobias noted that a legislative proposal to suspend executions for a year was still pending in the Illinois House of Representatives. "How fearfully awful if on March 17 Andrew Kokoraleis was executed and then the moratorium was put in place?"

At the end of the hearing, the board met and sent their recommendation to me—the vote was no to clemency.

Meanwhile, the business of being governor had to go on, even if it involved the mundane.

On Saturday, March 13, I was in Chicago marching in the 44th annual St. Patrick's Day parade, walking down Dearborn Street with Mayor Richard Daley as well as my lieutenant governor Corinne Wood, Attorney General Jim Ryan, Treasurer Judy Baar Topinka, and Secretary of State Jesse White. The Chicago St. Patrick's Day parade is a must for any politician, and I never missed it.

The following day, I was back in Springfield for the 43rd annual Sons and Daughters of Erin Dinner at the Knights of Columbus Hall on Meadowbrook Road.

On Monday, March 15, the day began with Illinois Supreme Court Justice Moses Harrison II issuing a stay of execution until the US Supreme Court ruled on the pending petition for a stay. But later that day, as I was heading back to Chicago for the American Jewish Committee's Judge Learned Hand award dinner, the Illinois Supreme Court voted four to three to overturn Harrison's stay.

That night, while I was at a Republican fund-raising event in Chicago, I learned that Republican State Representative Dan Rutherford of Chenoa, Illinois, who I had known for two decades, had conducted his annual tour for legislators and the media at the two prisons in his district—Dwight Correctional Center and Pontiac Correctional Center. And, I learned that Rutherford had been listening at Pontiac when reporters for the *Bloomington Pantagraph* newspaper had spoken to Kokoraleis. When I spotted Rutherford at the fund-raiser, I sent an aide to ask him to come to my table. As he knelt on one knee beside me, I peppered him with questions, looking for any last-minute intelligence that might help me reach a final decision.

"Danny," I said. "I understand you talked to Kokoraleis today. What was he like? Did he seem like he was remorseful?"

Rutherford explained that he had not spoken with Kokoraleis but was listening as the reporters conducted a brief interview with him. "I did not feel that," Rutherford said. "I do feel that he had resigned himself to what appears to be inevitable."

I nodded and Rutherford returned to his table. Not long after, I asked that he come back. Again, he knelt beside me. "Was he angry, Danny?" I asked.

"No," Rutherford said. "He was calm."

On Tuesday, while I was meeting with Heriberto Galindo, the consul general of Mexico, to talk about trade issues, Illinois Supreme Court Chief Justice Charles E. Freeman issued a statement saying that the court finished its formal conferences without ruling on a separate emergency motion to block executions filed by a group of legislators who opposed the death penalty.

"There are serious questions still to be resolved in connection with that petition, one of which is whether the petitioners have standing to bring the motion in this court," Freeman said.

Later in the day, the US Supreme Court refused to hear Kokoraleis's case. His appeals were finally exhausted.

Reverend Kantzavelos held a press conference at the Annunciation Greek Orthodox Cathedral to issue a plea directly to me. "We appeal to the governor's God-given conscience and humanity to commute the sentence from death by lethal injection to life in prison," he declared. Joining him was Dennis Williams, who had been exonerated from death row in Illinois in 1996. "I'm glaring evidence you need a moratorium on the death penalty in Illinois," he said.

Meanwhile, at Pontiac Correctional Center, inmates on death row heard the sounds of loud police radios and chains clanging on the concrete floor. The guards had come to transfer Kokoraleis to the Tamms Correctional Center in one of the deepest regions of Illinois. He was ordered to get dressed and to pack up any medications he would need for the day.

"Are you sure about this?" Kokoraleis asked. He was then told, for the first time, about the US Supreme Court's last decision.

His execution was back on.

Even so, Kokoraleis had good reason to believe I might halt it. He knew—everybody knew—that I was mightily affected by the high number of death row inmates who had been exonerated and freed from prison.

The numbers had become a mantra. Eleven had been exonerated. Eleven had been killed.

What kind of record is that?

For those exonerated, there had been new evidence clearing them or egregious mistakes at trial or incredibly bad defense lawyering. In addition, there were numerous media reports of inmates who were *still* on death row and claiming innocence because Chicago police detectives had tortured them to falsely confess to murders. This was real torture—electric shock machines hooked up to genitals, naked bodies pressed against scorching hot radiators, plastic bags pulled over their heads, and shotgun barrels placed in their mouths.

Kokoraleis was escorted in handcuffs and shackles onto a state plane and flown to Tamms. Until it was closed in 2012—because of state budget constraints—Tamms Correctional Center was unique among Illinois prisons. When it opened in 1995 with two hundred beds, it was the newest of the state's maximum-security facilities by more than one hundred years. Tamms was a state-of-the-art, computer-controlled penal showcase nestled against a hill on the edge of the giant Shawnee National Forest. The computer system allowed guards to control the prison without any physical contact with inmates—in effect, those confined here would have no human contact for the duration of their sentence. Tamms was among a handful of prisons nationwide that were constructed as "supermax" prisons, institutions designed to house the "worst of the worst"—gang leaders that persisted in running their criminal enterprises from their cells; chronic troublemakers; and inmates who posed a real danger to other inmates.

Kokoraleis, like all inmates arriving at Tamms, was processed through a reception area that resembled a warehouse loading dock and then was immediately escorted to solitary confinement.

Like all states with the death penalty, the Illinois Department of Corrections had developed a rigid set of procedures and rules to follow during an execution. Everything was planned down to the last detail. Witnesses, including members of the media, prosecutors, police, and relatives of the victims, would watch the execution through a window in front of the death chamber.

Corrections officials informed me that when the curtains shielding the window opened, onlookers would see the condemned lying on a gurney covered by a sheet pulled up to the neck. The order of execution—the one that was literally in front of me—would be read aloud. The inmate would be given an opportunity to say any last words. At the mandated time, a pump would start pushing a lethal cocktail of chemicals into the condemned. The first drug, sodium thiopental, would put the condemned to sleep. The second, pancuronium bromide, would paralyze the lungs. The third, potassium chloride, would stop the heart. Once the prisoner was declared dead, the curtains would close. The body would be removed and turned over to family members, if they wanted it. Unclaimed bodies were buried in a prison graveyard.

Corrections officials would then publicly report the basic facts about the execution and repeat any last words stated by the condemned. Any other details, including the reactions of witnesses, had to come from the witnesses themselves, if they chose to speak to the media.

This clinical approach had worked well for prior executions—even the media circus at Stateville Correctional Center in Joliet, Illinois, when John Wayne Gacy was executed for killing thirty-three young men and boys. The execution of Kokoraleis, if I let it go ahead, would be the first to be conducted at Tamms.

And so now, it was in my hands. The court appeals were exhausted. Only a gubernatorial order could delay the execution. I had never in my life felt such a weight on my shoulders.

In the end, after considering everything both sides brought to the table and after praying about it—I am a Methodist—I concluded that Kokoraleis deserved the sentence he got. I signed his death warrant because it was the right thing to do. I focused on the crime more than on the person or the process. I decided that Andrew Kokoraleis was not the case for stopping the death penalty.

Still, after all that had transpired in the prior ten weeks and all that had been said during the extensive and often heated discussions, I think there was more than a little surprise among my staff when I ordered the release of a statement saying that I would not stand in the way of Kokoraleis's execution.

At the same time, I remained troubled about all the exonerations of innocent men who had been sentenced to death. The word "maybe" resonated constantly, although I had concluded there was no possible way Kokoraleis was innocent.

My statement, issued on March 16, 1999, was concise and direct.

> I must admit it is very difficult to hold in your hands the life of any person, even a person who, in the eyes of many, has acted so horrendously as to have forfeited all right to any consideration of mercy.
>
> I have struggled with the pleas of our clergy and others who ask that I commute or stay the execution of Andrew Kokoraleis. I have struggled with the anguish that I know is part of each and every day for the family and friends of his victims; those who look for justice.
>
> I have struggled with this issue of the death penalty and still feel that some crimes are so horrendous and so heinous that society has a right to demand the ultimate penalty.
>
> To me, all the evidence at hand indicates that Andrew Kokoraleis is guilty of the gruesome murder of Lorraine Borowski. A jury has decided his fate according to the law of the land. His repeated attempts to appeal the verdict and his sentence have been considered and rejected many times by state and federal courts over the last 16 years.
>
> Accordingly, I will not stand in the way or alter the verdict or sentence handed down in this case.

Kokoraleis spent much of his last day praying, fasting, and calling a few select friends to tell them goodbye. As he talked to one of his brothers, he prayed and wept. He wrote a letter to Reverend Kantsavelos thanking him for his support and expressing hope that God would use his execution to end capital punishment.

That evening, as the prison staff prepared him for the short trip from a holding cell to the death chamber, he still wondered if the telephone would ring.

The telephone was on the wall of the death chamber at Tamms. It was a telephone that I could call to stop the execution at any time—even if Kokoraleis was strapped on the gurney and hooked up to the intravenous feed that would deliver the fatal mix of drugs. I had the number on a piece of paper in my pocket.

The execution was scheduled for midnight. I usually go to bed around 10:00 p.m., but that night Lura Lynn and I had a late dinner in the private quarters at the Executive Mansion in Springfield. We turned on the television and prepared to stay up. It was a sober evening. We spoke little, each keeping private counsel with our thoughts. Lura Lynn knew I was tense and anxious. I tapped the remote control as if I were sending Morse code, flipping through the cable channels from my easy chair. I kept hoping to find something that would distract me, but it was hopeless. My thoughts kept going back to what was going on in Tamms.

I told my staff I did not want to make a live appearance before the media. I made it clear that deciding to kill a man—even a serial murderer—was not a heroic act that should be trumpeted to score political points. I knew that if I didn't stop the execution and Kokoraleis was executed, the media would focus on Tamms. If I let him live, all eyes and ears would shift to where I was in Springfield. I would not make a last-minute call to the execution chamber.

A little before midnight, I called Newtson, who had remained in his office at the Capitol. He said corrections officials told him they would call him and give a verbal report after the execution.

"Do you think I did the right thing, Bob?" I asked. "Was this the right thing to do?" Even at the last minute I found myself reaching for assurance.

"He was a bad guy, George," he said softly. "This is the right decision."

Midnight passed. Ten minutes. Fifteen minutes. Thirty minutes. Forty-five minutes. The wait was excruciating. I wondered if something had gone wrong.

Finally, a few minutes before 1:00 a.m., the telephone rang.

"It's over," Newtson said. "He died about thirty-five minutes after midnight. There were no problems."

I breathed a sigh of relief.

"Before he went under, he apologized to the Borowski family and said that the kingdom of heaven was at hand," Bob said. "And then it was over."

"Thank you, Bob," I said.

"Get some sleep, George," he replied. "It's all over."

I said goodnight and hung up. I knew Bob was wrong. For me, it was just the beginning.

This had been one of the most difficult periods and one of the most difficult decisions of my life. I didn't get any sense of satisfaction or relief. Andrew Kokoraleis was a very, very bad guy. But I still was unsettled. There was the vague feeling—which would become very powerful over time—that this execution did not advance anything. It certainly did not bring his victims back. It was revenge, pure and simple.

And I figured that in the future not all the death penalty cases that would reach my desk were going to be like this one. Not all the cases would have the sort of overwhelming evidence that convinced a jury to sentence Kokoraleis to death.

I went to bed, but barely slept.

The eleven people who had been exonerated kept running through my mind. The evidence in those cases had led to convictions and death sentences too. But then, later, along came evidence that pointed to their innocence. How long does that take? How long must one wait?

I was certain that those eleven men exonerated and removed from death row were not going to be the last.

That night was the most emotionally draining night of my life. In the end, it was up to me to be the person who figuratively had to pull the switch.

That, I thought, was too much to ask of one person. Down the road, I would discover this wasn't just a one-night experience. And I learned that when you're responsible for putting a person to death, it sticks with you.

# 8

# ANOTHER EXONERATION

Before I ever heard of Andrew Kokoraleis or gave any serious thought to the death penalty, I thought my time as governor largely would focus on my plans to rebuild the state's infrastructure, expand the economy, and open up trade possibilities. But now, the death penalty began to increasingly dominate my time more and more as the year wore on.

My experience as the last court of appeal for a condemned man was personally gut-wrenching and mentally exhausting. But with Kokoraleis dead, I began to focus even more on the eleven men who had been executed before him. I wondered about the process in those cases and whether it had been corrupted or riddled with legal mistakes. The system I had placed my confidence in seemed full of flaws.

As I undertook my review, I certainly never forgot that I was the guy that put Kokoraleis to death. The night of the execution came back vividly when I learned that as prison guards were wheeling him into the death chamber, Kokoraleis was in a forgiving mood.

He told the execution team he understood my decision to let the execution go forward and that he wasn't angry with me. In fact, he said he forgave me for not stopping the execution. I'm a religious man—I pray every day. But still, that felt kind of odd. He's forgiving me? I was sure of his guilt. There was no question in my mind about that. What I wasn't sure about was the death penalty.

*Andrew Kokoraleis*, in one of his last breaths, forgave *me*.

That would ever stick in my mind.

By early summer, Kokoraleis, his crimes, and his fate had largely faded from public view as many news stories eventually do. As I had expected, police, prosecutors, and victims' rights advocates praised my decision to allow the execution as justice being served: a serial killer and rapist had gotten his just deserts—like Gacy had five years before. Death penalty opponents said they were disappointed that I believed that justice could be served by taking a life for a life. But at the same time, I think the death penalty opponents began to sense that the atmosphere was changing after, and perhaps even because of, my attention to the Kokoraleis case.

Eleven men had preceded Kokoraleis to the death chamber in Illinois and all the death warrants were signed by men, who were, like me, Republican governors.

The first execution, that of Charles Walker, who volunteered to be put to death, was overseen by my good friend Jim Thompson of Chicago. The others occurred during the administration of Thompson's successor, Jim Edgar of Charleston, a college town in East-Central Illinois. Thompson was unusual among politicians in Illinois because he had no political experience prior to gaining the state's top job. The first and only elective office he had ever sought was governor. He built up his political muscle as a corruption-busting US attorney for the Northern District of Illinois, which included Chicago. During his fourteen years in office, there were few pieces of anticrime legislation or new laws lengthening prison sentences that Thompson didn't support or sign into law. In 1977, at the beginning of his tenure, Thompson had signed into law the reinstatement of the state's death penalty.

So, it was a given in 1990—at the end of his administration—that Thompson would not stand in the way of Walker's execution. If an ex-con who murdered a young couple for a measly twenty dollars in beer money wanted to end his life, as Walker did, Thompson would not throw any moral roadblocks in his way.

Edgar, like me a former member of the Illinois House and Illinois secretary of state, had few qualms with the death penalty. He had been elected to a second term as governor in 1994 partly on the strength of a relentless advertising campaign that labeled his Democratic opponent, State Comptroller Dawn Clark Netsch, as "soft on crime."

It wasn't surprising to anyone following Illinois criminal justice issues in the 1990s, that when inmates sentenced to die more than a decade prior started to run out of opportunities to appeal their sentences, Jim Edgar barely thought twice about it and did nothing to stop most executions, with one notable exception. In 1996, Edgar commuted the sentence of Guinevere Garcia just fourteen hours before she was scheduled to die for killing her husband. Garcia, who would have been the first woman executed in Illinois in fifty-seven years, had suffered a life of alcoholism and sexual molestation and she had said she wanted to be executed. Edgar said Garcia's crime did not justify execution and that her husband's murder was not premeditated.

I believe I handled the Kokoraleis case and the larger question of the existence of a death penalty system differently than Thompson or Edgar. I not only spent more time focusing on it, but I also agonized over it—privately and publicly.

There was a larger debate than saying yes or no to a single execution.

As I said on the day I signed the death warrant for Kokoraleis: "The real issue for discussion is whether or not our society continues to approve of the death penalty as a legitimate means for society to ensure justice. I ask the citizens of Illinois for your prayers that I have acted wisely and in the interests of our state and in the interests of justice. I find no comfort in this position."

I think my shifting attitude on the death penalty surprised a great many people. It didn't sound like the George Ryan they knew—or thought they knew.

In the days after Kokoraleis's execution, it seemed as if Illinois had gone task force crazy. First, Illinois Attorney General Jim Ryan announced he had put together a twenty-six-member group to study the death penalty. Two days after that, the Illinois Senate's top Democrat—my old friend Emil Jones—formed a seventeen-member task force to reform the criminal justice system. "We need to have qualified individuals take a close look at the criminal justice system and provide us with a proposal that could be the basis to reform and improve the system," said Jones, the Senate minority leader. The Illinois House then formed a task force of its own.

At the same time, Coy Pugh, a democratic state representative, reissued a call for a six-month moratorium on the death penalty while the review took place. Pugh, who was himself an ex-convict represented a district on the South Side of Chicago where numerous convicted felons who had served their time now resided. His district also contained many families with relatives still in prison and many young people who unfortunately were destined for gang life and prison.

My spokesman, Dave Urbanek, issued a statement saying that I opposed a six-month moratorium. "At the end of that period, will Coy Pugh be satisfied if executions are allowed to continue? I don't think so," Urbanek declared.

And then, on April 6, Illinois Supreme Court Justice Charles Freeman announced the court would form its own committee to study the death penalty. This group was comprised of seventeen trial court judges. "Even the best system can be improved upon," Freeman said. "But improvements cannot be made without the dissemination of constructive and critical comment."

Two things are worth noting: all these groups were going to talk about improving the death penalty system, not abolishing it. And there was no sense of urgency. Ryan's group met once, did not reach any conclusions, and was not clear whether it would meet again. Emil's committee wasn't going to meet until later in the spring and the House task force wasn't going to convene until after the legislative session ended in June. Justice Freeman's committee had no timetable.

Justice James Heiple called Justice Freeman's move "a public relations gesture, pure and simple." He added, "So far as procedures and process are concerned . . . it is doubtful if any area of the law has received more intense and careful scrutiny over such a long span of time. It would be difficult, perhaps impossible, to say anything new or different on the subject."

Heiple suggested Freeman was playing to the media. "A common topic of discussion among Supreme Court members is how they can be made to look good in the press," he said. "A bandwagon psychology has developed, and the Supreme Court doesn't want to be left off the wagon."

The Illinois State's Attorney's Association pushed back. "If the law stays as it is today, and there is not one more 'i' dotted, this association does not believe that a moratorium would be appropriate," declared association president Kevin Lyons, chief prosecutor in Peoria County.

Task forces or not, the machinery of death continued its schizophrenic operation on May 17. Ronald Jones became Illinois death row exoneration number twelve when Cook County prosecutors dismissed rape and murder charges against him. Jones had been convicted in 1989 of the 1985 rape and murder of twenty-eight-year-old Debra Smith on the South

Side of Chicago. Her body was discovered in an alley, and a trail of blood led back to the abandoned Crest Hotel. Detectives believed that the thirty-four-year-old Jones had assaulted her and then took her into the alley where she died. About ten weeks later, a woman reported she had been raped at knifepoint. Ultimately, she had identified Jones as her attacker. Jones was arrested, but released because the prosecutor, although believing that Jones was guilty, deemed the evidence insufficient.

Because of the similarities in the two attacks, Jones was picked up again in October 1985. Following an eighteen-hour interrogation, he signed a confession that he immediately recanted. He consistently maintained it had been beaten out of him by Chicago police detectives. Jones testified at his 1989 trial that one of the detectives struck him with a "small black object, about six inches long." A photo of a bump on his head was shown to the jury. Police asserted the confession was voluntary and a physician testified that the lump was "a textbook picture of a sebaceous cyst."

Forensic tests included Jones as a "possible" source of semen recovered from the victim and prosecutors argued that it was in fact his. After the jury found Jones guilty, Cook County Circuit Court Judge John E. Morrissey sentenced him to sixty years for aggravated sexual assault and to death for murder. The Illinois Supreme Court affirmed the conviction in 1993.

In 1994, Jones sought DNA testing. Judge Morrissey refused to grant it, asking Jones's lawyer: "What issue could possibly be resolved by DNA testing?" When his lawyer, Dick Cunningham, responded that prosecutors originally had contended Jones was the source of the semen recovered from the victim, Morrissey told him, "Save arguments like that for the press. They love it. I don't."

However, the Supreme Court disagreed and overturned Morrissey in 1995. The testing went forward and in 1997, Jones was excluded as the source of the semen. Prosecutors waited nearly two years before dismissing the charges.

And just like that, the tally was even—twelve men had been executed and twelve men had been exonerated.

Two weeks later, Illinois House Speaker Mike Madigan, a Chicago Democrat, announced yet another task force. This committee was assigned the job of studying legislation requiring videotaping of confessions.

In August, I signed a bill that the General Assembly had enacted that one of its principal sponsors, Republican Representative James Durkin, a former prosecutor, asserted would "go a long way to restore the faith in the criminal justice system in the people of the State of Illinois." The legislation created a Capital Litigation Trust Fund to make funding available for the prosecution and defense of capital cases. The fund would use state money for extraordinary attorneys' fees as well as for investigators, expert witnesses, and forensic testing. Estimates put the cost as high as $20 million annually. The desired effect was to expand the imposition of the death penalty. Since being enacted in 1977, defendants in just fifty-five of the state's 102 counties had been sentenced to death. Republican senator Carl Hawkinson, also a former prosecutor and a sponsor of the bill, said that some counties had not sought the death sentence because it was too expensive.

"This bill is about seeking truth," Hawkinson said. "It's about equal justice under the law. It's about making sure that adequate resources are available at the trial court level not only to the defense, but also to the prosecution."

The measure had passed the House and Senate unanimously.

At about the same time, the Illinois Supreme Court also enacted new rules establishing minimum standards of experience for attorneys representing capital defendants, requiring special training for judges involved in capital litigation, and laying down ethical rules for prosecutors. These particularly noted that the job of a prosecutor was to seek justice—not win convictions.

The House task force met in late August and only four of the ten members showed up. Among the witnesses testifying was Bud Welch, whose daughter died in the bombing of the Oklahoma City federal building in 1995. "As long as we have juries, judges, and attorneys that are human beings, we are going to make mistakes," Welch said. "And we cannot make mistakes when it comes to taking someone's life."

Afterward, the task force chairman, James Brosnahan, a former Cook County prosecutor who was elected to the House as a Republican in a district in a Chicago suburb, noted that abolition was not on the table. He said that, like him, most of the legislators supported capital punishment. Brosnahan's task force met again in September where speakers included Sister Helen Prejean, whose book *Dead Man Walking* detailed her experiences counseling death row inmates in Louisiana, and Cardinal Francis

George, Catholic archbishop of Chicago. Both testified in opposition to the death penalty. Both were reminded that the purpose of the task force was not abolition.

The most emotional testimony came from U'reka Winder. The *Chicago Tribune* reported her as saying, "When I was six, two men came into my house and killed my whole family. They killed my mom, my sister, my mom's friend and they left me for dead."

Winder said one of the two men had been executed after the other was sentenced to life in prison. "I don't have a mom. I've got a big giant scar on my stomach, and I can't have a baby," she sobbed. "I feel as if they killed me. I don't know how anybody can consider that not using it is okay."

# 9

# SYSTEMIC FAILURE

In November, the *Chicago Tribune* published a series of articles titled "The Failure of the Death Penalty in Illinois," which examined every death penalty conviction in the state since the reinstatement of the death penalty in 1977.

The articles were deeply unsettling.

"Capital punishment is a system so riddled with faulty evidence, unscrupulous trial tactics and legal incompetence that justice has been forsaken," the newspaper reported. "The *Tribune* has identified numerous fault lines running through the criminal justice system, subverting the notion that when the stakes are the highest, trials should be failsafe."

*Tribune* reporter Steve Mills and Ken Armstrong reviewed 285 death row cases in Illinois and identified many of the same flaws that had contributed to death row exonerations not only in Illinois, but also across the nation. In the year since the conference at Northwestern, when the national tally of death row exonerees was seventy-four, the total had grown to eighty-four. Three of those exonerations were in Illinois.

The newspaper reported that 40 percent of the 285 Illinois death row convictions contained one or more of those red flags. Some had all of those dubious elements. The series was based upon an exhaustive analysis of appellate opinions and briefs, trial transcripts, and lawyer disciplinary records as well as interviews over several months with scores of witnesses, attorneys, and defendants. Their investigation found:

- At least thirty-three times, a defendant sentenced to die was represented at trial by an attorney who had been disbarred or suspended at some point—sanctions reserved for conduct so incompetent, unethical, or even criminal that the lawyer's license was taken away. In Kane County, an attorney was suspended for incompetence and dishonesty, but in 1997, ten days after his law license was reinstated, he was appointed to handle a death penalty defense.
- In at least forty-six cases, prosecutors relied upon a jailhouse informant—a form of evidence that had been proven time and time again to be unreliable.
- In at least twenty cases, the prosecution's case was based in part on a microscopic hair comparison, a category of forensic evidence that not only was unreliable but was frequently exaggerated or outright falsified by crime lab analysts. In one case, hair that was said to be human was subsequently discovered to be dog hair!
- Nearly two-thirds of the inmates on death row were black. In at least thirty-five cases, black defendants were convicted or sentenced by all white juries.

As an example of a case that contained all of these flaws, the newspaper cited the case of four black men—known as the "Ford Heights Four"—who had been convicted and exonerated in 1996 by DNA testing following another investigation by Northwestern University journalism students.

Kenneth Adams, Dennis Williams (who had urged me to commute Kokoraleis's death sentence), Willie Rainge, and Verneal Jimerson were convicted of sexually assaulting and murdering twenty-three-year-old Carol Schmal and murdering her fiancé, twenty-nine-year-old Lawrence Lionberg. Williams and Jimerson were sentenced to death. Rainge was sentenced to life in prison without parole. Adams was sentenced to seventy-five years. Their convictions were based on part on the testimony of Paula Gray, a seventeen-year-old mildly intellectually-disabled woman who testified that she held up a lighted disposal lighter while the four men raped Schmal seven times. Williams was sentenced to die by an all-white jury after he was convicted on evidence that included a jailhouse informant and hair comparison. His defense attorney was later disbarred.

The case of the "Ford Heights Four" was one that just screamed injustice, practically from top to bottom. Years after the convictions,

Northwestern University journalism students like the ones that later helped free Anthony Porter, began working on the case. They discovered a police file that revealed that within a week of the crime, a witness told police that they had the wrong men. The report said this witness also knew who committed the crime because he heard gunshots and saw four men run away from where the crime occurred. The next day, the report added, the witness saw these same four men selling items taken from the robbery of the victims. None of those four men were Adams, Williams, Rainge, or Jimerson.

After I met Rob Warden, he gave me a copy of his 1998 book, coauthored with David Protess, *A Promise of Justice*, which recounted how Williams and Rainge got a new trial because their defense lawyer was incompetent. At the retrial in 1987, which ended in convictions again, prosecutor Scott Arthur had countered defense arguments by saying: "Maybe the police made up all this evidence. . . . That's too far-fetched. If you find the defendants innocent . . . . Do it because you believe the police framed these men—because that's what you would have to believe now."

Following the journalism students' discoveries, Williams, Adams, Rainge, and Jimerson were exonerated and three of the real killers—men who had been identified at the time of the crime—were convicted. The fourth man who had been identified had died by then.

DNA, I was learning, was an incredibly powerful tool in the criminal justice system. Originally used by the prosecution to confirm guilt, defense lawyers quickly realized it had the power to exclude the innocent as well.

The first two DNA exonerations in the United States occurred in 1989, and one of them—Gary Dotson—was in Illinois. The Dotson case was hugely important in the evolution of the innocence movement. Just three years later, in 1992, Barry Scheck and Peter Neufeld cofounded the Innocence Project in New York City to focus solely on exonerating defendants with DNA testing. In 1996, the Ford Heights Four exonerations had increased the total of DNA exonerations nationwide to thirty-nine. Ronald Jones, who was exonerated just months earlier, was the eighth man to walk off death row in the United States as a result of DNA testing. The first had been Kirk Bloodsworth in 1993 in Maryland.

After Adams, Williams, Rainge, and Jimerson were released, my predecessor, Governor Jim Edgar granted them pardons. Just before Kokoraleis was executed, the Ford Heights Four settled their federal lawsuit against Cook County for $36 million in damages—at the time the largest wrongful conviction settlement in US history.

Although I did not favor a moratorium, I still had questions. My unease was centered on the fairness of the system in Illinois. I had supported the concept of the death penalty, or at least I thought I did, but it was becoming clearer that the process used to determine who the state was going to kill didn't meet the highest of standards that should be met. The outcome of the process, the conclusion, was irreversible, so as far as I was concerned, there should be no room for error. Yet there were errors all over the place in Illinois.

The issue was further complicated by the emotion that is attached to capital punishment. When you get past the black-and-white of the law, emotions on both sides take over. And there were compelling stories on both sides of the argument. In my mind, I went back and forth every time I was confronted with another horrid crime that prompted family and friends of the victim to scream that justice required the death penalty. And then just as quickly there would be another capital case that screamed injustice and incompetence on the part of police and prosecutors.

The false confession of Ronald Jones was troublesome to me. In the background was Jon Burge, who had been a Chicago Police Department lieutenant when he was fired by the City of Chicago in 1993. Burge, a decorated Vietnam veteran, had been in charge of a violent crimes detective unit that covered a large portion of the city's South Side.

The unraveling of Jon Burge and the detectives who worked under him was preceded by a horrible crime. On February 9, 1982, officers William Fahey and Richard O'Brien made a traffic stop. One of two men in the car took Fahey's gun and shot him in the head and then shot O'Brien in the chest. Both officers died. They were the third and fourth officers killed in just a few weeks.

Five days after the shootings, police brought in two brothers, Andrew and Jackie Wilson, for questioning. Thirteen hours later, both confessed. Medical evidence would later show that Andrew Wilson had a torn retina, numerous bruises, burns on his chest and thighs, and other odd-shaped marks on his body.

They were tried together and both were convicted. Andrew Wilson was sentenced to death. Jackie was sentenced to life in prison without parole. The convictions were vacated by the Illinois Supreme Court. Andrew Wilson's conviction was vacated after the court held that his confession was the result of physical coercion. "The inescapable conclusion is that [Wilson] suffered his injuries while in police custody that day," the Court said. Jackie Wilson's conviction also was reversed on other grounds. Both were reconvicted and both were sentenced to life in prison without parole.

Andrew Wilson then sued the City of Chicago, Burge, and other detectives. During the proceedings, he testified that Burge and one of his detectives attached electroshock devices on his ears, fingers, nose, and his groin while he was handcuffed to rings on a wall next to a radiator that burned him.

Although detectives denied employing torture, other convicted inmates began recounting similar stories of physical torture, including claims that they had been "bagged," in which detectives put plastic bags over their heads to nearly suffocate them. Some inmates recalled mock executions in which they were driven to a remote area and a shotgun barrel was put in their mouths and they were told to confess or they would be killed.

Wilson was ultimately awarded $1 million. Over the next several years, more than one hundred men would raise claims that Burge and his men had tortured them. Burge and his officers had been suspended without pay for more than a year. In 1993, the detectives were reinstated. Burge was fired. (Andrew Wilson died in prison in 2010. Jackie Wilson, who asserted that Burge detectives put a gun in his mouth, beat him over the head with a phone book, used electroshock, and kicked him, was granted a new trial in 2019 and released.)

Meanwhile, more lawsuits were filed. Inmates who called themselves the "Death Row 10" accused Burge or his detectives of torture to force them to confess.

That was troubling to me. If people are on death row because of a tortured confession—something is not right. There is something wrong with a system that's willing to put someone to death and ignore these problems.

I had always believed that the police in general are good people and they've got an extraordinarily difficult job to do and they do what they have to do. But I also realized that they're human and they make mistakes and at times engage in gross misconduct. And I was putting it together that when it comes to the death penalty, you can't afford mistakes. You're talking about taking somebody's life.

Learning about Jon Burge and the torture of suspects with all kinds of almost medieval devices to confess to crimes—some of which they committed and some of which they didn't—was especially terrifying. It raised the question of who was guilty and who was innocent. After that, how can you tell?

The allegations of torture against Burge and others became the most troubling question surrounding the use of the death penalty in Illinois. This was police and prosecutors—there were prosecutors assigned to police stations—bending and breaking the rule of law and order to win a conviction. I kept wondering how Burge got away with what he did for so long. More worrisome was the question of whether Burge was a standalone problem or was he the tip of an iceberg?

But still, for every time I heard Burge's name and had to think about the effect his crimes had on the administration of justice, it wasn't long before my brain balanced it out with the memory of a horrendous murder case that started, literally, in my backyard in Kankakee in 1987.

# 10

# CLOSE TO HOME

Lura Lynn and I and our kids lived in a two-story home with a finished attic on a tree-shaded street in the Riverview neighborhood of Kankakee. Our house had a detached garage adjacent to an alley and a neighboring garage. That garage belonged to Steve Small, whose father and uncle had owned newspapers throughout Illinois, including the *Kankakee Daily Journal* as well cable companies and television stations. Steve's mother, Reva, had been a family friend for decades. Steve and his wife, Nancy, would babysit my children when Lura Lynn and I wanted a night out.

Steve was a husband and a father. He was a good businessman, owned the local radio station, and had a great number of interests in the community. Among those was the preservation of an old home that had been designed by Frank Lloyd Wright. Steve spent a lot of money on the home and employed a number of painters and laborers and others in the restoration project. He spared no expense in the effort, such as going to Europe to purchase special windows.

At about 12:30 a.m. on September 2, 1987, Steve got a telephone call at home warning him that someone had broken into the Wright house. The caller said he was a police officer and asked Steve to go down there to sign some papers. Steve got dressed and hurried out his back door to his garage. The police said he never made it to his car.

He was abducted by a local man named Danny Edwards who was an electrician and had worked on the Wright home. While working on the house, Edwards decided that Small was the perfect target for a get-rich-quick scheme. And although his intention was to release Steve after the money was paid, the plot soon went awry.

Edwards tied up Small and drove him to a secluded area in one of the farm fields outside of Kankakee. Steve was forced to get into in a box buried in a shallow pit. The box contained an electric light and a pump designed to keep fresh air flowing.

Around 3:30 a.m., a man called the Small residence and told Steve's wife, Nancy, "We have your husband." Nancy then heard her husband say that he had been handcuffed inside a box underground. Small told his wife to obtain $1 million in cash. Although the caller told Nancy not to report the matter to the police, she did anyway. Police attached equipment to the Small family telephone line to record incoming calls and determine the location of the caller.

At 5:03 p.m., the same man called again and asked Nancy how much money had been collected. Police determined this call was placed from a telephone located at a Phillips 66 gas station in the nearby city of Aroma Park. Witnesses recalled seeing a man there in the company of a blonde-haired woman.

At 5:40 p.m., Jean Alice Small, Steve Small's aunt, telephoned the Small residence. She said a male had called her and said that he knew that Nancy's phone line was tapped. The man told Jean that Steve was buried and threatened to kill Jean's husband.

The man called Nancy again at 11:28 p.m. This call was traced to a telephone at a Sunoco gas station in Aroma Park, where an FBI agent saw a white male at a telephone and a blonde-haired woman in a car that was later identified as belonging to Nancy Rish, who had blonde hair. Her boyfriend was Danny Edwards. This time, the caller played a tape recording of Steve Small's voice. On the tape, Steve provided instructions for delivering the ransom.

Nancy Small received one more telephone call from the kidnapper at 11:46 p.m., eighteen minutes later. The call was placed from a Marathon service station in Kankakee. The caller accused Nancy of having notified the police and refused her offer of the ransom. Minutes later, at 11:50 p.m., an Illinois state police officer saw Rish's car, with its trunk partly open, driving from Kankakee toward Aroma Park.

Law enforcement officers, who had Danny Edwards's home under surveillance, saw a dark-colored Buick, with its trunk partly open, arrive at the house in Bourbonnais where Edwards and Rish lived. Edwards and a white woman with blonde hair left the car and went inside.

Officers searched the home later that morning, September 3, and arrested Edwards. Later that day, he led law enforcement officers to the site where Small was buried. There, officers dug up a plywood box six feet long and three feet wide. Inside, they found Small's body.

A medical examiner later concluded that Small died of asphyxiation caused by suffocation. The medical examiner believed that Small probably did not survive more than three or four hours.

The search of the Edwards's residence turned up a Kankakee telephone book with the name "Small" circled. His boots were found behind a washer and dryer at the residence and soil on the boots was similar to a sample from the location where the box was buried as was soil in the Edwards's van. White caulking material on gloves found in his trash had the same chemical composition as the caulking material used to fill in the seams of the wooden box. His fingerprints were found on PVC pipe and duct tape recovered from the box.

In 1988, Edwards and Rish were convicted of murder and kidnapping. Edwards was sentenced to death. Rish was sentenced to life in prison without parole.

Before I was elected governor, I would talk about Steve Small's murder whenever the subject of the death penalty came up. Steve had been kidnapped practically in my own driveway—a stone's throw from my own back door. This murder was not like watching a sixty-second news report on television and then moving on to the latest news about the economy.

For my family, this was a murder that didn't go away. Every time we looked at the Small's garage and driveway, we were reminded of how my friend was killed in such a cruel and horrifying way. A young man with a family, Steve was murdered by an idiot. As far as I was concerned, Edwards deserved what he got.

But as the evidence of the precarious nature of the death penalty system continued to pile up, I found myself listening and learning.

Just before Thanksgiving, the Supreme Court's commission issued recommendations that included appointment of a screening panel to require minimum training and experience for both prosecutors and defense attorneys handling death penalty cases. Prosecutors would be required to give notice of their intent to seek the death penalty within 120 days after a defendant was arraigned. Defense attorneys would be allowed to question prosecution witnesses under oath prior to trial. In addition, the group recommended that police interrogations—not just the confessions—be videotaped.

On November 30, Representative Coy Pugh introduced a bill in the House calling for an eighteen-month moratorium on the death penalty and yet another commission. He noted that none of the task forces had produced any substantive changes—just recommendations from the Illinois Supreme Court's group. Earlier in the year, the House had passed Pugh's resolution seeking a six-month moratorium, but it went nowhere—just like an earlier attempt to get a bill passed requiring a moratorium and a resolution for a twelve-month moratorium.

I capped the year on December 28 appearing with Mayor Richard Daley to urge Republican state senators to break away from Senate president James "Pate" Philip and help restore the Safe Neighborhoods Act's provision that illegal use of a weapon was a felony, even for first-time offenders.

"You don't hunt deer or ducks with an Uzi or a Glock," I said.

It went for naught, however, the following day. I thought we had the votes, but then we discovered that two senators who had promised to vote for my compromise bill—one Democrat and one Republican—were on vacation. Philip realized we didn't have the votes and decided to call the bill for a vote. But just as he was getting ready to pound his gavel, the lights went out in the Senate. An hour later, the power was restored amid whispers of sabotage. The vote was taken and the bill was defeated.

"The criminals, the felons, the gunrunners, the gun dealers, the gangbangers all won today," I said. "And the honest people of Illinois, the law-abiding citizens of Illinois, lost."

The capital litigation fund and these other bills were good measures, I believed, even though the gun law did not pass. At the same time, I remained unconvinced that a moratorium on executions was the correct response. There was no sense of urgency anyway, there were no executions scheduled.

I didn't have another Andrew Kokoraleis looming before me.

# 11

# TIME TO ACT

Four days into 2000, Ronald Jones, who had been convicted and then exonerated of murder, asked me to grant him a pardon. The criminal justice system—or what appeared to be a system of injustice for some people—continued to be a constant presence in my life. I wondered if this was going to be a common request.

I had just completed my first year as governor during which I engineered passage of a $12 billion construction program (Illinois First) and the higher taxes and fees necessary to pay for it. Tough on crime bills had been enacted and because of my efforts, 51 percent of all new revenue was being funneled to education. We passed tuition tax credits for parents with students in private and public schools and health maintenance organization reforms.

I had visited Cuba—the first state governor to do so since Castro came into power there in 1959. Our delegation received approval as a humanitarian mission and hauled along $2 million worth of pharmaceuticals and medical and educational supplies. I spent seven hours with Castro and called for an end to the US trade embargo with Cuba. After a Cuban representative came and addressed the legislature, we became the only state at the time to pass a bill to urge Congress to end the embargo.

Two weeks after Jones asked for a pardon, Cook County prosecutors dismissed murder and armed robbery charges against Steve Manning, who had been sentenced to death in 1993, largely on the testimony of a notorious jailhouse informant named Tommy Dye as well as testimony from the victim's wife, who claimed that on the day her husband disappeared, he told her that if he didn't come home to call the FBI and blame Manning, his business partner.

In 1998, the Illinois Supreme Court had vacated Manning's conviction, ruling that the testimony from the victim's wife never should have been admitted and that the introduction of evidence of other crimes by Manning was unfairly prejudicial.

The *Chicago Tribune* had highlighted Dye in its series on Illinois death penalty cases. The newspaper said Dye was "a con man and chronic liar who fabricated stories even under oath and that his testimony incriminating Manning was undercut by the FBI's own investigative reports."

Dye testified at Manning's trial that the FBI had given him a body recorder to wear during conversations with Manning when both were in Cook County jail. Dye claimed that Manning had twice admitted he killed his business partner, but the alleged admissions were not on the tapes. The tapes had two gaps, which Dye said occurred at exactly the time when Manning made the admissions. That was either a mind-boggling coincidence or a huge and convenient lie.

The dismissal of the charges brought the total of death row inmates who had been exonerated since I voted "green" in 1977 to thirteen!

Twelve had been executed.

Then, on Thursday, January 27, 2000, the Illinois Supreme Court tossed out the conviction and death sentence of Murray Blue for killing a Chicago police officer with a bullet to the head and wounding another officer. The court ruled that even though the evidence of guilt was "overwhelming," the prosecutor in the case, James McKay, had egregiously overstepped his boundaries and made a naked appeal to the jury's emotions. He had wheeled in a headless mannequin clothed in the dead officer's uniform that was stained with blood and brain matter.

The ruling pushed the number of Illinois capital cases reversed for a new trial or sentencing hearing to 131, slightly more than half of the 261 death-penalty cases that had completed at least one round of appeals.

I wondered if this would ever stop.

My good friend and advisor, Pete Peters, had begun quietly advocating for a moratorium after the *Chicago Tribune* published the series exposing the deep fissures in the Illinois death penalty system. Meanwhile, the antideath penalty groups were issuing calls for moratoriums of varying lengths as well as for outright abolishment.

And Dennis Culloton, who was my media spokesman, also was working behind the scenes. Dennis had checked with our legal office to try to find out if a governor even had the power to declare a moratorium. No governor had done such a thing in the United States. Was it even possible?

It was.

In fact, the Illinois constitution gave me broad power to act in the interest of justice. Dennis had presented me with a one-page summary of the *Tribune* reporting, which concluded with the fact that I did have the power to declare a moratorium. I started reading the bullet points—thirteen inmates exonerated, inmates convicted solely by jailhouse snitches, lawyers who were disbarred or disciplined representing defendants, black defendants convicted by all-white juries—and after each one, I asked rhetorically, "How does that happen?"

That question, which sprang from me organically as a reaction to these stunning revelations, became the foundation of my speeches and public statements over the next three years. It sprang from my honest, immediate impression of the mess that was the criminal justice system. And really, it was a mess.

While we were sitting in my private office, my secretary came back and said that Attorney General Jim Ryan was on the phone.

"Cuz," I said, a name I used because we had the same last name, although we were not related.

Ryan got straight to the point. "There are more than ten death row inmates whose cases are in the pipeline," he said.

"Uh-huh, is that right?" I replied.

"Yes," he said. "They are either out of appeals or about to exhaust their last appeal."

Ryan paused.

"It's time to start setting some execution dates," he said.

"You might want to hold off on that," I told him. "I think I am going to have something to say."

And that is how it happened. I instructed my staff that we had to meet on an important and urgent matter—I wanted to declare a moratorium.

Dennis wanted me to approve giving advance notice to the *Chicago Tribune* so the paper could have an exclusive story in its Sunday edition about the forthcoming announcement. So, that Saturday afternoon, I gave

Dennis the nod to contact the *Tribune* and to plan for the Monday news conference at 10:00 a.m. As we were talking, I began chuckling.

"What's so funny?" Dennis asked.

"Pate's gonna love this," I laughed.

And so did Dennis.

Pate, of course, was Pate Philip, the architect of the defeat of the Safe Neighborhoods Act just a month earlier. Philip was deeply conservative and came from DuPage County, where death row exonerees Rolando Cruz and Alejandro Hernandez had been wrongly convicted.

On Monday at 10:00 a.m., I walked into the fifteenth floor conference room at the State of Illinois Building in Chicago. The room was packed with reporters. They knew what was coming. They just didn't know what the words were yet.

"I now favor a moratorium," I began. "Because I have grave concerns about our state's shameful record of convicting innocent people and putting them on death row. How do you prevent another Anthony Porter—another innocent man or woman from paying the ultimate penalty for a crime he or she did not commit? Today, I cannot answer those questions."

"I have grave concerns about our state's shameful record of convicting innocent people and putting them on death row," I continued. "It is a system so fraught with error and has come so close to the ultimate nightmare."

I said that while I still considered the death penalty a proper societal response to crimes that shock sensibility, I believed that Illinois residents were troubled by the persistent problems in the death penalty system. I called for a review of the system and said I would appoint a commission to undertake a full examination. "It's not going to be a stacked panel one way or the other.

"Until I can be sure that everyone sentenced to death in Illinois is truly guilty, until I can be sure with moral certainty that no innocent man or woman is facing a lethal injection, no one will meet that fate."

I pointed to the *Tribune* investigation. "Disbarred lawyers, jailhouse informants—those kinds of problems are in the system, and we've got to get them out," I said.

"There's going to be a lot of folks who are firm believers in the death penalty who may not agree with what I'm doing here today," I said. "But I am the fellow who has to make the ultimate decision whether someone is injected with a poison that's going to take their life."

I took note of the various task forces already studying the issue, saying, "As governor, I am ultimately responsible, and although I respect all that these leaders have done and I will consider all that they say, I believe that a public dialogue must begin on the question of the fairness of the application of the death penalty in Illinois."

And with that, Illinois marched into the history books. What I didn't realize was how much more history there was to write.

# 12

# LIGHTING THE COLOSSEUM

I knew the decision to impose a moratorium was significant, but the reaction caught me completely off guard.

In Rome, Italy, the lights at the ancient Colosseum shone golden in honor of my decision. This was the place where gladiators once fought to the death and it had become, to my surprise, a focal point of the antideath penalty movement. I learned that beginning in 1999, the Colosseum lights, which were usually white, were gold for a two-day period each time someone was spared execution or a country abolished the death penalty. Now, the lights were burning gold for the eighth time already this year. There were scores of demands to be interviewed by media in the United States and around the world, particularly in Europe, which had long ago banned the death penalty and considered us barbarians for continuing to exercise it.

My decision meant that Illinois was the first of the thirty-eight states with the death penalty to formally suspend executions. At least six states had considered the idea in 1999, but none had actually done it. Nebraska came the closest—a bill calling for a two-year moratorium was passed by the legislature, but Governor Mike Johanns vetoed it in May 1999, saying it was "poor public policy" and would only inflict more pain on the families of the victims. He said that a moratorium would "at a minimum be utilized to advance further unnecessary criminal appeals by those currently sentenced to death in Nebraska."

The reaction to my decision was mixed and some of it was expected.

Kirk Dillard, an Illinois Republican senator, said, "The person who stands behind the final lethal injection and the prison is George Ryan. He's the final stopper, and if he's not comfortable with the process, then I would support his efforts to have experts make him comfortable with the process.

"My guess is virtually every member of the Senate Republican caucus supports the death penalty," Dillard said. "And I don't know how any of us could oppose the governor wanting to make sure that the death penalty system, the most important cornerstone of Illinois criminal law, is working."

US senator Patrick Leahy, a Vermont Democrat and member of the US Senate Judiciary Committee who was preparing a package of death penalty reforms called my decision "courageous and timely." He predicted it would be a "catalyst for a similar review in Washington."

However, Illinois state senator Ed Petka, a Republican, said, "I believe in capital punishment and I think the quicker we get on with the business of getting rid of hard-core, cold-blooded killers who are truly guilty, the better."

The prevailing thought on the prosecution side seemed to be if someone was convicted erroneously, that's what the lengthy appeals process was for. The courts would catch the mistakes and right the wrongs in their own good time.

DuPage County State's Attorney Joe Birkett, who in 1995 had prosecuted Rolando Cruz a third time for the murder of Jeanine Nicarico despite the evidence that Brian Dugan was responsible for the crime, said, "By setting aside all executions, Ryan is standing in the way of victims' families seeing criminals put to death who have been found guilty beyond a reasonable doubt by the legal process. They have a constitutional right to be treated with dignity and respect." Birkett added, "There is no chance an actual innocent will be executed. It doesn't exist."

Ronald Tabak, a New York City attorney who headed up a death penalty committee at the American Bar Association (which had urged a national moratorium three years earlier), said, "When a conservative Republican governor in a large state with a large death row recognizes that there are so many systemic questions about the death penalty, it strongly buttresses the need for a moratorium in all the other states. As great a need as there is for a moratorium in Illinois, the need is even greater in Texas, Florida, Louisiana, and many other states."

Cook County Public Defender Rita Fry said, "I assume that he's doing it for all the right reasons. I think he realizes that this is an embarrassment to Illinois and that the system, while not perfect, could certainly be better. I think he's trying to do the right thing."

Dan Curry, a spokesman for Attorney General Jim Ryan, whose phone call about setting execution dates had spurred me to act, said that Ryan supported the idea of a moratorium. "Everyone is working toward the same goal," Curry said. "And if the governor believes the process should continue in an execution-free environment, the attorney general supports that."

Chris Lauzen, a conservative Republican Illinois senator, said that though he supported the death penalty, "What else could we do? Nobody wants to put innocent people on death row."

The moratorium received headlines everywhere; not because I wanted it to be or because I had mapped out a grand strategy to generate support for the issue, but because I came to realize there was a growing groundswell of uneasiness about the death penalty all across the country. But it had been a quiet unease because the supporters of the death penalty have always owned the debate. Being "tough on crime" and supporting the death penalty is always easier in the public debate because the opposing position is automatically "soft on crime," and nobody wants to be soft on crime.

Bill Ryan, head of the Illinois Death Penalty Moratorium Project, a coalition of antideath penalty groups and people, called the moratorium "a very courageous step. This says Illinois leadership is sensitive and has the courage to address its faults."

Larry Marshall, the Northwestern University law professor whose conference on the death penalty and whose personal counsel had helped me immensely, called my decision "a wonderful, wonderful statement" of my moral ground. "Even if a person looks guilty, he now knows from our lessons in Illinois that looks can deceive." Marshall added, however, "The real question is going to become: What happens? What does the commission look like and how seriously do they take their job?"

There certainly was no magic solution to the problems with the death penalty in Illinois, but I truly believed that a moratorium was a middle ground that was acceptable to abolitionists and more-or-less acceptable to law enforcement and victims' families.

We needed time to separate fact from fiction and take a thoughtful look at where we were and where we wanted to be.

I was hoping a moratorium would get the approval of the public simply because of the math—more men had been exonerated from death row than had been executed. Every time the issue drew media attention, the moratorium idea had been raised again and again and again. It had happened in the days leading up to the execution of Andrew Kokoraleis. It happened when Ronald Jones was exonerated. It happened when Steve Manning was exonerated. It happened when anyone in the United States was exonerated.

Still, I was fully aware that a moratorium was not universally welcomed, especially among some elected officials and some families of victims. Aside from African American and Hispanic lawmakers in the House and Senate, few legislators were interested in supporting a moratorium, even when confronted by the facts.

Some state's attorneys told the media the moratorium was unconstitutional and that I didn't have the authority under the Illinois Constitution to issue a blanket moratorium on all executions.

I knew I didn't have the authority to prevent the prosecutors from seeking the death penalty. I couldn't stop the courts from sentencing someone to death. And I couldn't stop the Illinois attorney general from scheduling an execution date.

But under the law, I still had to sign off on any and all executions. That was my power and mine alone. What I'd have to do was deal with each death case individually as it came to my desk. My position, simply, was that you send me one case with an execution date, I'll hold on to that and I won't sign the death warrant. You send me ten cases and I won't sign any of the ten death warrants. That's how it was from the get-go.

Even before I decided to impose a moratorium, I had decided I needed to hire an expert on criminal justice issues. So, I brought in Matthew Bettenhausen, a veteran of twelve years in the US Attorney's Office, as my deputy governor for public safety to oversee criminal justice and law enforcement policy. I wanted him for his knowledge and experience, and his first task was to organize the commission to study the death penalty system in Illinois.

A poll that had been commissioned in 1999 by the Death Penalty Education Project found that 70 percent of Illinois citizens supported a moratorium on executions. What was more, that support was broad-based. Not only did Democrats and self-described liberals support a moratorium, but so did Republicans and a lot of conservatives too. But prior to making my decision to declare a moratorium, I never consulted the opinion polls. That wasn't my concern. My concern was the system in Illinois. It was obviously riddled with error and the innocent were being convicted and condemned along with the guilty.

I knew we couldn't abolish it. I didn't have the votes and I couldn't get any more in the General Assembly. But as long as I had the executive power to say that we were going to stop the death penalty for a time and as long as I was governor, I was determined that there would be no more executions until we found out what was wrong with it and got it fixed.

I likened it to flying an airplane from Chicago to Boston. If we flew the airplane from Chicago to Boston seven days a week and it crashed four days out of a week, would we continue to send planes every week? The best thing to do would be stop the flights, identify the problem, and fix it.

I wanted the commission to take a critical look at the death penalty law and see how it was used, who it was used against, and to suggest reforms and changes for what wasn't working. The fourteen-member commission that Matt put together included prosecutors and defense attorneys. It also included the well-known—such as best-selling author Scott Turow, who was a former federal prosecutor and also had defended a death penalty case—and the virtually unknown—Roberto Ramirez, a Mexican immigrant who founded a commercial janitorial firm in a Chicago suburb.

Frank McGarr, former chief US district judge in Chicago, was the chair. The vice chairs were Paul Simon, who had served Illinois in the US Senate, and Thomas Sullivan, who had served as US attorney in Chicago and also was a veteran criminal defense attorney.

I decided at the outset to give them a lot of latitude, including the authority to recommend abolition. With Bettenhausen's help, we purposely structured the commission to eliminate, as much as possible, any belief that the outcome of the panel's work was a foregone conclusion that would just back up what I already had done.

On March 7, 2000, the *Chicago Tribune* reported that a poll it had commissioned showed that support for the death penalty in Illinois had dropped from 75 percent in 1994 to 63 percent in 1999 to 58 percent in 2000. The numbers on the death penalty versus life in prison without parole were even starker: 43 percent supported the death penalty and 41 percent supported life without parole.

Two days later, I held a press conference in Chicago to announce what we called the Death Penalty Moratorium Commission.

"The system has proved to be so fraught with error that thirteen innocent people almost faced the ultimate nightmare of being wrongly convicted of a crime for which they had been sentenced to die," I said. "I can draw only one conclusion: our system is broken."

I introduced or described the members of the commission, including former federal judge and FBI and CIA director William Webster. "His name is synonymous with integrity and public service," I said.

I ticked off the names in addition to Simon, McGarr, Turow, Sullivan, and Ramirez. Cook County public defender Rita Fry, Lake County state's attorney Michael Waller, chief of staff for the Chicago police (and former Cook County prosecutor) Thomas Needham, criminal defense attorney (and former Cook County prosecutor) William Martin, private attorney Donald Hubert, Illinois state appellate defender Theodore Gottfried, former federal and Cook County prosecutor Andrea Zopp, and Montgomery County state's attorney Kathryn Dobrinic. Bettenhausen would also be part of the commission.

"This will be an extraordinary undertaking," I declared. "Each of the commission members is aware of that. This is a complicated issue, but there is nothing more important. It is serious business.

"Not only were thirteen innocent men nearly executed, there are some other facts that I find remarkable brought to light in the recent *Chicago Tribune* reports: half of the nearly three hundred capital cases had been reversed for a new trial or sentencing hearing, thirty-three death row inmates were represented at trial by an attorney who had been disbarred or suspended at some point, thirty-five African American death row inmates had been convicted or condemned by all-white juries, and prosecutors used jailhouse informants to convict or condemn forty-six death row inmates.

"And these are just a few of the issues that have raised questions about the fairness of the administration of the death penalty in this state," I said.

"So, my only direction to this commission is to remind them of what I said on January 31: until I can be sure that everyone sentenced to death in Illinois is truly guilty; until I can be sure with moral certainty that no innocent man or woman is facing a lethal injection, no one will meet that fate. We must ensure the public safety of our citizens, but in doing so we must ensure that the ends of justice are served. This concept is fundamental to the American system of justice."

The panel had three main tasks:

- Study and review the administration of the capital punishment process in Illinois to determine why that process had failed in the past, resulting in the imposition of death sentences upon innocent people.
- Examine ways of providing safeguards and making improvements in the way law enforcement and the criminal justice system carry out their responsibilities in the death penalty process—from investigation through trial through judicial appeal and to executive review.
- Make any recommendations and proposals designed to further ensure the application and administration of the death penalty in Illinois is just, fair, and accurate.

I stepped aside while Judge McGarr made a brief statement before taking questions from the media. "Our first task has to be to focus on the problem, fully understand it, gather all the evidence," he said. "We don't know what our timetable is, we haven't had our first meeting. . . . We've got to find out why it's flawed, in what way it is flawed . . . and how it can be corrected."

The mix of prosecutors and defense attorneys, members of law enforcement, lawyers who had both been prosecutors and criminal defense lawyers, as well as people with extensive experience in politics and government was designed to prevent any objections of bias—one way or another. Along with Turow's celebrity, Simon and Webster added considerable weight. I thought it was a well-rounded group of very bright, hardworking people with unassailable reputations for integrity.

Nonetheless, there was criticism.

I had anticipated some criticism from death penalty supporters who feared that the commission was only going to rubber-stamp the moratorium and automatically call for the end of the death penalty because they thought that's what I wanted. That didn't happen, though. I am sure that was blunted by the fact that nine of the fourteen members were prosecutors or former prosecutors.

Instead, some antideath penalty activists actually accused me of stacking the commission with death penalty supporters. That dumbfounded me. I was the one governor in the history of Illinois who was seriously listening to them about their concerns and had enough gumption to actually declare a moratorium because I thought the system was broken. I decided that these criticisms were just a "told you so" strategy in case a commission they couldn't control didn't agree whole-heartedly with what they were after. I could see that after years of getting nothing but lip service, these people really didn't trust anyone in power and were still unsure whether I ultimately would bend to political pressure and end the moratorium. They were afraid that I would use the commission as a justification to return Illinois back to the old days.

In fact, I was serious about what I wanted this commission to accomplish. I didn't think this could be overstudied or that too much information could be gathered. I also didn't want them to automatically agree with me; I wanted the truth. I wanted a detailed look at the problem and concrete ways to fix it. If the system could be fixed, that was fine with me. I just didn't want Illinois fumbling along with a process that got things wrong on a life-or-death decision more times than they got things right. If we continued down that road, I was convinced that, one day, the state would put an innocent man or woman to death. As long as I had some power to help make sure that didn't happen, I was going to do my best to fix things.

Later that day, the Chicago Council of Lawyers issued a fifty-eight-page report suggesting several reforms aimed at preventing wrongful executions. It was a jump-start of sorts. The recommendations included videotaping of all interrogations, not just confessions, in murder cases.

I couldn't help but wonder what a difference such a requirement would have made in the cases of Gary Gauger and Rolando Cruz and Alejandro Hernandez.

# 13

# POLITICS OF DEATH

There were some deep political considerations that made me nervous. I was the Illinois chairman of George W. Bush's presidential campaign. Although my chairmanship was a figurehead role, the moratorium and my questions about the system ran headlong into W's views.

He was a two-term governor, first elected in 1994 and reelected in 1998. By the time he left the governor's office in Austin in December 2000, a total of 152 executions had been carried out in the State of Texas. At that time, it was the most executions under any governor in the history of the state—a state known to have the busiest death chamber. I now understood the process—the cases come to the governor as the last stop before the needle is inserted and the poison injected.

W, I learned, was criticized for failing to take clemency petitions seriously. After my experience with Kokoraleis, I couldn't conceive of someone who would blow off these petitions.

In other words: W was *very* pro-death penalty. In 2000, that's what conservative Republicans wanted and he played to the base. And, according to him, all those defendants were convicted and sentenced after fair trials. They were all guilty and no mistakes had been made. He had repeatedly rebuffed requests for a moratorium. The death penalty wasn't the only thing we differed on—I had raised taxes and promoted gun control legislation while he cut taxes and signed into law legislation allowing some citizens to carry concealed weapons—but the death penalty was the most obvious difference.

In the days leading up to the March primary elections, W came to Illinois and during stops at fund-raisers and rallies in Springfield, St. Charles, and Wheaton, we talked about the death penalty. How could we not? He told me he was confident of the system he had in place in Texas and that it worked well.

I told him that I, too, once thought our system was fine, but that I also never spent a lot of time looking at it. I suggested that someday, someone, even students or journalists, might find a case that would make him think twice about what he was saying.

Bush didn't back down and neither did I.

I was speaking for Illinois and he was speaking for Texas. In the end, that's what it came down to, I suppose. I did think, though, that it wasn't smart for him to tell the world every time the subject came up that there was no possibility that an innocent person would be put to death in Texas. In my experience, just as soon as you say something like that, you're proven wrong.

Four years later, in 2004, the *Chicago Tribune* presented compelling evidence that Cameron Todd Willingham had been wrongly executed earlier that year for arson that killed his three children. The evidence strongly indicated the fire was an accident. And in 2006, the *Tribune* reported on the wrongful execution in 1979 of Carlos DeLuna for the robbery and stabbing murder of a gas station clerk in Corpus Christi, Texas. The newspaper identified the real killer who had subsequently died in prison for stabbing someone else.

There had always been a little edge to my relationship with Bush. I knew we were never going to be friends. And I wasn't going to stand down on an important issue just for the sake of his presidential ambitions. My decision to impose a moratorium wasn't a political consideration, it was an important decision on an issue that I felt brought dishonor to my state and made it a symbol of injustice. I didn't want that.

But because Bush had national political ambitions, he looked at things differently. I'm sure he saw me as a pain in the neck. My decision to impose a moratorium was used by the media—which weren't friendly to him anyway—to paint him as some sort of mad executioner because so many defendants had been put to death in Texas. You could almost predict what would happen: the media would say, "Why couldn't he be as enlightened as Ryan?" Then they would couple that issue with my visit to Cuba—which wasn't well received with Hispanics in South Florida, a key voting bloc—and you could see what I mean. Bush and his chief strategist Karl Rove never had any use for me because it seemed that every time they turned around, I was going in the opposite direction from where they wanted everybody to go.

I did worry that if he were elected president, when Illinois was eligible for federal funding, he would think of me and freeze the state out of money. That would be petty, of course, but that's what happens in politics. I took some comfort at the time in the fact that Illinois Republican congressman Denny Hastert was still Speaker of the US House of Representatives. I hoped he could help soften any hard feelings, but I suspected that even Hastert probably would not be enough.

I'm sure it didn't help things when, in June, just three months later, the *Chicago Tribune* published an article documenting the examination of 131 executions that had been carried out by that time under W.

The article, "Flawed Trials Lead to Death Chamber," was blunt.

"Under George W. Bush, Texas has executed dozens of Death Row inmates whose cases were compromised by unreliable evidence, disbarred or suspended defense attorneys, meager defense efforts during sentencing and dubious psychiatric testimony," it began.

"While campaigning for president, Bush has expressed confidence in the fairness and accuracy of the death penalty system in Texas, the nation's busiest executioner. He has said he sees no reason for Texas to follow Illinois' lead by declaring a moratorium on executions," the article said. "But an investigation of all one-hundred-thirty-one executions during Bush's tenure found that the problems plaguing Illinois are equally pronounced in Texas and that additional flaws undermine the state's administration of society's ultimate punishment."

George Bush had never been a friend of Illinois. I don't know if that sealed it, but it was hard to not say I told you so. In fact, a few years later, Illinois lost a multibillion-dollar Superconducting Super Collider project, even though Illinois was the best site for it. The project would have fit perfectly with FermiLab National Accelerator Laboratory in the western suburbs of Chicago. But instead, it went to Texas.

At that moment, I was thinking about the future of the death penalty in Illinois. I had stopped executions and now the commission was beginning its comprehensive look into how the capital punishment system was administered. A moratorium did not alter the verdicts or sentences imposed on any prisoners. I felt it gave us a chance to get to the real truth behind some of the more questionable convictions that had placed men and women on death row and possibly to build a public case for major reforms of the system—possibly even the abolition of the death penalty.

Larry Marshall wasn't afraid to weigh in. During a speech before the Sangamon County Bar Association, he said that my stand "wasn't one that everybody expected, but [Ryan] realized that the good people of Illinois wanted it fixed." He noted that he was "unabashedly" opposed to the death penalty, but considering that "generally speaking, the American people support the death penalty . . . let's see if we can fix it, at least."

He ticked off ten reforms, including barring anyone from being executed solely on the testimony of a single eyewitness or being executed solely on the basis of a police officer claiming the person confessed as had happened in Gary Gauger's case. No one should be executed on the testimony of a jailhouse informant or on the testimony of an accomplice, he declared.

# 14

# EMOTIONS FLARE

A thin-skinned politician generally doesn't last too long. And after more than thirty years as an elected official, I had learned that sometimes you have to endure some things in quiet stoicism. But we are all human and there are times when the emotion of the moment gets the better of us. That happened to me in early May.

On May 10, I fulfilled a promise by meeting with Northwestern journalism professor Dave Protess and his students, some of whom had worked on the Anthony Porter case. I think they were a little stunned when I arrived by helicopter, touching down on the southern edge of campus near Fisk Hall, the school's journalism building. But in a state as large as Illinois, I spent a lot of time in planes and cars and yes, a helicopter, hopscotching from here to there and back again.

The students were smart and inquisitive, as you would expect them to be at an institution like Northwestern University. They wanted to know why I waited nearly a year after Anthony Porter's release to declare the moratorium and, of course, they wanted to hear my view on the death penalty.

"I don't think an execution will ever happen again while I'm governor," I said. "I'd rather err on that side." I also repeated my support for the death penalty for heinous crimes. At the same time, I said the Death Penalty Moratorium Commission had to confront issues such as tortured confessions, jailhouse informants, and prosecutorial misconduct in determining what recommendations to make.

"But I may never be satisfied with what they come up with," I said. "I'm not sure that anybody can come back and say, for a fact, that the death penalty provisions have been fixed."

Asked about my interactions with George Bush when he campaigned in Illinois, I told them that George expressed confidence that no innocent person had been executed during his watch. "George told me he's confident of the system he has in place in Texas and that it works well," I told the students. "Now, I thought our system was okay too. But I never spent a lot of time looking at it. Maybe you can find a case that will make him think twice about what he is doing."

Well, the headlines that came out of this off-the-cuff session raised some eyebrows. The *Bloomington Pantagraph*, relying upon an Associated Press wire story, declared: "Ryan says death penalty is needed." The *Chicago Sun-Times* headline read: "Ryan open to end of death penalty." The *Chicago Tribune* reported: "Ryan virtually shuts door on executions."

This was something I would run into over and over again—the media were trying to discern from each and every syllable that came out of my mouth exactly what I was going to do. I wasn't even sure what I was going to do, let alone tell them. But that didn't stop them from trying to read the tea leaves or studying my words like an archaeologist poring over a potsherd. The *Tribune*, which was pushing on this issue because of how its reporting had influenced my decision to impose the moratorium, said my comments were "the strongest to date" on the death penalty.

But the initial reports sent reporters scurrying after me, apparently in the hope that I would issue some sort of death penalty edict that would give them a big scoop. They were after me that night at a Republican fund-raising dinner. I tried to be clear.

"What I said was unless this commission can show me the system is perfect, I won't execute anybody and I don't know if that will happen during my term, at least this term, as governor. I don't know whether that will happen or not."

The next day, during a two-hour town-hall style meeting at the University of Illinois in Chicago, I repeated that I would not feel comfortable approving an execution until I could be sure that the system had been fixed. The *Chicago Tribune* headline declared: "Ryan still noncommittal on ban for death penalty."

I knew that it was pointless to argue. I remembered the old saying, supposedly first uttered by Frank Branigan, who would become governor of Indiana: "I never quarrel with a man who buys ink by the barrel."

So, this was the background leading up to a meeting on Friday, May 12, 2000, in my office in Springfield with some members of the Illinois Conference of Churches. They had been seeking time with me to talk about the commission. And I knew that among them would be Reverend Demetri Kantzavelos from the Greek Orthodox Diocese of Chicago, who had been Kokoraleis's spiritual advisor in the days before the execution. Honestly, as a man of faith myself, I felt Reverend Kantzavelos had been particularly critical of me in his dealings with the media prior to and after the execution, notwithstanding that Kokoraleis said he had forgiven me.

As they filed into the office, I greeted each one with a handshake—Bishop Joseph Imesch, from the Catholic Diocese of Joliet; Reverend David Anderson, the executive director of the Conference of Churches; Peter Beckwith, the bishop of the Episcopal Diocese of Springfield. And then came Reverend Kantzavelos.

"I want you to know," I said, gripping his hand, "that you are lucky to be here. I did not want you here, but you are here and you need to know that you are just lucky to be here."

We took seats at a conference table. They were there to discuss several issues, including welfare reform, health care, and the death penalty. At some point during the conversation, Reverend Kantzavelos said he had "a concern and a question. My concern is that while we are grateful for the declaration of the moratorium, some of us are haunted by the fact that you have called the moratorium *after* the execution of Andrew Kokoraleis."

That ticked me off. It struck a nerve and, I confess, I lost my temper.

"That animal got everything he deserved," I snapped. "He butchered a woman—Let me tell you something. I have always been in favor of the death penalty and I always will be. I reviewed everything and I have absolutely no remorse for what I did. I have no regrets. I read everything about his case. And let me tell you something else, I read all of your nasty letters."

The fact is that I was torn in those days. My long-held belief in the death penalty was being challenged by the way the system was operating—more people exonerated than had been executed. It was as if I deliberately waited until after Kokoraleis was executed to declare the moratorium just so I could let the guy die on the gurney.

Reverend Kantzavelos seemed unphased. "My question, Mr. Governor, is with regard to the commission you have appointed. It seems that the majority of the members are from the legal profession. Do you have an intention of making the commission more inclusive and include representatives from the religious community, the medical community, ethicists, social services professionals, not to mention representatives from diverse minority groups?"

"Absolutely not," I said. "Are there any more questions?"

Bishop Imesch had one.

"But, Governor, you were quoted in the media yesterday as saying that if the commission came back to you with the suggestion of abolition that you would support it."

So, there it was.

"Your excellency," I said. "Don't believe everything you read in the papers and more importantly, don't believe everything you believe you have read."

The meeting had turned south for everyone in the room and by then, the allotted time was up and everyone quietly filed out after we took a group photograph.

I was trying to grapple with what was turning out to be one of the most difficult issues of my entire life. I was trying to be honest about it. And I couldn't help that the media were, in the pursuit of a story, going to push the envelope in a way that might influence the public one way or another.

Later, I learned that Kantzavelos complained to Bill Ryan, the head of the Illinois Death Penalty Moratorium Project, that the commission was merely a "smokescreen." And to Bill's credit, he told Kantzavelos that he believed I was sincere when I halted executions and established the commission and that I did what I did because it was the right thing to do. Bill said he believed (rightly) that I had moved substantially from where I was when I allowed Kokoraleis's execution to go forward. Bill told Kantzavelos that he understood that Kokoraleis had repented for his horrible crimes and was a changed man at the time of the execution. He urged Kantzavelos to consider the moratorium a memorial for Kokoraleis and to move past the execution.

"Let's move on," Bill told Kantzavelos. "Let's not be like Pogo, who once said we have found the enemy and it is us."

Days later, the Illinois Supreme Court upheld the death sentence for Ike Easley, who had been convicted of helping beat and stab a superintendent to death at the Pontiac Correctional Center in 1987. The attack on Robert Taylor apparently was triggered by the death of an inmate, a gang member named Bill Jones, who died when he swallowed a plastic bag of cocaine when guards were moving him from one cell to another. Easley was convicted with two other inmates, Michael Johnson and David Carter, the gang members who ordered the killing. Unlike Easley, Johnson and Carter were sentenced to life in prison without parole. The Supreme Court rejected Easley's claim that it was unfair that Carter and Johnson, who instigated the murder, should live and he should die. The court also rejected Easley's contention that he had mental problems, which his defense lawyer had failed to fully develop—which, had they been, might have persuaded a jury to impose life instead of death.

Justice Freeman noted, "As this court's opinion on direct review indicates, this was not a perfect trial. However, a defendant is entitled to a fair trial, not a perfect one."

The same day, Cardinal Roger Mahony of the Catholic Diocese of Los Angeles publicly supported renewed efforts for a national moratorium on the death penalty in the states and in the federal system. Speaking at the National Press Club in Washington, DC, he mentioned "the courage of Illinois Governor George Ryan." Mahony said he had written to California governor Gray Davis asking him to halt executions there. With a death row population of 565, California had the largest death row in the nation.

"Simply put, we believe that every life is sacred, every life is precious—even the life of one who has violated the rights of others by taking a life," he declared. "Human dignity is not qualified by what we do. It cannot be earned or forfeited. Human dignity is the irrevocable character of each and every person."

I felt as if I were on a roller coaster, emotionally and physically.

# 15

# AFRICA BECKONS

I was going to meet Nelson Mandela. And I had Fidel Castro to thank for it. Well, sort of. On May 23, 2000, I led a delegation of about one hundred people, including politicians and business people, to establish a trade office in Johannesburg, South Africa. The trip had been in the planning for more than a year and when I inquired about meeting with Mandela, I was told that he "only meets with heads of state." Joseph Hannon, my director of the Illinois Department of Commerce and Community Affairs, made a phone call to Cuban diplomat Fernando Remirez, who was a friend of Mandela. Remirez talked to Castro and what do you know? We were in!

It made a lot of sense to set up a trade office there. South Africa had imported $272.5 million worth of Illinois products in 1999, more than half of it in computer hardware and machinery. I was hoping to boost the imports of pharmaceuticals, technology, and farm products. It was not lost on me that meeting Mandela, a man who had been imprisoned for twenty-seven years for conspiring to overthrow the South Africa's apartheid government, might give me insight into the criminal justice system that I couldn't get anywhere else.

Lura Lynn and I were joined by my old friend, Senate minority leader Emil Jones and his wife, Patricia, as well as Illinois democratic senator James Clayborne from East St. Louis and Illinois democratic representative Monique Davis from Chicago. We were moved just by being in the presence of the man in his home in Houghton, Johannesburg.

There are moments in your life when you are able to touch history, and talking to the man who endured apartheid, fought apartheid, and beat apartheid was one of those moments. It truly was an honor to sit in Mandela's living room and hear him speak about his life without a scintilla of bitterness. They beat the hell out of him, and this great man kept telling us how honored he was to meet *us*. I couldn't believe how I felt. I was teary-eyed. How could you not, hearing him talk about spending all those years in prison and how, when he walked out, he felt the anger and resentment fall away? I thought back to Anthony Porter and the years he spent imprisoned after being wrongly convicted.

This visit was in stark contrast to my time with Castro in 1999. Castro was a dictator. Mandela was a liberator. When I met with Castro, he was strident and kept talking politics. Mandela talked in human terms. Castro was angry. Mandela was not. Mandela talked about the education of his people and the HIV-AIDS epidemic that was decimating them. I couldn't help but think that what Castro had done to his people was what apartheid had done to Mandela. He told me that my trip to Cuba was a brave move.

We brought gifts: a bust of Abraham Lincoln, a baseball signed by Chicago Cubs slugger Sammy Sosa. Mandela signed two baseballs for us to take back: one for Sosa and one for Cubs manager Don Baylor. Mandela also inscribed Lura Lynn's copy of the autobiography of Mandela's life: "Best wishes to an outstanding governor."

At the end of the half-hour meeting, Mandela walked us to the front porch for a group photograph. I grabbed his arm to help him down the stairs, but he said we were staying right there because his knees were in bad shape. He stayed in the shade, about a foot behind the line of sunlight. His eyes couldn't take the brightness after being damaged during his imprisonment.

I remember that Monique had tears streaming down her face when we left. She later said, "It's just something to realize that this man spent all of these years in prison that his people could be free, and then to get to sit and talk with him. . . . He leaves all of us with an awesome responsibility."

After the meeting, I walked backed to the guard's gate of Mandela's compound, rang the buzzer, and asked officials to accept one more gift: a Cubs jersey with the number one and Mandela's name emblazoned across the back. When I handed it over, I said, "Tell him he can play first base the next time he is in Chicago."

The next day, the full impact hit me when we visited Robben Island, where Mandela spent eighteen of his twenty-seven years and from which he had been released in 1990. We stood in silence outside Mandela's cell with the bucket for a toilet and a bowl and a spoon like the ones he used to eat his meals.

Later, after I pointed out what a difference one man, Mandela, had made, Davis said that the moratorium showed what one man could do as well. I appreciated the comment, although there was no way I could compare myself to Mandela.

It wasn't long after I returned that I was confronted by more death penalty news in the form of the most damning study yet. Columbia University Law School professor James S. Liebman looked at all capital trials between 1973 and 1995—a total of 4,578 cases. He not only examined the original trial records, but the appeals as well. He found that 68 percent of the trials that resulted in a conviction and a sentence of death were reversed by appellate courts because of serious errors. But, shockingly, his research found that 82 percent of those defendants did not receive the death penalty when they were retried. Even more amazing, 7 percent of the accused were acquitted at their retrials.

The Liebman study, "A Broken System: Error Rates in Capital Cases," underscored the facts that confronted all government officials in death penalty states in 1999. Illinois ranked second only to Florida in the number of death row inmates that had been exonerated since 1973. Twenty-four states other than Illinois had been forced to exonerate at least one inmate scheduled to die, meaning that more than half of the states that allowed the death penalty had experience with convicting innocent people.

Illinois just had more experience, it seemed.

There were 161 prisoners on death row in Illinois. On June 16, the Illinois Supreme Court affirmed the death sentences of three of them. Andre Jones had been sentenced to death in 1979 for the murders of three people in East St. Louis. Paris Sims's death sentence was upheld for the 1994 murder of a woman in Belleville, Illinois. A moratorium couldn't stop all the machinery of death, just the last stage—the execution chamber. Ulece Montgomery's death sentence for the 1981 murders of two women in Robbins, Illinois, was upheld despite arguments from his lawyers that he had agreed not to contest the prosecution's evidence in return for a life prison sentence if convicted. But after he was convicted, the trial judge sentenced him to death.

At the same time, I granted pardons based on actual innocence to three former Illinois death row prisoners. After reviewing the recommendations of the Illinois Prisoner Review Board, I believed that it was right to pardon Perry Cobb and Darby Tillis, who had been freed thirteen years earlier after being acquitted at their fifth trial. And I granted a pardon to Ronald Jones, who had filed his request just after the first of the year.

I didn't have much time to think about these cases, though. I was on my way to Washington, DC, to testify before the US House of Representatives Judiciary Committee relating to a bill—the Innocence Protection Act—introduced by Illinois Republican congressman Ray LaHood and Massachusetts Democratic congressman Bill Delahunt. The bill would grant all prisoners a chance to obtain state-funded DNA testing of biological evidence in an attempt to prove their innocence. It also called for minimum competency standards for court-appointed lawyers in death penalty prosecutions.

During my testimony, I was asked about other pardons and I said I would grant them to other freed death row prisoners if they asked for them. "There's no reason not to," I said.

My presence was not to endorse the bill, though I did support it and had participated in a press conference back in March when LaHood and Delahunt introduced the bill. I noted that five of the thirteen freed death row inmates had been exonerated by DNA testing and that some of the others had had a terribly inadequate legal defense.

"It's about fairness," I said. "It's about right and wrong."

I said that Illinois had been at the forefront of forensic testing and that I supported the National Forensic Science Improvement Act as well as a measure to help states reduce DNA evidence testing backlogs in crime labs. That bill would create $768 million in block grants over five years to improve the quality, availability, and timeliness of forensic services nationwide.

"In Illinois, these block grants could help us catch up with a ten-month backlog of cases from Chicago and across the state of Illinois. That is a backlog of 2,500 cases," I said. "That means investigators can't match evidence from unsolved crimes against updated records. That means, in some cases, innocent people are sitting in jail waiting for the evidence that clears them to be processed by the crime lab. It also means some criminals continue to walk the streets."

Several congressmen tried to draw me into commenting on George Bush and Texas, particularly because of the *Tribune* report on the problems in that state. "I'm not here to second-guess George Bush," I said.

But I was there to talk about the "shameful record" in Illinois of convicting innocent people. I told how I had appointed a commission to study the death penalty system. "Unless they can report back to me that there are precautions we can take to build a flawless system, I am not sure anyone will be executed again in Illinois."

I said I believed there were a growing number of people who shared my concerns. "I also believe there is a deep wellspring of fairness in the people of Illinois and in the United States of America. They want a system that is fair, that will not convict and execute the innocent."

Upon my return, I signed legislation that took the first step to create a uniform statewide evidence retention policy after a conviction of a defendant. The bill required police departments and sheriff's offices to preserve all physical evidence in cases and to maintain records to be able to locate the evidence. "I have made a commitment to do all that I can to improve the truth-seeking ability of the criminal justice system," I declared. "We are taking an important step in ensuring justice through modern technology."

Meanwhile, DuPage County state's attorney Joe Birkett decided to go on the attack against the moratorium by emphasizing the case of Walter Thomas, who had been convicted and sentenced to death for a 1986 murder in Aurora, Illinois. His appeals were basically exhausted. "He's waking up every day and eating three square meals because of the governor's moratorium," Birkett said. "The execution of Walter Thomas should go forward. There is no claim of actual innocence. He's had his due process."

I wasn't happy with comments like that. Mike Waller, the Lake County state's attorney, said he agreed that two men sentenced to death in his county—Hector Sanchez and Johnny Neal Jr.—should be executed. But as a member of my commission, he had the common sense to say, "The issue has been made larger than individual cases." And so, until the commission had completed its mission and system-wide problems were fixed, he could wait.

And, so would I.

# 16

# INTERNATIONAL ACCLAIM

When the Italians lit up the Colosseum in Rome after I declared the moratorium, I thought I got a sense that this was a big deal. But really, I didn't know the half of it. Yes, I was the first governor to declare a moratorium. And yes, I did it not because I was morally opposed to the death penalty—I supported it. I made that clear.

It was that I said I didn't trust the system to kill the right people—that was what really struck a chord. I didn't realize it was going to erupt into the international debate that it actually became. I really didn't. I had no idea.

The American media came calling in droves. From the print media came the big boys—the *New York Times*, the *Washington Post*, and the *Los Angeles Times*. Of course, the two major Chicago papers, the *Tribune* and the *Sun-Times*, were on it all the time. The *St. Louis Post-Dispatch*, the Peoria *Journal Star*, and the *State Journal-Register* in Springfield were joined by the *Washington Times*, the *Sacramento Bee*, the *Miami Herald*, *Newsweek*, *Time*, and *Brill's Content*.

The moratorium was discussed and I was interviewed on the CBS News programs *60 Minutes* and *The Early Show*; the ABC news programs *Good Morning America*, *This Week* with Sam Donaldson and Cokie Roberts, and *Nightline*; the NBC news program *Today*; the HBO program *Dennis Miller Live*; National Public Radio's *Morning Edition* and *Talk of the Nation*; PBS's *The News Hour with Jim Lehrer*; CNBC's *Geraldo Live*, the BET Network, and the Courtroom Television Network.

In addition, I had been interviewed for radio and television programs in Switzerland, France, England, Germany, and Canada.

Anna Quindlen, in her column "The Last Word" in *Newsweek*, said that while DNA had helped show innocence, "it really is the character of one elected official that has turned the capital punishment debate on its head. God bless Gov. George Ryan of Illinois. Faced with the astonishing statistical news that more people on the state's death row were being exonerated then executed, he instituted a moratorium. Though the governor is a conservative Republican and a death penalty advocate, he has said he doubts anyone else will be executed during his term."

Ted Koppel devoted four hours of prime-time specials on the death penalty during September 2000. That was really unheard of. Koppel praised my decision to impose a moratorium as "an act of courage."

The moratorium drew praise from the governments of South Africa and Mexico and accolades from the Italian Senate.

Paula Bernstein, a spokeswoman for the Death Penalty Information Center, a Washington, DC-based nonprofit organization that tracked all manner of statistics and rulings and developments in the death penalty, declared, "There is no question the moratorium has touched off a nationwide examination of the death penalty." She said that just over a year after my declaration, more than 1,500 local governments and institutions passed moratorium resolutions. "Proposals to temporarily halt executions or to abolish them altogether have been introduced in nineteen states, and legislators in at least thirty-one are proposing bills to revise the way convicted prisoners are placed on death row."

In New Hampshire, for example, the legislature voted to abolish the death penalty, although Governor Jeanne Shaheen vetoed the bill. Indiana governor Frank O'Bannon ordered a review of that state's death penalty system. And of course, there was heightened pressure on Governor Bush, who steadfastly maintained the system in Texas was just fine.

Journalists across the country were beginning to tackle the death penalty in their own states in the same manner as the *Chicago Tribune* had—by examining every case instead of cherry-picking egregious examples. In addition, legislators and policy makers across the country were following Illinois closely.

Illinois Supreme Court Justice Moses Harrison II, an outspoken critic of the death penalty, had taken some action as well. He created a special commission to create new rules for capital cases in Illinois that were designed to even the playing field for people accused of a capital crime.

If I were ever to get complacent—and I wasn't—the Illinois Supreme Court seemed to be ready to remind me that the death penalty system was broken. In August, the Supreme Court reversed or remanded six death sentences. Six! The *Tribune* accurately summed it up, not that I needed a summary, noting that the rulings "highlighted nearly every problem plaguing the state's criminal justice system."

Two of the rulings remanded the cases of Aaron Patterson and Derrick King for hearings to present evidence that they were tortured into falsely confessing by Chicago police detectives working under the notorious Lieutenant Jon Burge, who had been fired in 1993. Patterson, who was sentenced to death for the murder of a couple in 1986, had long claimed that he was beaten by detectives and that a plastic typewriter cover was put over his head, suffocating him. His case was particularly notable because while he was alone in the interrogation room, he had scratched his claim of torture on a metal bench, using a paper clip. King, who was condemned for an armed robbery and murder in 1979 in Chicago, claimed detectives struck him with a baseball bat twenty to forty times.

The court also sent two DuPage County cases back to the trial court. Ronald Alvine, convicted of a 1992 murder of a police officer from the suburb of West Chicago, was granted a new sentencing hearing—his third. The court held that a judge erroneously failed to grant Alvine a complete hearing before sentencing him to death. In the case of Darryl Simms, the court ordered a hearing on defense claims that prosecutors, including the current DuPage County state's attorney Joe Birkett, knowingly allowed three witnesses to testify falsely. Simms had been sentenced to death for the rape and murder of a woman in Addison, Illinois, in 1985.

Daniel Ramsey's conviction and death sentence for a shooting spree in 1996 was set aside and a new trial was ordered. The court held that the insanity law used at Ramsey's trial had been voided because it violated the Illinois constitution. Ramsey had been sentenced to death for shooting two young girls to death and wounding three other people.

The court ordered new legal briefs to be filed in the case of Milton Johnson, who had been sentenced to death for murdering four women in a ceramics shop in Joliet, Illinois, in 1983. The court said that Johnson's attorney had done such a terrible job that the defense had to file new briefs. The briefs that the attorney, Louis Redmond Jr., had filed were lacking in citations to the record and the law. The court noted that the case number had been incorrectly listed, then was crossed out and the correct number was written in by hand. The court also noted that Redmond's claim that he was worried about the brief being too long was ridiculous—the brief he filed was twenty pages under the limit of seventy-five pages.

At the same time, the court upheld the death sentences in two other cases. Still, the track record of half of all death cases being reversed continued. I could only shake my head in disbelief.

On a Sunday in September, nearly one thousand people gathered at the First United Methodist Church in Evanston to call for a nationwide moratorium on the death penalty. Democratic US representative Jan Schakowsky, who had sponsored a bill calling for a national moratorium, declared, "The system is so flawed. In my view, it is irreparably flawed. There is no way to craft a system that is infallible.

"What a sea change there has been on this issue," she said, noting that more and more congressmen and congresswoman were seriously considering supporting her proposed moratorium bill. She also recalled how, when she first ran for office, her opponent called out her opposition to the death penalty. "That would not occur today," she said, "because the sentiments are different in [public opinion] and in legislative bodies."

At least one judge weighed in against the moratorium. Illinois Supreme Court Judge James Heiple, who was retiring and apparently felt compelled to criticize it, gave an interview to the *Kankakee Journal*, my hometown newspaper, during which he said the moratorium was illegal.

"The governor has no authority to declare a moratorium on capital cases," Heiple said. "He can grant pardons. He can grant stays. He can grant reprieves in individual cases. But to declare a blanket moratorium on executions is something wholly outside his authority."

Heiple, who had survived a threat of impeachment years earlier for allegedly using his position to avoid traffic tickets, said the exoneration of the innocent men was proof that the system worked. There was no proof an innocent person had been executed, he said. The real problem, he declared, was that the system took too long to execute the condemned.

Clearly, I disagreed with Heiple and my legal team told me I was on very solid ground. It was this sort of thing that seemed to take away from the real story—which was how to fix a broken system.

I refrained from a public response. I would now let my actions speak for themselves.

Northwestern's Larry Marshall felt no compunction about addressing the assertion that exonerations showed that the system worked.

"That's complete and utter hogwash," Marshall declared. "Those innocents who survive are the result of dumb luck, serendipity, even the hand of God."

I hadn't been seeking the spotlight in January, but having been thrust into it as a result of my decision, I had decided it was important that I explain and talk about the issues the moratorium had raised, such as fairness and innocence.

In September, I met with Mexican president Ernesto Zedillo during a trade mission to Mexico, a country that has no death penalty. "I congratulate you on your death penalty moratorium," Zedillo declared.

"I may not go back to the death penalty as long as I'm governor," I said. "I don't know. The worst nightmare can be executing an innocent man."

Zedillo replied, "It took courage."

"Our system was flawed," I said. "We were one hour away from executing a man we had already fed his last meal. The United States is one of the only countries left among major industrial nations to have the death penalty."

Invitations began arriving requesting me to speak at antideath penalty events. In October 2000, I traveled to Atlanta, Georgia, to deliver an address with former First Lady Rosalynn Carter at an American Bar Association (ABA) event: Call to Action: A Moratorium on Executions. Among those present were New York University law professor Anthony Amsterdam, who had been described as the most distinguished law professor in the United States and who had argued the case (*Furman v. Georgia*) that had resulted in the US Supreme Court declaring the death penalty unconstitutional in 1972.

The conference was an attempt by the ABA, on behalf of its four hundred thousand members, to galvanize lawyers nationwide to work for suspension of executions until the death penalty system could be reformed. The ABA had first called for a moratorium in 1997 and ABA president Martha Barnett said it was only in the past year that the call was gaining momentum.

The conference was going to focus on racial discrimination in the administration of the death penalty, the execution of juveniles and the mentally challenged, and the need for better defense representation.

Mrs. Carter preceded me at the podium and called for a "thorough examination" of the death penalty. "I am morally and spiritually opposed to the death penalty," she said. "Even for those who do not share my belief, the questions that have been raised about the unfairness of the system, the conviction of the innocent, poor quality of legal representation, racial discrimination, and the imposition of the death penalty on mentally ill or mentally retarded people and even children clearly call for a moratorium."

I began by praising Mrs. Carter for the contributions that she and former president Jimmy Carter had made to the country during and after his presidency through Habitat for Humanity. I used the occasion to note that Lura Lynn had helped build a house for Habitat for Humanity in Springfield. "I know she was impressed by all the volunteers who followed your example, Mrs. Carter, and gave of their time to work with a family to build them a home and a chance to live the American dream."

And then, I got to the matter at hand.

"Ten months ago, I don't think any of us thought we would be together here today in Atlanta to talk about the death penalty," I said. "I've been in politics for more than thirty years; most of that time as a county board member, legislator, or executive office holder.

"I was a death penalty supporter. Like many other elected officials, I have believed there are crimes so heinous that the death sentence is the only proper, societal response for the criminals convicted of those crimes in a court of law," I said.

"But a lot has happened to shake my faith in the death penalty system. I know a lot more about the administration of the death penalty in Illinois—and the more I learn, the more troubled I've become.

"You may not know that earlier this year, in addition to declaring the death penalty moratorium, I established a commission to do a complete reevaluation of the forty-year-old Illinois Criminal Code," I said. "A study of the imposition of sentences can certainly lead any reasonable person to see the discriminatory disparities in the system.

"I may be a recent convert, but I have committed myself and my administration to the development and establishment of a system of justice that is truly just," I declared. "I wanted you to know this so that you would know my concern with the entire system of justice."

I recounted the story of the release of Anthony Porter, freed through the work of journalism students so close to his execution. I told of my review of the Kokoraleis case and how I ultimately allowed his execution to go forward. "I double-checked and then triple-checked," I said. "I wanted to be absolutely sure and, in the end, I was.

"But it was a gut-wrenching, exhausting experience," I said. "It all came down to me—a pharmacist from Kankakee, Illinois, who became governor—to make the final decision. Quite frankly, that might be too much to ask of one person to decide whether you owned a drug store or you were a Harvard-educated lawyer—we are only human."

Regarding Porter, I said, "How do you prevent another Anthony Porter—another innocent man or woman from paying the ultimate penalty for a crime he or she did not commit? I said then and I say today, I cannot answer that question. What I do know is there is no margin for error when it comes to putting a person to death."

In closing, I said, "It is a question of fairness. What I learned as governor is that the view changes when the buck stops with you. It is easy to be an ardent death penalty supporter when you don't have to make the final decision about who will live or die. But when you sit in judgment, when you have the power to decide who will live and who will die—it is an awesome responsibility.

"In this country, governors have to make that ultimate decision. They must shoulder that awesome burden," I said. "Since I made the decision I have made, I have endured my share of political attacks from people who don't agree with me. That hasn't deterred me one bit. I would make the same decision again.

"Many other people have told me it was courageous," I said. "I haven't let that get to my head either. That's because I simply tried to do the right thing, regardless of whether it was popular. I will not tell other governors or elected officials what to do. All I can do is share what we have done in Illinois. We recognized that there were questions—far too many questions."

On my way home, I had a recurring thought—I wished I could swallow some of the words of unqualified support for the death penalty that I had uttered in the past.

# 17

# DEATH MARCHES ON

On November 16, 2000, the Illinois Supreme Court issued two more reversals in death penalty cases. The court overturned the conviction and death sentence of Cecil Sutherland and the death sentence of Hector Nieves.

In Sutherland's case, the court ruled that his lawyer failed to present compelling evidence that would have cast doubt on his guilt. The court ruled 6 to 1 to overturn the conviction and sentence, saying that his defense lawyer had caused him "substantial prejudice" and because the prosecutor improperly misstated the significance of some of its evidence during arguments to the jury.

Sutherland had been convicted in 1989 of kidnapping, rape, and murder in the death of ten-year-old Amy Schulz, whose body was found in a ditch near Dix, Illinois, a few miles from where Sutherland lived and about eighty miles east of St. Louis, Missouri. The prosecution's case relied heavily on tire tracks and boot prints found near the girl's body. The prosecution said its experts concluded the impressions matched Sutherland's car and boots at the time of his arrest. However, the Supreme Court noted that there was evidence that Sutherland had purchased his boots and changed his tires *after* the girl was killed, but the defense attorney never presented it.

Nieves had been convicted in Chicago in the 1992 murder of Louis Vargas in the Humboldt Park neighborhood. While the court upheld Nieves's conviction, it ordered that Nieves be resentenced and that a death sentence was off the table. The trial judge who had imposed death had considered evidence that should have been excluded at the time of sentencing, the court concluded.

These decisions meant that 135 Illinois death penalty convictions or death sentences had been reversed—more than half.

Two days later, I was attending a conference in San Francisco to receive an outstanding public service award. The conference, "Committing to Conscience: Building a Unified Strategy to End the Death Penalty," was at that time one of the largest antideath penalty conferences ever to be assembled. It was the first time that a broad array of antideath penalty groups convened jointly.

The dignitaries included Sister Helen Prejean, whose personal story inspired the movie *Dead Man Walking*; Mike Farrell, an actor *(M*A*S*H)* and president of Death Penalty Focus in California; US senator Russell Feingold from Wisconsin, who introduced legislation to abolish the federal death penalty; and officials from groups such as the National Coalition to Abolish the Death Penalty, Amnesty International USA, and Citizens United for Alternatives to the Death Penalty. Other groups included the American Civil Liberties Union, American Friends Service Committee, Murder Victims' Families for Reconciliation, and Journey of Hope.

I also met Bud Welch, whose daughter, Julie Marie, was killed in the 1995 Oklahoma City bombing committed by Timothy McVeigh and Terry Nichols. Welch had been opposed to the death penalty, but in the aftermath of what was then the worst act of domestic terrorism in US history, for a time he was so angry at McVeigh that all he wanted was to be put in a room alone with him. That lasted about six months and then Welch returned to his abolitionist view. Ultimately, he forgave McVeigh before he was executed.

I met with some of the Italians who were opposed to the death penalty who had come to Chicago and who I would later meet in Italy. Although Italy had no death penalty, they were studying the criminal justice system. They would ultimately meet with United Nations secretary-general Kofi Annan to present an international petition containing more than three million signatures calling for an international moratorium on the death penalty.

It was heady company and I received a lot of encouragement from these antideath penalty advocates. To each and every person, I maintained my position—I was awaiting the conclusions of the Death Penalty Moratorium Commission before I made any decisions.

I was honored at Northwestern University Law School's Center on Wrongful Convictions, founded by Larry Marshall and Rob Warden, and gave a speech that went just a little further than others from the past. And I voiced a thought that was increasing in volume in my head as I talked about my lifelong support for the death penalty.

"I was part of that great body of Americans who saw a nation in the grip of rising crime rates, inner cities becoming armed camps and ever-growing violence in our streets, our schools, and even our places of worship," I said. "Tough sentences, longer prison terms, more jail, and strict imposition of the death penalty. During the debate on the death penalty, those of us who supported the death penalty, we were asked by those who opposed it, who would be willing to throw the switch? Would you be willing to throw the switch? It was a sobering question, and I wish now that I could swallow the words of unqualified support for the death penalty that I offered."

I praised the *Chicago Tribune* reporters whose work had shaped my thinking and decision to impose the moratorium. "Your reporting and columns crystalized my thinking," I said. "One of the highest callings in journalism is to save the life of an innocent person on death row. You have achieved that and you are to be commended."

Later, in talking about the moratorium, I went off my prepared remarks.

"I'm not only concerned about the death penalty, but I'm concerned about the whole criminal code we have here in Illinois," I said. "There is, without question, a lot of people sitting in prison today that didn't commit the crimes they are there for. They may not be facing the death penalty, but we've shortened their lives by putting them in prison for a crime they didn't commit."

This really was the most damning thing I had said to date about the criminal justice system in Illinois because it went beyond just death penalty cases. My education, if you want to call it that, had been continuing and my eyes were really starting to open up. Afterward, when a reporter asked me how widespread the problem of mistakes in the criminal system was, I said, "Frankly, I think it's pretty bad."

By the end of November, the Illinois Supreme Court had upheld the convictions and death sentences in five more cases, putting five more prisoners a step closer to execution should the moratorium be lifted.

The death sentence was affirmed for Reginald Chapman, who was convicted of beating his girlfriend to death with a bat and murdering his infant son in 1994 in Alsip, Illinois. He tried to hide the crime by tying weights to their bodies and dumping them in a canal.

The court also upheld the death sentence for William Kirchner, who had been convicted of killing an elderly couple and their adult daughter in 1997 near Decatur, Illinois. The case was somewhat memorable because family members of the victims wrote a letter to the *Chicago Tribune* in February decrying the moratorium.

"Not all Death Row inmates are innocent," the family members wrote. "So far, no one in the state of Illinois has been wrongfully executed due to the fact that the appeals process, already in place in our state, does what it is supposed to.

"We challenge Gov. Ryan to support the victims and surviving family members of violent crimes by taking actions other than a moratorium on the death penalty. We feel that spending our tax money to prolong the lives of killers on Death Row is wrong."

The Supreme Court also upheld the death penalty for Anthony Hall, who was convicted of murdering a kitchen worker at Pontiac Correctional Center. Hall had been sentenced to death but was granted a new sentencing hearing by a federal judge. At the second hearing, Hall was again sentenced to death.

The court also approved a death sentence for David Smith who was convicted in the 1987 rape and murder of a Chicago woman who was babysitting her four-year-old cousin.

And the court also affirmed the death sentence for Anthony Enis, who was condemned for the 1988 murder in Waukegan of Merlinda Entrata, a nurse who was going to testify in an upcoming trial that Enis had raped her.

The first week in December, I found myself, almost unbelievably, at Harvard Law School, delivering a speech to law students. I joined a distinguished list of Speakers who preceded me, including Anita Hill, Supreme Court Justice Stephen Breyer, Reverend Jesse Jackson, Reverend Al Sharpton, Johnny Cochran Jr., and—of particular significance to me—retired Supreme Court justice Harry Blackmun, who had so famously said he would no longer tinker with the machinery of death.

"In my heart, I knew I couldn't go any further, and that I couldn't live with myself if I did," I said. "When it came to the death penalty in Illinois, there was no justice in the justice system."

I encouraged the students to consider a career as public servants and to do pro bono work if they wind up at a private law firm. "I hope you will remember that the criminal courtroom is not an arena to compete for victory," I said. "You've got an obligation to go out and make sure that there is fairness in the system."

The very next day, I was in Manhattan addressing the New York City bar association, prompting the Associated Press to publish an article quoting Robert Jones, spokesman for the antideath penalty group, Moratorium 2000, as saying that the Illinois moratorium had re-energized the movement. "I'd say it's probably been the largest energizing event in the last twenty years," he said.

The following week the Death Penalty Moratorium Commission held its third public hearing in Springfield, and during the proceedings the commission chairman, former federal judge Frank McGarr said that the commission could possibly recommend eliminating the death penalty.

"Our conclusion, I suppose, could be that we can't reform the system enough and we should make a recommendation," Frank McGarr said, but noted that only the legislature could abolish it. "Whether we will ultimately make a recommendation or not, I don't know. I don't rule out the possibility." The commission's primary focus, he said, was to deal with other issues such as prosecutorial misconduct and inadequate legal defense. Former US senator Paul Simon, a commission vice chairman who had opposed the death penalty for decades, added that he would support "whatever we can do in the way of restricting the imposition of the death penalty and making sure innocent people are not put to death."

During this third and final hearing, commission member Scott Turow asked parents of murder victims who testified in favor of the death penalty if sentencing the murderers to life in prison without the possibility of parole—a sentence already on the books in Illinois—would satisfy them; bring them peace.

George Hartman, whose twenty-six-year-old son was murdered in 1998 by a man who was convicted of second-degree murder and was scheduled to be released on parole in 2005, said that although he supported the death penalty, he might have accepted a natural life sentence. "If you knew that he was never going to get out . . . I'd have to say, 'Probably,'" he said.

Commission member Roberto Ramirez noted that when he was eight years old, his own father was murdered and then Ramirez's grandfather avenged the murder by killing the murderer. "It didn't bring any closure," Ramirez said.

At the same time, news was breaking in Florida that DNA testing confirmed the innocence of Frank Lee Smith, who had been sentenced to death for the 1985 rape and murder of an eight-year-old girl. Unfortunately for Smith, he had died of cancer eleven months earlier while still on death row. He had been scheduled to be executed in 1990 but won a stay. Had he not won that stay, Smith would have been an innocent man executed and no one would probably ever have known.

Reporters asked me about the McGarr statement leaving the door open to a recommendation of abolition. I said it was becoming more of an option to consider. "I just think people have come to realize that maybe there could be errors in the execution of people and rather than take the chance, they're better off putting them in jail without parole," I said.

The *Chicago Tribune* did it again just before the end of the year, publishing a report titled "Executions in America." The newspaper examined three cases where prisoners had been executed: Alvin Moore in Louisiana, Bennie Demps in Florida, and Wilburn Henderson in Arkansas.

"The cases of these men are bound by a common element—all went to their death accompanied by doubts about the evidence against them, while their claims of innocence received scant public attention," the article said.

By that time, a total of 682 people had been executed since the return of the death penalty in the United States. About 120 were still asserting their innocence as they were wheeled to the death chamber, the newspaper said. These were just three of the cases.

How does this happen? I wondered.

The year was coming to a close. My commission was still working and there was no timetable for their report. Meanwhile, five other states—Indiana, Maryland, North Carolina, Arizona, and Nebraska—had begun reviewing their death penalty systems.

Richard Dieter, director of the nonpartisan Death Penalty Information Center, said, in issuing the center's annual report, that "the big story this year is the change in the atmosphere of the death penalty."

Asked why the state would continue with a system that resulted in twelve executions and thirteen exonerations, I said, "Why would we continue with a system like that? I don't think that's okay. People in public service try to do what's right. You may not get everybody to agree you've done the right thing—whether you build a road or whether you tear down a bridge, whether you set policy, whatever you may do. Anybody who serves in an office like the governor's office tries to do the right thing, what they think is the right thing, based on the counsel they get."

If I had a New Year's resolution, it was that it was important to keep delivering a message that I had concluded people needed to hear regarding the death penalty. Too many people were, like I was for many years, ambivalent about it.

How do you get the message across, I wondered, to people who feel that law and order is the first priority and that means the death penalty?

I wondered what they would think if they had to go to bed every night contemplating the possibility that they would be responsible for saying whether someone should live or die.

The more I thought about it, I started to wonder what would happen to the prisoners already on death row if the commission were to recommend abolition. I had told the *Tribune* in a year-end interview that the commission "may come back and say that everybody who sits on death row is entitled to review based on these rules, based on these recommendations, based on these changes. I would hope that's what they do. I don't know why you wouldn't. If there is some doubt about the system prior to our stopping it, then those folks must have all been convicted based on that system and that system is in question, then I would think that they would all have an opportunity for review."

Little did I know what was about to unfold.

# 18

# DEATH ROW EXPANDS

The machinery of death kept cranking along in 2000 despite the moratorium. The Illinois Department of Corrections reported that fourteen people were added to death row that year—the most in any year since 1990. Eight were sentenced to death after I declared the moratorium on January 31, 2000.

One of the more vocal critics of the continuing push to send defendants to death row was Dick Cunningham, a Chicago lawyer who had represented death row inmates since 1989. He was the lawyer for Ronald Jones, one of the thirteen men exonerated from death row in Illinois.

"I'm disappointed that the prosecutors in many counties have gone forward as if there's no problem," Cunningham said.

There wasn't anything I could do about it. That's what prosecutors were doing. My position was that if people were going to be sentenced to death, I wasn't going to execute them. I told the *Chicago Tribune* during an interview one year after the moratorium that if the system didn't work the way it was supposed to, then it probably ought to be ended.

"If you're going to put innocent people to death, then it doesn't work and it ought to be abolished. We're one of thirty-eight states that have it. There are twelve states that don't believe we ought to have the death penalty, and I don't know that society is any worse because of that. Unless that commission can come back to me and say, 'Look, this system is solid, with checks and double-checks on it and works fine,' then I may say OK. But I don't know if we can do that."

This was a high hurdle, I had to concede.

I said I didn't know how that happened. I kept coming back to that punch line. Although I knew it was starting to sound repetitive, the fact was, it was true. In fact, I was starting to wonder if some of these problems were even correctible at all.

I was asked what would happen to the inmates already on death row if the commission I appointed made recommendations that became law and the system was improved to the point where I decided to lift the moratorium.

"It depends on how the laws are written and what changes the commission recommends," I said. "They may come back and say that everybody who sits on death row is entitled to review based on these rules, based on these recommendations, based on these changes. I would hope that's what they do. I don't know why you wouldn't. If there is some doubt about the system prior to our stopping it, then those folks must have all been convicted based on that system and that system is in question, then I would think that they would all have an opportunity for review."

I had always believed that people in public service try to do what's right. But while you may not get everybody to agree you've done the right thing whether you build a road or tear down a bridge or set policy—whatever you may do. Anybody who serves in an office like the governor's tries to do the right thing, what they think is the right thing, based on the counsel they get.

Some of my comments didn't sit well with at least one member of my commission, even though I felt my comments had not only been consistent, but weren't an attempt to influence commission members. Lake County state's attorney Mike Waller told the media, "He's kind of given us an impossible mission, based on some of the comments he's made. He's asked for recommendations or improvements and at the same time doesn't seem to indicate the death penalty can be fixed. He ought to allow the commission to complete its work."

But I had been consistent and I was not trying to influence the commission. What I wanted was a system that would allow me to be sure with a moral certainty that the right person was going to be executed.

Meanwhile, nearly a year to the day that I declared the moratorium, the Illinois Supreme Court went ahead with significant reforms of the death penalty system. The court, based on recommendations by a panel of seventeen judges appointed in 1999, imposed minimum standards for both prosecutors and defense attorneys. Defense attorneys and prosecutors would now be required to have at least five years of experience handling criminal cases, including at least eight felony trials, of which at least two were murder trials. It just seemed incredible to me that until now no experience was necessary. None!

The new reforms also required judges who would preside over capital cases to attend training seminars every two years. In addition, prosecutors would now be required to promptly inform defense attorneys of their intention to seek the death penalty—within 120 days of arraignment—and about any DNA testing that was done in the cases.

Chief Supreme Court judge Moses Harrison II conceded that the court was hamstrung in its ability to change the law. "There are no easy solutions to the problems presented by this state's death penalty law," he said. "Ultimately the fate of the state's death penalty statute will be a matter for the General Assembly and the governor to resolve."

I welcomed the new rules as a step in the right direction, but I also knew—and agreed with Justice Harrison—that they did not speak to many of the problems that had led to thirteen innocent men being sentenced to death. Harrison's commission also suggested that the role of prosecutors be redefined to "seek justice, not merely to convict." And trial judges would decide whether to let defense lawyers question witnesses prior to trial and that prosecutors make "a good faith effort" to disclose prior to trial any evidence that was favorable to a defendant. In addition, the rules called for the Supreme Court to screen lawyers for admission to what would be called the Capital Litigation Trial Bar to assure that attorneys met the requirements needed to handle a death penalty case instead of allowing judges handling the trials to make that assessment.

The rules were touted as among the most progressive in the country. James Coleman, a Duke University law professor who had studied the death penalty nationally for the American Bar Association, said, "When Illinois establishes standards like this, I think that it says to other states this is necessary to avoid the kinds of problems that Illinois has had."

Dick Cunningham, Ronald Jones's lawyer, remained critical. "The fact is that we're kidding ourselves if we think this is going to fix the vast amounts of problems we've seen," he declared.

Justice Thomas Fitzgerald, who chaired the seventeen-judge committee, allowed that the reforms were just the beginning of the process of recalibrating the system. "I don't suggest for a moment that, by what we have done, we have finished the job. Maybe we have just started the job. It's absolutely true that this is part of a larger piece, certainly an important part, but only part of that piece of continual improvement."

On the anniversary of my declaration of the moratorium, Russ Feingold, a Democratic senator from Wisconsin, introduced legislation to halt all federal executions and to urge states to also impose moratoriums. "Illinois should be a model for the federal government and all the other thirty-seven states that authorize the use of capital punishment," he said. "Governor Ryan's decision set off a yearlong, nationwide debate on the death penalty. During the past year, we have seen far too many examples of the death penalty system gone wrong. In the last year alone, eight innocent people were exonerated and released from Death Row."

Feingold added, "Before executing even one more person, the federal government and the states must ensure that not a single innocent person will be executed, that we have eliminated discrimination in capital sentencing on the basis of race of either the victim or the defendant, and ensure that we provide for certain basic standards of competency of defense counsel."

Meanwhile, in Illinois, Republican senator James Durkin introduced a bill that would allow judges to assess the credibility of jailhouse informants—snitches—prior to trial. I saw this as vitally important since five of the thirteen exonerations involved false jailhouse snitch testimony. Another piece of the legislation would allow prosecutors and defense attorneys to take sworn statements from witnesses, except for law enforcement, crime victims, or crime victims' families, prior to trial.

At the end of January, the Illinois Death Penalty Moratorium Project, an antideath penalty organization headed by Bill Ryan, who was not related to me, issued a report titled "A Broken System at Work: A Preliminary Report on the State of the Death Penalty in Illinois in the Year of the Moratorium." The report said that racial bias remained a persistent problem. "Eighty percent of this year's condemned are non-white, an increase from the already disproportionate sixty-seven percent non-white population of death row at the moratorium's beginning," the report concluded. In addition, the report said, minorities continued to make up disproportionately small numbers on the juries in death penalty cases. The report noted that Raul Ceja, a Hispanic man, was sentenced to death in DuPage County by a jury of eleven white people and one black person.

In Jefferson County, an all-white jury sentenced JoJulien Hicks, who was black, to death.

The report noted that while ten more defendants had been added to death row, the Illinois Supreme Court had vacated or remanded fourteen other death penalty cases. "The same issues continue to infect death penalty cases and result in their being overturned as in prior years: prosecutorial misconduct, ineffective assistance of counsel, coerced confessions, judicial corruption," the report said.

In addition, the report noted that public opposition to the death penalty had been growing in Illinois. The report cited a 2000 poll saying that 47 percent of Illinois residents favored a sentence of life without parole instead of the death penalty and that 70 percent of Illinois residents approved of the moratorium.

What really caught my eye was the estimate that Illinois spent $25 million on death penalty cases in 2000 that would not have been spent if the ultimate punishment was life without parole. That was money that could have been well spent elsewhere in the criminal justice system, I thought.

On January 31, during my State of State address, I touched only briefly on the moratorium. And I was startled, I admit, when the legislators—men and women who generally hide their feelings behind a safe, tough-on-crime facade, actually applauded. Members of the black democratic caucus ignited the outpouring by leaping to their feet, clapping loudly. The applause spread to fellow Democrats and finally to Republicans. The result was an extended standing ovation. It was, for me, no small moment.

In late February a group of legislators announced the introduction of a bill to abolish the death penalty. Bill Ryan, chairman of the Illinois Death Penalty Moratorium Project, said the bill was

> in keeping with the results of the annual report developed by our moratorium project that clearly documents that we have a system that is so badly flawed it can only be fixed by repealing current death penalty provisions and substituting life without parole. Until we can make sure that mistaken identification doesn't result in an innocent person being executed, until we can remove racism from Illinois, until we remove arbitrariness, until we can remove prosecutorial misconduct and police torture and until we recognize the alternative of a life sentence without the possibility of parole provides a meaningful clo-

> sure to the family of murder victims, I don't think we can have moral certitude.

Art Turner, a Chicago Democratic state representative, said he didn't expect any action on it until after my commission had made its recommendations.

I didn't think it had a chance to pass at all, but I remained quiet.

On March 1, I was stunned to learn that Dick Cunningham, the vocal critic of the death penalty and a long-time defender of death row prisoners, was murdered in his home on the North Side of Chicago. Tragically, he was stabbed to death by his own son, Jesse, in the kitchen of Cunningham's home. Jesse, who was twenty-six years old, had fought depression and schizophrenia for years. He was talking with Dick at about 1:00 p.m. when he suddenly grabbed a knife and stabbed his father in the head, chest, and back. Dick staggered outside, calling for help. When a neighbor who was an off-duty police officer rushed over with his gun in one hand, Dick shouted, "Don't hurt him. My son, Jesse, he's sick."

One detective told the *Chicago Tribune*, "There was no argument, zero arguing. He had no idea it was coming."

Just one day earlier, Cunningham had been in my office, accompanying his exonerated death row clients, Steven Smith and Ronald Jones, as they testified at a session of my moratorium commission. I found it unsettling to think that this man, whom I had come to know as a tireless worker and steadfast champion for the case of justice, was silenced at such a critical time in Illinois.

On March 29, the Illinois House passed a package of reform legislation designed to crack down on prosecutorial misconduct and prevent wrongful convictions. If approved by the Senate (and signed by me), the legislation would strictly limit the testimony of jailhouse informants. In cases where prosecutors failed to turn over evidence to defense lawyers, the prosecutors would have the burden to show that the evidence would not have changed the trial or sentencing results. And equally significant, the defense would be allowed to take pretrial sworn depositions of nonpolice witnesses in cases where the possible sentence was either death or life in prison without parole.

"If you're injured in a fender bender at the corner of State and Madison, you can depose everyone who's at that location at that time and ask them what their observations were of the accident," Durkin declared.

"However, if you are accused of a terrible crime—murder—in which you are subject to capital punishment and you are identified by one or two witnesses as the person who pulled the trigger, you don't have an opportunity to depose those witnesses."

Durkin noted that five of the thirteen Illinois death row exonerees were convicted, in part, by jailhouse informant testimony. "We've come dangerously close in Illinois over the past three years of executing innocent individuals. We have a legislative and a moral obligation to make changes to this system. Also, in the long run, it's going to make cases better so the culpable person will be prosecuted and the innocent man won't have to wait fifteen years to be exonerated."

Unfortunately, I figured that this would go nowhere in the Senate, which was under the control of Pate Philip. He told the press, "We'll look at it. We'll give it a hearing." But then he tipped his hand, saying the legislation was "like giving ammunition to the enemy."

And in fact, the legislation died a quiet death in committee. The work of my commission took on even more significance.

# 19

# PONDERING ABOLITION

In April, I was back on the road, talking about the moratorium and the death penalty. I was honored to be asked to speak and I was eager to tell my story. First up was a visit to the West Coast. UCLA School of Law was the initial stop and Pepperdine University School of Law was next—sandwiched around visits to the Richard Nixon Presidential Library in Yorba Linda and the Ronald Reagan Presidential Library in Simi Valley.

At UCLA, I told the law students:

> Since I declared the moratorium last year, I have received more attention around the world than I ever imagined. I've received awards for courage. In fact, tonight, I am receiving the Act of Courage Award from Mike Farrell's Death Penalty Focus Group. I don't know that courage is the best word to describe what I did. I just call it doing the right thing.
>
> That is why I wanted to come here to speak with you. You are law students. You've been very fortunate and you have tremendous opportunity before you. Someday you will be lawyers. Some of you will try cases as prosecutors or defense lawyers. Some of you may become law professors. Even others may become lobbyists or elected officials.
>
> But you also have an obligation. Because someday, you may find yourself representing a man or woman accused of a capital crime—facing the death penalty. Maybe you will be a prosecutor, seeking the death sentence for someone you've convicted.
>
> Or perhaps you will find yourself in my situation.
>
> Maybe you'll be elected governor and have resting on your shoulders the enormous weight of having to decide whether a death row

> inmate should live or die. It could happen. I'll tell you I never thought I would be here today talking to you in this lecture.
>
> I never thought I would be in the position of making life or death decisions. I had to make that decision once and then I came to learn the indisputable facts—that the administration of the death penalty in Illinois was just not fair and our record was shameful.

As I always did in these presentations, I told the story of Anthony Porter and how journalism students helped save his life and prove his innocence. I recounted my agonizing over my decision to allow the execution of Andrew Kokoraleis to go forward. And I reiterated my intention for the commission to study the system.

"Until I can be sure that everyone sentenced to death in Illinois is truly guilty, until I can be sure with moral certainty that no innocent person is facing a lethal injection, no one will meet that fate," I declared. "I am comfortable knowing that I did the right thing.

"Someday you will no longer be living the life of a law student," I said. "You will graduate, pass the bar—trust me, you will—and practice law. You owe it to your client and to the entire justice system to be engaged in the relentless, passionate search not for victory at all costs but for truth. Embrace that search. Engage in that quest for truth. And never, ever compromise it."

My message the following day to Pepperdine law students was similar. I found these moments exciting—and worthwhile. I felt that I was delivering a message that people needed to hear about the death penalty, especially people who might be ambivalent about it—like I was for all those years.

The more I thought about this, I was concluding that our prisons were full of people whose cases probably should have a second look. In my travels, I was finding, not surprisingly, that most people felt that law and order comes first and that meant getting convictions and sentencing people to prison and to death. But I also discovered that the idea of the criminal justice system is abstract to most people. They don't have to go to bed every night with the death penalty.

It really was impressive to be honored by Death Penalty Focus. Mike Farrell, in his personal invitation, said, "We're aware that it is not easy in today's political world to carefully examine issues and positions often characterized as unpopular, and the ability and willingness of a political leader to maintain a position of such integrity reassures, invigorates and energizes those who often tend to think they're alone in the struggle for human dignity."

He said that an important goal of Death Penalty Focus was to demonstrate in public events such as their awards dinner the "breadth and depth of the community of individuals committed to social progress through the advancement of human rights." He added that my acceptance of the award would "lend great strength to the work of our organization and to the social justice movement as whole."

Among others honored that night was Cardinal Roger Mahony of the Los Angeles Archdiocese of the Roman Catholic Church. Mahony had taken a stand earlier in opposition to the death penalty, saying, "This is a time for a new ethic—justice without vengeance. We cannot restore life by taking life. We cannot practice what we condemn. We cannot contain violence by using state violence. In this new century, we join with others in taking prophetic stand to end the death penalty."

I couldn't say I was ready to abolish the death penalty, but increasingly, I had an open mind to what people like Cardinal Mahony and Mike Farrell were saying.

In my speech that night I talked about courage and how there was nothing courageous about what I did. I had found myself at a fork in the road. I either had to let innocent people die or declare a moratorium—a decision I hoped anyone would have made.

"Courage," I said, "is Nelson Mandela, a man who spent decades in prison, in harsh conditions, simply because he believed his people should be free and equal.

"Courage is to be exiled from your country for advocating for democracy, like President Kim of South Korea, who I met this year.

"Courage really describes the young men and women I have met and presented with awards for their acts of heroism as police officers or firefighters, running into burning buildings or putting themselves in harm's way to protect us.

"Courage describes what it takes to endure being wrongfully convicted and sentenced to be killed by the state for a crime you did not commit, only to be exonerated at the eleventh hour—as we have done thirteen times in Illinois. That is a shameful record," I said.

"There have been a few naysayers, but they are pretty easily drowned out when you hear the Colosseum in Rome has been illuminated in light in your honor," I said.

Declaring the moratorium, I said, was not a courageous thing. "But I know as sure as I am standing here tonight that it is the right thing."

Days later, I was on my way to Yale Law School in New Haven, Connecticut. My speech to law students there was timely. The Connecticut legislature was debating a moratorium on the death penalty as well as a ban on executing mentally disabled defendants. I took the occasion to deliver a message: don't kill someone unless you can be sure that person is guilty.

I was greeted as a hero, although I certainly didn't feel like one. And back in Illinois, it didn't take long before I wound up in the crosshairs of the media and Pate Philip, who increasingly was a personal nemesis.

In a speech at Loyola University in Chicago, I spoke candidly about my growing doubt about being able to support the death penalty even if the system was flawless. I said I didn't know if I could personally throw the switch on Oklahoma City bomber Timothy McVeigh, who was scheduled to be executed at a federal prison in Indiana in June.

When a student asked if I could support a perfect death penalty system, I was honest. "I don't know," I said. "I'm still struggling with it." I went on to say I couldn't give the go-ahead to execute McVeigh, who I considered a terrible human being.

"He thought this thing out and went out and killed a whole bunch of people and said that children were collateral to the event and it didn't matter," I said. "He's shown no remorse. I think there may be cause for the death penalty for a guy like him, but I don't know."

What I was trying to say was that while I thought McVeigh probably deserved to be executed, I was glad I didn't have to be the one making the final decision.

Less than twenty-four hours later, Philip told the press that he would be willing to execute McVeigh if I didn't have the courage to do so. "For this horrendous crime, I'll pull the switch," Philip said. "In case he hasn't got the courage, I'll volunteer."

I am sure there were people more than a little gleeful at Philip's cheap shot at me. I tried to make it clear it wasn't about McVeigh. This was about my feeling that I couldn't approve another execution. Period.

At the same time that the legislature was refusing to pass reform legislation, it was actually approving a bill which would potentially *increase* the number of people sentenced to death. The legislation would expand the death penalty law to allow death sentences to be imposed on people convicted of murder if the crime was committed as part of street gang activity. This was referred to as an "aggravating factor" that could qualify a murder conviction as eligible for the death penalty. Illinois already had twenty of these aggravating factors, one of the most expansive lists in the nation.

I came in for personal criticism from a different source in June when Will County Circuit Court judge Herman Hasse sentenced Timothy Cunningham to life in prison for killing his wife in 1999 and another twenty years in prison for the attempted murder of his wife's stepfather.

"If we can't put serial killers or the murderers of police officers to death, how can we give it to someone who committed murder in a family situation?" Hasse asked and went on to question whether I had the authority to halt executions.

"I don't think he does have the authority," Hasse said. "As a result [of the moratorium], vicious killers who have been sentenced to death are sitting on death row today and their sentence is not being carried out. We need the state legislature, the state Supreme Court, and the governor to decide whether we are going to have death penalty or not."

I was getting used to this kind of criticism and just put it to the side. As long as my commission was still meeting and taking testimony, I did not want to publicly respond and risk being interpreted as trying to influence the commission. Above all, I wanted the commission to be above reproach; to be fair and to come back with the best course of action—not for me—but for Illinois.

While I stayed quiet, others did not. Sensing that momentum was on their side after years of little, if any, success, death penalty opponents began talking publicly about their preferred option short of abolition: the need to commute all capital punishment convictions to life in prison. To them, it was the only viable option any governor had to deal with a broken system. They began voicing arguments that with such a high error rate among capital cases, the system's fundamental flaws made any conviction under the existing rules at the least suspect and at the most, unjust.

What I didn't know at the time was that earlier in the year, at the annual death penalty conference convened by the NAACP Legal Defense and Educational Fund in Airlie, Virginia, a group of Illinois lawyers, including Northwestern's Larry Marshall, had met privately to discuss a plan to begin seeking commutations for death row prisoners—all of them.

Soon, they would begin lobbying heavily for me to use my authority to empty death row.

The commission, to their credit, ignored the lobbying efforts that were pushing both sides of the issue. They were working to meet the expectations that I had set for it. I wasn't pushing them, but in my heart, I was more than ready for them to go public.

# 20

# END OF AN ERA

The month of August in Central Illinois can be withering. The sun is intense and the humidity chokes the life out of even the hardiest of souls—particularly those who would sit in such heat for more than an hour on a weekday afternoon. In the stillness of the midafternoon heat, you can almost hear the corn growing.

Wednesday, August 8, 2001, was no exception. The media as well as a crowd of about one thousand people were sweltering when I arrived at the Kankakee County Courthouse that day with Lura Lynn and the other members of my family—my six children and their spouses and fourteen grandchildren.

The television cameras were set up—a row of electronic sentinels aimed at a podium that had been pushed to the center of the top step and draped with American flag bunting. A placard with my name graced the front, although there wasn't a soul present who didn't know who I was or my job.

The word had gone out that I was going to make an important announcement and now I was ready to face a coterie of state, county, and local officials along with friends and supporters. In fact, I was going to say that I would not run for reelection. My life as an elected official was going to end as governor after winning statewide elections ten times—more than any other elected official in state history. Before I ran for governor, Lura Lynn and I had decided that I would serve only one term if elected. After one term it would be time for us to be together more often with our families and not to spend virtually every day crisscrossing the state or the country. We had kept this to ourselves because I didn't want to be a lame duck any sooner than I had to be. In fact, it wasn't until just before I stepped before the podium that I told my staff members of my decision. My lieutenant governor, Corinne Wood, learned of my decision when I said the words aloud.

In the end, I also felt running for re-election would be too divisive for the Republican Party. I had become increasingly progressive and the Illinois Republican Party was veering ever further to the right.

"Thanks for being here," I said to acknowledge the rolling applause. "It's hot. Thanks for all the wonderful support."

"I know we've all be sitting around here in this hot weather waiting for some important news," I said. "I am going to get right at it and get it out of the way at the beginning of this conversation so there isn't any more to talk about."

Pausing only slightly, I picked up a white card. "The Cubs won two to one. That's a final score. And they now lead the division by three games." Behind me, my family was laughing and in front of me people were clapping and cheering. Hand-held fans fluttered in vain attempts to cool brows coursing with beads of sweat. I moved to the matter at hand.

"In the political season that's soon to come, some may say the greatest thing I did was launch Illinois First," I declared. "You all know that's the comprehensive rebuilding of the state and all its promise. Some may say it was working to open the door to Cuba, a nation that is as close to America as South Bend is to Chicago. And others may say it was acting decisively to halt a series of executions that threatened the rule of law that everyone in this hallowed land of Lincoln holds so dear.

"I don't know of anybody who wants to execute an innocent person," I said, prompting the crowd to erupt in applause again. "I leave it to others to determine what is the greatest thing my administration has accomplished. But there can never be any doubt in my mind about the best thing I ever did in my life." Turning to Lura Lynn, I hugged her close. "And that was to marry this woman right here. We've been together for fifty-three years and we are still in love."

After thirty-four years in public office, I said that I was proud of what I had accomplished but that I still had work to do. I knew I was speaking to more than just the hundreds of state workers, department directors, lawmakers, lobbyists, party officials, and hometown friends who had gathered to hear my announcement. I reminded them that I had taken on and supported controversial issues—including gun control, public funding for abortions for the poor, and gay rights.

"So, I say to you now, this is my record as governor of this state—the record on which I would ask the voters of this state to judge my performance," I said. "I've done my best and I am proud of what we have been able to accomplish by working together.

"I've been criticized by some in my party—the hard right wing if you will—for doing some things they don't agree with. I led a humanitarian mission to Cuba. We pressed Castro on human rights. We also explored new opportunities to feed both the needy and to open markets and minds with the food that grows here in abundance. We brought two ailing children back to the United States to find new hope from the greatest medical system in the world. I would do it again in a heartbeat. It was the right thing to do.

"We tackled these challenges not because they were easy, but because they were hard," I said. "And I was always grateful you supported me, even when I had tough decisions to make.

"Some of you may recall that in my early days of my term in the General Assembly, I voted to reinstate the death penalty in Illinois. But during the past three years, I have talked with people from all over the world about the shocking condition of our system of capital punishment. We nearly executed innocent men. Not once. But thirteen times in this state. Not once, but thirteen times we almost made that mistake. And I don't know how that happened. But I knew then as I do now that I had no choice but to call a halt to what was obviously a deeply flawed process.

"And I tell you today that I will continue to lead the fight to reform our criminal justice system. Looking back, it wasn't a tough decision. The death penalty moratorium was quite simply the right thing to do.

"My conservative right-wing critics deride me for being in favor of equal and fair treatment for everyone, regardless of who they are as a person," I said. "I am not in favor of special treatment for anybody, but I am for fairness for everybody and equality.

"And I would make all of these decisions again because they were the right thing to do," I declared. "I can take the heat. But I worry for the Republican Party—the party of Lincoln—under whose banner I have proudly served all of my life. If we are to be successful, we need to listen more and shout less. We need to moderate our positions. People of Illinois want to reach out to their neighbors. They want new markets for their farmers, not outdated ideology. They want compassion for the poor and I learned a long time ago that winning public office is about addition and not subtraction. I would hope that the party folks are listening. We need to be a party of inclusion.

"There are challenges ahead that will require all of our talents," I declared. "We have a lot of work to do to continue to fight to bring excellence to our schools and to reform the death penalty, to fight for safe neighborhoods, to spark economic growth. . . . These all mark efforts that deserve passion, commitment, and the full attention of the government. The work ahead is important. It's important to me. It's important to you and it's important to Illinois.

"These challenges require serious debate—a dialogue free from rancor or personal attacks about motives or character. And that's why the governorship should not become mired in the political divisions of a campaign year. And that's why, over the next seventeen months, I will devote every ounce of my abilities to the challenges that Illinois faces and the duties of high office that you hired me to do.

"And that's why I will not be a candidate for Republican nomination for governor in 2002. I want to tell you my friends, the hopes of Illinois, the real working of governing still lie ahead. And that's as it must be. The priority today and in the months to come must be those priorities we work on now. Important challenges remain. They remain for me and for all of Illinois. The journey is far from done. Our pact is a four-year contract to do my very best for the state—to fulfill the sacred trust you placed in me in 1998. This decision today is not about my future. It's about the future of Illinois."

I patted the head of one of my grandsons. "It's about the future of these young people here today."

And after a reiteration of thanks to various legislative leaders and elected officials, I was done. The speech was over. I loosened my tie. I was drenched in sweat. I had pulled the trigger and now, more than ever, I could focus on the tasks at hand without the distraction of a political campaign. More than ever, I could focus on doing the right thing.

Although Lura Lynn and I had previously decided I would be a one-term governor, this was still a difficult day. But in my heart, I knew this was the right decision. I also suspected I would face much harder choices in the future.

One of the first tasks was to confront the bill that passed overwhelmingly in the General Assembly adding an additional "aggravating factor" to the twenty such factors already in place in the death penalty statute that made an offender eligible for the death penalty. In this instance, lawmakers fed up with the gang-related murders in their districts, engineered a bill that allowed prosecutors to seek the death penalty if a murder was committed as part of gang activity.

I vetoed that bill without a second thought. While it may have been well-intentioned, I thought expanding the reach of the death penalty moved things in the wrong direction. It certainly wouldn't have curtailed gang activity, I thought. I issued a statement saying that our past history of erroneously sentencing individuals to death was evidence that officials should be questioning rather than expanding use of the death penalty.

"By changing the law to make more and more crimes eligible for the death penalty, we introduce more arbitrariness and discretion, and edge ever closer to our previous capital punishment system that was effectively held unconstitutional by the US Supreme Court in 1972," I said.

At least one person agreed with me—Chicago democratic senator Barack Obama. "There's a strong overlap between gang affiliation and young men of color," Obama declared. "I think it's problematic for them to be singled out as more likely to receive the death penalty for carrying out certain acts than are others who do the same thing."

The measure had passed the House 77 to 32 and the Senate 44 to 9. These were vote totals that were sufficient to override my veto. But the veto remained in place. I thought that was a good measure of how many members of the legislature were listening to the concerns I had with the death penalty system and how uneasy they were with expanding it before it could be fixed.

Without the moratorium in place, my veto probably would have been overridden.

And who knows how many more wrongful convictions and wrongful death sentences would have occurred?

# 21

# CRITICS EVERYWHERE

It didn't take long for the political season to begin with people announcing their candidacies and calling for an end to the moratorium. Republican state senator Patrick O'Malley, who actually had declared his candidacy for the Republican nomination for governor back in June, weighed in almost immediately.

"We have a governor who is apparently confused or indifferent as to what the law in Illinois is," O'Malley said. "He does not have the right to ignore the law by a process of executive nullification." Moreover, O'Malley claimed I had dreamed up the moratorium as a public relations maneuver when all I had to do was just stay any executions that came up.

O'Malley also went after Illinois attorney general Jim Ryan, who was also running for the Republican gubernatorial nomination. "By not seeking dates of execution of persons justly convicted of capital crimes, Attorney General Ryan is not providing for 'timely disposition' of these cases. As such, the families of these crime victims are not getting justice," O'Malley declared. "Attorney General Ryan should no longer hide behind the governor's moratorium, nor should the governor hide behind the attorney general's failure to seek execution dates."

O'Malley quoted Will County Circuit Court judge Herman Haase, who had criticized me during a sentencing hearing earlier in the year, saying, "If we are going to have a death penalty and a death sentence law that is not carried out as to the most vicious serial killers, to killers of police officers in the line of duty, to multiple murderers, then I think we have to ask ourselves a question: What are we doing?"

O'Malley said that if I wanted to get rid of the death penalty, I should go to the General Assembly. It was a cheap shot and he knew it. I wasn't trying to get rid of the death penalty system—I had appointed a commission to try to fix it.

I refused to sit on my hands on this issue. I fired right back.

"If this fella wants to be governor of the State of Illinois, he ought to have his facts straight, and he hasn't," I said. "It would be the worst thing to ever happen to Illinois if he ever got elected governor of the state. He's an ideologue that's got tunnel vision and doesn't understand what it takes to be governor of the State of Illinois. And I would certainly hope nobody would support him."

Joseph Birkett, the DuPage County state's attorney who announced he was running for the Republican nomination for Illinois attorney general, also said it was time to lift the moratorium.

"I know that we have the fairest system of capital punishment in the nation. I think it is time to move on with capital punishment," Birkett declared at a news conference. Birkett, of course, had been a critic of the moratorium since the day I imposed it. He said I could have individually halted executions and that there was no need for a moratorium. In any event, now he was saying that the system had been fixed and the flaws had been corrected.

He also was strongly in favor of a legislative proposal designed to combat terrorism. The bill would create a new crime of terrorism that would be eligible for the death penalty.

"I believe it's critical that everybody in America, including local law enforcement and local state's attorneys, be part of the war on terrorism," Birkett said. "The federal government cannot do the work alone."

These calls to end the moratorium didn't bother me. I was patiently waiting for the commission to do its job. And they were working long hours and taking testimony from a wide variety of individuals. It was clear that the moratorium was going to play a significant role in the 2002 race for governor. O'Malley was definitely trying to play the tough on crime card against his primary opponent, Jim Ryan, because Jim supported the moratorium. Birkett had four people sentenced to death while he was the DuPage County state's attorney and I presumed he wanted to be about the business of seeing them killed.

Meanwhile, in late October, the Illinois Supreme Court ordered a new hearing for Howard Wiley, who had been sentenced to death in Cook

County in 1990 for the murders of three women. The court held that Wiley's attorney could have presented evidence of Wiley's need for psychiatric counseling and his history of mental illness. Such evidence "might have provided the sentencing judge with additional information that could have influenced the choice of sentence," the court declared.

And the court noted that Wiley's attorney could have called better witnesses from the family. Instead, Wiley's brother had testified, but only after he was subpoenaed and then said that Wiley was "not his role model" and that he didn't like Wiley's friends.

At the time of sentencing, the judge said that the brother was a better witness for the prosecution than for Wiley and that they couldn't have called a better witness "if they wrote the script themselves."

Meanwhile, another death sentence was handed down. Just before Thanksgiving, Luther Casteel was condemned to die by lethal injection in Kane County for a shooting spree in JB's Pub in Elgin, Illinois, seven months earlier. He was convicted of two counts of first-degree murder and fifteen counts of attempted murder. The jury gave him what he wanted, apparently. On the witness stand, Casteel said he wasn't afraid of anything, that he had no remorse, and he didn't want any mercy.

The *Chicago Tribune* did it again in December, publishing a series of articles titled "Cops and Confessions."

The first paragraph was particularly riveting: "Substituting interrogation for thorough investigation, police in Chicago and Cook County have repeatedly closed murder cases with dubious confessions that imprison the innocent while killers go free."

The reporters documented 247 cases in ten years where defendants were said to have confessed to murder but either were acquitted at trial or the charges were dismissed. Now, 247 cases over a decade may not have seemed like a very big number, but in fact that averaged out to a murder case with a confession failing to stand up once every two weeks for ten years!

The newspaper reported how children as young as seven and eight were said to have confessed after being questioned without their parents or a legal guardian present as required by the law. Police had obtained a confession from people who were in jail at the time of the crime and could not possibly have committed the killings. In some cases, suspects said they told the police what they wanted to hear because they thought they could go home, which, of course, was not what happened. One suspect said he thought he could go to court and tell the judge the truth—that he did not commit the crime—and the judge would let him go. That was so not what had happened.

It reminded me of the Gary Gauger case and how the police got him to falsely confess to killing his own parents. Meanwhile, the bikers who had committed the murders were laughing at Gauger being sentenced to death.

Although the series ran for five days, I kept returning to the last four words of that first paragraph of the first article: "while killers go free."

How could O'Malley and Birkett possibly think the system was fine? This was political posturing at its best.

And that antiterrorism bill Birkett was pushing? I vetoed it in part because I was concerned about expanding the death penalty eligibility factors. In fact, I really didn't think terrorists were going to be deterred by the threat of a death sentence if they were caught.

"It sure didn't stop the fellows that flew into the World Trade Centers," I said. "In fact, it would be difficult to imagine a scenario under which a terrorist act resulting in death would not already qualify for capital punishment under our current statute. Moreover, terrorism is currently a death-eligible offense under federal law."

Just as important, I said that I didn't want to do anything that was going to influence my commission. "If I sign that bill with the death penalty in it, it might indicate what I'd like to have in the report," I said. "I've done my best in two years not to signal how I may or may not feel about it."

# 22

# A NEW WRINKLE

When I could get away from my duties as governor, I continued to accept invitations to speak about my decision to declare a moratorium and to establish the Capital Punishment Commission.

On March 1, 2002, I was among thirty-five men and women with death penalty experiences who gathered to speak at a conference at the Wayne Morse Center for Law and Politics at the University of Oregon Law School in Eugene, Oregon. The conference was titled "Law and Politics of the Death Penalty: Abolition, Moratorium or Reform?" and was organized by Charles Ogletree Jr., who had heard me speak at Harvard. Ogletree was becoming one of America's most preeminent criminal justice scholars. The conference featured numerous luminaries in the death penalty trenches, including Sister Helen Prejean.

When my turn came, I recounted my thought process that led me to declare the Illinois moratorium. "We freed thirteen innocent men who were nearly strapped to a gurney in the state's death chamber so that fatal doses of poison could be injected into their bloodstreams," I said. "That is the ultimate nightmare." And I stressed that even 99 percent accuracy was not enough. "If the government can't get this right, it ought not be in the business of passing such final, irreversible judgment," I said.

Afterward, during a question and answer session, Joshua Marquis, district attorney in Clatsop County, Oregon, and a strong supporter of the death penalty, asked me pointedly: if my faith in the system was so deeply shaken, why didn't I consider commuting the death sentences of the 163 men and 4 women then on death row to sentences of life in prison without parole?

I did not expect that question.

The truth was that I had been thinking about that possibility. I was faced with 167 prisoners on death row put there by a criminal justice system that had gotten things wrong more than 50 percent of the time. It was like flipping a coin. To me, the seeming chance nature of how the system operated carried greater weight than the fact that there were that many men and women on death row. If you drew out the problems that we knew about and applied them to the men and women on death row, number-wise there might be dozens of innocent people.

But how would you know which was which?

That was the problem.

This was the first time I had been directly asked about the issue of clemency.

"I just might," I said. "We are looking at that. I just this week received a file on every one of them. I got two big books. And it's going to take a good deal of time to review it, but I'm going to do that."

My comment streaked through the stratosphere back to Illinois where it unintentionally gave some ammunition to the supporters of the death penalty, especially prosecutors around the state who, as a group, were smarting over having sent innocent people to death row. I don't know how many times in the previous two years prosecutors and police expressed their opposition to the moratorium. To some, I was undermining the rule of law and I was giving comfort to criminals. One prosecutor, Bill Haine, from downstate Madison County, accused me of committing "treason against the state and the constitution" I had sworn to uphold. Haine said commutations would be "a slap in the face to every police officer, every victim of every murderer, every juror who ever rendered a verdict."

Now that I had brought the possibility of clemency out into the open, it clearly was a matter that I had to seriously consider.

It wouldn't be easy. In fact, it was going to be fraught with difficulty. How does one go through these cases and decide which ones are worthy of commutation to life in prison without parole? Deciding if any of them were innocent was probably an impossible task. If the thirteen exonerations taught us anything, it was that sometimes the evidence of innocence is not readily apparent or not discovered until years—decades—later.

Anthony Porter wasn't exonerated until Alstory Simon confessed. Ronald Jones wasn't exonerated until DNA tests were performed on the evidence. Gary Gauger wasn't fully exonerated until after federal agents discovered that the Wisconsin motorcycle gang members were responsible.

Northwestern's Larry Marshall pointed out, "The thing to remember is this—when Anthony Porter was about to be killed, no one thought that was a case that raised any questions of factual innocence. And lo and behold, it turns out we couldn't have been more wrong. When you have bad lawyering or you have no investigations, how can you look at a record and say you know a guy is guilty?"

And the *Chicago Tribune* was quick to note that governors in other states had commuted death sentences in cases where the lawyers for the condemned presented evidence of mental illness or diminished mental capacity or evidence that the defendants were raised in environments where they were abused, either physically or emotionally, by adults with serious mental problems or were seriously addicted to drugs or alcohol or both. It was determining who was mentally ill or had a diminished mental capacity that was the hard part. Invariably, prosecutors had experts who said there was no such evidence of mental shortcomings while the defense experts said just the opposite.

This task would almost consume me.

Nine days later, I was at the podium again—this time at Saint Josephat Church on Chicago's North Side to receive an award named for Dick Cunningham, the death penalty lawyer murdered by his mentally ill son, and for Jack Carey, a veteran public defender who had tried numerous death penalty cases before succumbing an at early age to cancer. This was a two-day event with sessions on various aspects of the death penalty featured such notables as Sister Helen Prejean, Mike Farrell, Cardinal Francis George of the Chicago Catholic Archdiocese, Larry Marshall, and Bud Welch, the abolition advocate whose daughter was killed in the Oklahoma City bombing. I was getting to be a regular part of the anti-death penalty circuit.

I took the opportunity to reemphasize how, since imposing the moratorium, I had rejected two separate attempts by the state legislature to expand the death penalty.

"Twice I have used my constitutional authority to veto those measures," I said. "The measures would have expanded the death penalty to include murders committed by gang members and terrorists—even though those criminals would be eligible for the death penalty today. With so many questions, so many difficult questions about the fairness of capital punishment in Illinois, I believe it was not the time to expand our flawed and shameful system.

"In this new era, after the horror and tragedy of September 11, lawmakers have been hearing from their constituents a desire to strike back, to do something to hold terrorists accountable," I continued. "People want to feel safe in their communities. I remember those same inflamed passions from more than twenty-five years ago, when my colleagues and I voted to reinstate the death penalty.

"We all want to punish the guilty," I said. "But in so doing, we must not also punish the innocent. And with our mistake-prone system in Illinois, we were doing just that."

After more than two years of public speaking and listening to experts and exonerees and defense lawyers and—yes—prosecutors, I was determined that Illinois would be a model for the rest of the world.

"We must strive for a system in which those accused of capital offenses or other serious criminal charges can be afforded the best defense with competent, trained counsel," I said. "That means the only lawyers that can sleep will be at home in their beds, not in the courtroom."

As I accepted the award in the name of Carey and Cunningham, I recalled how Cunningham had been in my office testifying before my commission on the day before he was murdered. He had given a passionate speech about the wrongs committed by the system. He had spoken of the twenty-two capital cases that he had handled on appeal. He had shared with the commission stories of his clients, including ones who had been beaten and tortured to confess, and one client who had been sentenced by a judge who was taking bribes.

I didn't know Jack Carey, but I had heard from many of his friends and colleagues what a great lawyer he had been. And I thought about what it must have been to work for the public defender's murder task force, hamstrung by budget cuts and always being up against the state with its limitless funds.

"God took Dick and Jack from us too soon," I declared. "There was so much more work for them to do. But maybe God had other plans. And this award can keep their memory and their passionate fight for justice alive."

Later that day I began seriously thinking about what course of action to chart. I could continue as I had been, encouraging new reforms of the system, but not seeking to have any of them apply retroactively.

Or we could study every case and try to separate out the ones that fell into the categories where there had been the most problems—all-white juries, incompetent defense lawyers, jailhouse snitches, and prosecutorial misconduct.

Soon I would get files on everyone on death row, each with a one- or two-page summary of the case. The fact is that each of these cases likely had a room full of documents—police reports, witness statements, defense motions and prosecution responses and appeals decisions, let alone transcripts of trials and various evidentiary hearings. Something that Larry Marshall said stuck in my mind about the Anthony Porter case: judges had sixty-one different chances to catch something wrong in the case of Anthony Porter and they had not.

And commutation didn't mean anyone was going free. Life in prison without parole is no walk in the park. In fact, I—and many others—considered it a fate worse than execution.

Three days later, on March 13, 2002, the Clarence Darrow Commemorative Committee met—as they did annually—at the Darrow Bridge at the Chicago Museum of Science and Industry to mark the sixty-fourth anniversary of the legendary Chicago lawyer's death. The committee presented me with the Governor John Peter Altgeld Courage in Government Award.

Governor Altgeld, who had been dead for one hundred years, was probably best remembered for his pardons of three of the people who were convicted of the murders of those who died during the infamous Haymarket Square Riot on May 4, 1886. What had begun as a peaceful labor demonstration to support workers striking for an eight-hour work day ended in bloody chaos when someone tossed a dynamite bomb at police. Seven police officers were killed and so were four citizens. Dozens of people were wounded.

Ultimately, eight anarchists were convicted, although there was no proof any of them threw the bomb. Seven were sentenced to death and one was sentenced to fifteen years in prison.

Before leaving office in 1889, Governor Richard Oglesby commuted two of the death sentences to life in prison. Of the remaining five sentenced to death, one committed suicide in prison and the other four were hanged. In 1893, Governor Altgeld, after conducting a review of the case, concluded that guilt had not been proved and the men had been convicted based upon prejudice and hysteria. He pardoned the remaining three defendants and released them from prison. At the time, Altgeld suspected his actions would cost him his political career. And he had been right.

At least that was something I didn't have to worry about. I had already voluntarily ended my political life seven months earlier on the steps of the Kankakee County Courthouse.

I did have to figure out what I was going to do. For now, I was sitting tight until my commission completed its work. Asked by reporters about the process, I said I had not decided how or whether I would review each of the cases of everyone on death row. "I'm not sure I'm going to do all of that yet," I declared. "I'm just not sure how I'm to handle it."

I was conflicted once more.

# 23

# HISTORY LESSON

Sometimes a good history lesson from an unexpected source can be quite revealing. I had been candid all along that my education on the death penalty system had come from a variety of sources—the media, defense lawyers, policy makers, abolitionists, and death penalty supporters and the exonerees themselves.

In the immediate aftermath of the raising of the issue of commutations, I received a most interesting letter from Seymour Simon, a former Illinois Supreme Court justice who, during his tenure on the bench from 1980 to 1988, wrote nearly two hundred majority opinions and authored about 174 dissents. He particularly dissented in death penalty cases, believing that the death penalty was constitutionally defective because it was arbitrarily applied. His letter was an appeal to commute everyone on death row to life in prison without parole.

"I commend you upon your wisdom in imposing a moratorium on executions, and on your willingness and courage to consider which, if any, of the inmates on death row in Illinois should have their death sentences commuted," he wrote from his office at the Chicago law firm of Piper Marbury Rudnick & Wolf. "The errors evident in the thirteen cases of persons released from Illinois penitentiaries after being on death row for lengthy periods clearly require, at the very least, a reappraisal of the sentence imposed on each individual to determine whether he was properly convicted and sentenced. I respectfully suggest, however, that there is another approach to determining the propriety of carrying out executions imposed under the Illinois death penalty statute which does not require individualized appraisals of the circumstances which brought each person to death row."

He suggested that I take a look at the "incongruity" of the Illinois Supreme Court decisions dealing with the constitutionality of the death penalty statute—the statute I voted for when I was in the General Assembly. He said that the statute should have been held unconstitutional in 1981 in a case involving a man named Cornelius Lewis. As a pharmacist by trade, I was not experienced in the law. I found former justice Simon's analysis to be quite interesting.

It began with the case of Ronald Brown.

Cook County Circuit Court judge William Cousins Jr. had presided over the trial of Brown, who was accused of the armed robbery, kidnapping, and murder of Charles McGee on the Southwest Side of Chicago. McGee had been found shot to death in an alley and Brown was seen driving McGee's car later that day. There really was little doubt that Brown was guilty. The murder weapon, a .22-caliber revolver, was recovered in Brown's home along with three tires and a citizen's band radio from McGee's car. Brown was carrying McGee's watch, and his fingerprints were found on McGee's car. When questioned by police, Brown said he and another man, Andre Walker, had robbed McGee and that Walker was the one who shot McGee. With no proof linking Walker to the crime, he was never charged.

Judge Cousins heard the trial without a jury and convicted Brown. After the verdict, the prosecution requested that a jury be empaneled to hear evidence and decide whether—as the state wanted—Brown should be sentenced to death.

Judge Cousins denied that request. He ruled that the section of the death penalty that "vests the prosecution with unlimited discretion to trigger death sentence proceedings" essentially caused the death penalty to be "wantonly and freakishly imposed." Judge Cousins concluded that the statute contravened the due process clause as well as the prohibition of cruel and unusual punishment by the Eighth Amendment to the US Constitution.

The prosecution appealed Judge Cousin's ruling and in 1979 the Illinois Supreme Court overturned it by a vote of four to three. The three justices in the minority, Joseph Goldenhersh, Howard Ryan, and William Clark, dissented and said the death penalty was unconstitutional. They wrote that the death sentence could not be imposed fairly and uniformly because of the absence of sufficient standards to guide the 102 Illinois state's attorneys in deciding whether to request the death sentence. As a result, the three justices said, the determination was left to the discretion of each individual state's attorney. Brown's case was remanded back to Cook County for a death penalty hearing and ultimately, he was sentenced to eighty years in prison.

Simon explained that he came onto the Supreme Court in December 1980 after the Brown decision. He replaced Justice Thomas Kluczynski, who had been one of the four justices who supported the death penalty statute in the Brown ruling.

Subsquently, the first death penalty case to reach the court after Simon came onto the bench was the case of Cornelius Lewis, who had been convicted and sentenced to death for fatally shooting a security guard during a 1978 robbery of tellers at the Citizens National Bank in downstate Decatur, Illinois.

Simon, like the three justices who had held the death penalty statute unconstitutional in the Brown case, believed the statute was unconstitutional. And he expected that the Lewis case would be the one that would overturn the statute.

That did not happen. Instead, two of the dissenters said they believed that the Brown decision set a precedent that could not be overturned, notwithstanding the view they had previously expressed that the statute was unconstitutional. The third dissenter said he still believed the statute was unconstitutional, but that he preferred that the US Supreme Court make that decision. Of course, it never did.

Simon noted that in 1984, Justice Ryan—one of the original dissenters—called Simon out in the death penalty case of Charles Albanese, who was sentenced to death for poisoning his father, his mother-in-law, and his wife's grandmother with arsenic to obtain the family fortune.

"My colleague, Justice Simon, in three capital cases, has emphasized that three members of this court, Justice Clark, Justice Goldenhersh and I, originally dissented from the holding of the majority in [the Brown case], which case upheld the constitutionality of our death penalty statute," Justice Ryan wrote. "It is, apparently, my colleague's position that his vote against our death penalty statute, added to that of the three who dissented [in Brown] means that a majority of this court, as now constituted, is now of the opinion that our death penalty statute is not valid.

"In these cases, my colleague has chided the three dissenters . . . for continuing to adhere to the holding of the majority in that case despite our 'belief that the death penalty statute is unconstitutional,'" Justice Ryan declared. "My colleague errs when he asserts that I now believe that our death penalty statute is unconstitutional. That was my opinion at the time the opinion in [Brown] was adopted. I stated in my dissent the reason for my belief. Four members of this court did not agree with my reasoning and held that the statute was constitutional. I must accept the fact that my opinion was wrong because four members of this court said it was wrong. In reality, the judicial process does not deal in abstract propositions of right and wrong."

Justice Ryan went on to say that the decision of the majority in the Brown case was "binding not because of the concept that it is right or correct as a proposition of law, but because it is the final statement on that issue made by the highest judicial tribunal that has considered it. That is the nature of the appellate process. That is the manner in which cases and issues are decided. Simply because I dissent in a case does not mean that I must forever insist that I was right and the majority was wrong, or that 'everyone was out of step except me.'"

Simon wrote in his letter to me, "I was astounded by that simplistic description of the judicial process because I believe that it is the responsibility of the highest judicial authority in a forum to get it right, to do justice, especially in cases involving death sentences or restraints on freedom, and that in cases involving constitutional issues each judge of a reviewing court owes allegiance to the constitution itself rather than the gloss that has been put upon the constitution by the rulings of his predecessors."

Simon noted that at the time, he replied that Justice Ryan's statement "implies that ours is a system of footrace justice in which the first opinion entered prevails simply because it is first in time, and not necessarily because it is correct. . . . If a correct constitutional position were rendered forever incorrect merely because four judges once said it was, then our system of justice would not be one of laws, but one of men; not one of principle, but one of chance."

The idea of chance particularly resonated with me. I had compared the Illinois death penalty system to flipping a coin.

Simon then drove his point home.

"An experience with our judicial system I recommend you consider is that of Girvies Davis. His case reached the Illinois Supreme Court five times. If you were searching for individual death row occupants who were deserving of having their death sentences commuted, he would be a leading candidate were it not for the fact that he has already been executed," Simon wrote. "I invite your attention to Girvies Davis for two reasons. The first is that unlike other defendants whose exonerations resulted from fortuitous circumstances, Girvies Davis was executed, but his execution, like the exoneration of many of those who were released, happened because of chance.

"It came about in this way: the Illinois Supreme Court reversed a death sentence which had been imposed on Davis and remanded his case for a new death sentencing hearing. Following the remand, the State's Attorney of St. Clair County, Dick Allen, filed a petition with the Circuit Court requesting a re-sentencing hearing and stating that the State was waiving its request for the death penalty and instead would seek a term of natural life. Before the court acted on the petition, however, Mr. Allen was replaced as State's Attorney and the new State's Attorney withdrew Mr. Allen's petition and instead requested a death penalty hearing for Davis."

Davis was again sentenced to death and his appeal was denied in 1991—after Simon had left the bench and returned to the private practice of law. The denial was based upon the premise that the chief prosecutor had the discretion to seek the death penalty and that the new state's attorney therefore was within his rights to do so.

"So long as the initial decision to impose the death sentence is left to the individual 'prosecutorial discretion' of Illinois 102 state's attorneys, death sentences cannot be imposed uniformly and fairly in this state," wrote Simon. "Aberrations in the imposition of the death sentence between various individuals and various counties will continue in Illinois as they have in the past. I recognize that prosecutorial discretion plays a part in every decision to initiate a prosecution, but when life or death is at stake, uniformity and fairness require clear and strict standards to limit that discretion so that it will not be exercised arbitrarily.

"The absence of such standards in our present statute, together with the simultaneous presence of four Justices on the Illinois Supreme Court who had expressed the opinion that the death penalty was unconstitutional because of the absence of such standards is a compelling reason for you to commute all death sentences to life imprisonment," Simon declared.

Simon also noted that at the time of the Cornelius Lewis decision, he and the other dissenters objected to the statute's provision that did not require the prosecution to declare its intent to seek the death penalty until after a conviction. Defendants were put at a disadvantage by not knowing in advance of trial whether death was a possible outcome. This had finally been taken care of just this year, Simon noted, by the Illinois Supreme Court adopting a rule that advance notice to the defense was required.

"This belated action by the Court is justification for commuting the death sentences of all those on death row who did not have the benefit of that rule," Simon wrote.

He noted, "Some may view it as unseemly to commute all death sentences after twelve persons have already been executed." He said the best answer was given by former Second Circuit U.S. Court of Appeals judge Jerome Frank, a Chicagoan. Frank, in a ruling in 1956, said that "in criminal actions, where life or liberty is at stake, courts should not adhere to precedents unjust to the accused. It is never too late to mend."

That last sentence also resonated.

Girvies Davis had been executed in 1995. I discovered that like Anthony Porter, David Protess and his students had examined the Davis case and became convinced he was innocent. However, they had been unable to win his freedom. Protess had written an account of the last conversation with Davis—on the day he was executed—during which Protess and his students were listening as Davis said, "Try not to mourn for me. Move on with your lives. Just try to help people like me who get caught up in the system."

And then he asked Protess and the students to promise they would work on other death penalty cases.

"Of all the guys you know on the row, who do you think most deserves help?" Protess had asked.

Davis didn't miss a beat. He said that Dennis Williams was deserving of attention. "I'm certain he's innocent," Davis said.

And sure enough, Williams was one of the Ford Heights Four and along with Verneal Jimerson, Kenneth Adams, and Willie Rainge, was exonerated and freed in 1996.

I wondered if Girvies Davis should have been exonerated instead of executed.

Justice Simon had given me much to think about.

# 24

# CALL FOR CHANGE

As of Monday, April 15, 2002, the day the Capital Punishment Commission finally issued its long-anticipated report, 764 people (756 men and 8 women) had been executed in the United States since the reinstatement of the death penalty. During that same time, ninety-nine people had been released from death row nationwide. Florida had the most with twenty-two being released from death row. Illinois was second with our thirteen. In third place, Texas and Oklahoma each had released seven inmates from death row. The 100th death row exoneration—that of Ray Krone for a murder he did not commit—would occur nine days later in Arizona.

At the outset of its report, "a narrow majority" of the commission members said they supported abolishing the death penalty. At the same time, the commission concluded that if capital punishment remained in place in Illinois, reform was important to better ensure that it was fair, just, and accurate—although it could not be made foolproof.

"The commission was unanimous in the belief that no system, given human nature and frailties, could ever be devised or constructed that would work perfectly and guarantee absolutely that no innocent person is ever again sentenced to death," the report said.

The commission said that I and the next governor should consider the reforms that should be needed to be made to the death penalty system when considering clemency petitions in capital cases.

"It is entirely appropriate to consider how those changes might have made a difference to defendants when reaching determinations about whether or not a death sentence should be upheld on the merits or whether mercy should be extended in light of all of the circumstances," the report said.

The central question essentially went unanswered. There was no definitive verdict on whether capital punishment should be retained or repealed in Illinois. I didn't get the "moral certainty" I was looking for to help me decide the fate of current death row inmates. The commission said it was sure about just two things: the death penalty system in Illinois was broken and they couldn't find a way to make absolutely certain that everyone sentenced to death actually was guilty beyond any doubt.

I led off the press conference by thanking the commission members for their time and "extraordinary efforts to the public good. Their hard work and comprehensive study of this difficult issue is appreciated by all of us as citizens of this great state."

I promised to study the report and decide what to do. "I owe it to everyone who believes in justice and to everyone touched by our legal system to reflect upon this commission's findings," I said. "There are some who will be impatient, who will demand quick solutions now that I have this report. But our experience in Illinois with the capital punishment system has gained worldwide attention. What we do from this point forward may be an example to the rest of the country and the world."

Indeed, Richard Dieter, executive director of the Death Penalty Information Center, said, "People are looking to Illinois for what to do about this problem." He noted that of the thirty-eight states with the death penalty, twenty-two were considering moratoriums similar to the one I declared in Illinois, though it was unlikely that any would be enacted.

The report noted that had the recommendations been in place since the reinstatement of the death penalty in Illinois, at least 115 of the approximately 250 people sentenced to death by the end of 2001 would not have been eligible for the death penalty.

The commission's report not only underscored all the findings of previous investigations but proposed a number of concrete reforms for the current system—eighty-five recommendations in all. Some were minor and could be implemented by rule or a simple change of procedure. Other recommendations, however, would require real political muscle and a change in statute to be effective. All eighty-five of the recommendations, backed up by pages and pages of documentation, were solid, substantial improvements to Illinois death penalty law.

The conclusions and proposals addressed every one of the significant failings that had been identified by the media, by attorneys, or academics. The major recommendations were:

- Create a statewide panel that would conduct a pretrial review of all prosecutors' decision-making processes in capital cases. This panel, it was hoped, would curtail questionable decisions to seek the death penalty in cases where it really wasn't warranted.
- Reduce the number of legal factors making felons eligible for death from twenty to five.
- Ban the death penalty for anyone with diminished mental capacity (at the time the term was "mentally retarded").
- Prevent death penalty prosecutions when the prosecution's case was based solely on a single, uncorroborated eyewitness, the testimony of an accomplice, or the testimony of a jailhouse informant.
- Videotape the entire interrogation of a homicide suspect.
- Allow trial judges the power to reverse a jury's decision to impose the death sentence and impose a sentence of life without parole.
- Give the Illinois Supreme Court new power to vacate a death sentence if it is excessive or disproportionate to the penalties imposed in other similar crimes.
- Change the rules for police lineups to require that the officer conducting the lineup does not know who the suspect is and to obtain a detailed statement of the confidence level of witnesses who make identifications.
- Clarify the death penalty statute so juries fully understand their responsibilities when determining whether an accused is eligible for death and to ensure that judges fully explain to juries the range of sentences that a defendant may receive.
- Add as a mitigating factor for the jury to consider at sentencing information about a defendant's history of being abused physically or emotionally as well as reduced mental capacity that was short of the legal definition of mental impairment.

Death penalty opponents were disappointed. Some felt that a commission appointed by me should have at least leaned toward their views and done more to back up their beliefs. They questioned how the commission could remain deadlocked on this central question after spending two years poring over evidence that clearly revealed the flaws in the system.

But the commission had confirmed all the details others had uncovered about executions in Illinois. They had proposed meaningful changes to a broken system.

Rob Warden, the executive director of the Northwestern University Center on Wrongful Convictions, declared, "It comes to exactly the conclusions that anyone who studies the issue fairly comes to—that the system is not working and cannot work."

Legislators began weighing in on the possibility or probability that any of these reforms would be enacted by the General Assembly. Democratic state representative Barbara Flynn Curry, the House majority leader, said that some would be easy to support while others would require serious debate and significant infusions of money at a time when the state was laying people off due to a budget crisis.

Republican state senator Kirk Dillard told the *Chicago Tribune* that some of the recommendations, such as reducing the eligibility factors, would probably be "headed straight for the trash bin." He noted, "Legislators like to get tougher and tougher on crime. We ratchet it up, not down."

My response was simple: "We're talking about life and death. We're not talking about losing an election."

The commission said it had reviewed rulings in nearly three hundred capital cases and also reviewed the cases of the thirteen exonerations. The commission found there was very little solid evidence against the defendants. The disparities in the system were apparent. A review of a decade of cases revealed that people who killed white victims were more likely to get a death sentence than people who killed minorities. People convicted of murder in rural areas were more likely to get sentenced to death than people convicted of murder in urban areas.

Peoria County state's attorney Kevin Lyons emerged as a leading critic of the report. In a press conference, he contended that the commission's objective "was and is abolition of the death penalty. But they could not bring themselves to simply say that in a sentence or in a one-page report.

"It as an effort . . . to create more burdens and restrictions upon the prosecution, hoping they will say, 'Oh, the heck with it. What's the use? I'll just pursue it as a regular murder,'" he declared.

Chicago mayor Richard Daley, the former Cook County state's attorney, attacked the commission's recommendation of reducing the eligibility factors from twenty to five. He told the *Chicago Sun-Times* that eliminating the murder-for-hire factor was wrong. "Fabulous," he said sarcastically. "Just think, you plot it, you do it and you say to somebody, 'I'll give you $50,000. Go kill so-and-so.' You get the death penalty, but I will not. Very interesting. If that's the rule in Illinois, you'll have a big business in Illinois."

He added, "Think about a terrorist. If I sit back and I plot everything and I tell other people to do it, you're trying to tell me I'm not accountable? Then you'd better start thinking about history—what people did to people in the second world war—you don't think those generals should be held accountable? They'd better be accountable. And it's not just the person in those concentration camps. It's everybody being held accountable."

I thought that the commission understood the reality of the political situation in Illinois better than the death penalty opponents. A recommendation to repeal the death penalty right before an election would have been explosive throughout Illinois, and not necessarily in the direction that the opponents wanted. The reality was that endorsing an end to capital punishment at that time would become the major issue in campaigns all over the state. And regardless of the momentum the opponents thought they had built up, it was clear that a majority of Illinois residents—Illinois voters—still supported the death penalty. An official challenge to capital punishment from the commission might only serve to motivate supporters of the death penalty.

Also, if the commission called for the repeal of capital punishment, I would almost certainly have had to introduce that bill. There was absolutely no way that legislation abolishing the death penalty would survive the General Assembly in an election year.

From the very beginning of my questioning of the death penalty and how it was administered in Illinois, in the back of my mind two questions kept popping up—How is this going to end? What is at the end of the tunnel? At the beginning of my term, the answers to these questions were way in the future. I had four years. And when I declared the moratorium I still had three years left. I kept saying to myself that three years was plenty of time to find that conclusion. Now, with less than a year left, the "moral certainty" I was seeking had not yet materialized. I wondered if it ever would.

I had hoped that the moral certainty would, in large part, flow from the public. The public was beginning to see and understand the problems that I saw with the death penalty. They saw more men sentenced to death released from prison than prisoners on death row executed. The math was easy. The moral outrage at the injustice was easy. But, as I experienced from the beginning, there was moral outrage and math on the other side of the argument, as well. The math on the other side came from the number of victims of these crimes—many of them heinous, brutal murders. Families counted one less person at the dinner table at every holiday. And their moral outrage at the possibility that these men or women, convicted and sentenced by a court of law, might not be executed, was very strong and very certain.

With the report in hand, I started to list my options. And the first thing I had to confront was the distinct possibility that none or very few of the commission's recommendations would be adopted or enacted. If that were the case, and I ended the moratorium before I left office in January 2003, everything would just return to the way it had been. I decided I couldn't do that. Everything I had done and stood up for would be lost. A broken system would stay in place. There would be no reform, and police and prosecutors would just continue on as they had before 2000.

On the other hand, I could keep the moratorium in place, leave office, and do nothing else. That would throw the issue to the next governor. The next governor would either keep the moratorium or end it. There still was no guarantee of any reform at all.

The more I pondered this, neither of these options was acceptable. The attention that the issue had received had stimulated public debate. A vast number of people who previously had no opinion on the death penalty now did. But there still hadn't been any real reform of the system. Yes, the Illinois Supreme Court had issued new rules for capital cases and the state's attorney general had put some programs in place. It was a start, but I was certain those changes didn't go far enough.

And even so, the new rules and programs only affected future cases. They didn't do anything about the men and women that were already on death row—sent there, rightly or wrongly, by a broken system. The new rules wouldn't affect them. The problem I faced was really what to do about the past as much as it was what to do about the future—maybe more.

I knew I would push for the reforms recommended by the commission. I felt confident that the antideath penalty lobby had grown in strength since I became governor such that they would continue their fight in front of the public and before the General Assembly no matter what happened there. Nobody could flatly dismiss death penalty reforms any longer, I hoped.

The more I thought about it, I realized that I was coming to the conclusion that eventually capital punishment would be abolished in Illinois. How or when, I didn't know. It just seemed inevitable. But to deal with the past, well, that was up to me alone. And it was not a comfortable position. It was difficult. I had tremendous powers as governor to deal with the sentences of any person convicted of a crime in Illinois. These powers—to commute sentences and to pardon people completely for their crimes—were literally as old as the United States. From the beginning of the formation of the United States, the executive branch of the government had been given some authority to change the outcome of a criminal trial if it saw fit. And the thing about it was, there was no review of this power. It was my responsibility, and once I acted, that was it. No one could reverse me. I had the power to change the past.

The question was whether I would be able to. Could I bring myself to use it?

# 25

# GET ME A WHEELCHAIR

Exactly one month after the commission revealed its report and three weeks after I was a featured speaker at Harvard Law School, I proposed legislation aimed at enacting the reforms. The legislation included a ban on executing the mentally impaired, a reduction in the type of crimes that were eligible for the death penalty, and barring the death penalty when the conviction was based solely on the testimony of a jailhouse snitch.

"It is imperative that we move forward on all of the commission's recommendations to fix our broken justice system," I declared. "It is also imperative that through hearings and meetings, all of the key parties—the prosecutors, defense attorneys, victims, and the wrongfully convicted—are allowed an opportunity to offer their perspectives on these issues of life and death."

By the account of the commission, these reforms would make the system vastly more expensive and Illinois was already severely financially stressed. The budget hole was estimated to be $2 billion! The state was in crisis mode. And the system was already expensive. Prior to the moratorium, the average time from imposition of a death sentence and execution was more than thirteen years. There was no doubt that, based on prior studies, the cost of executing a defendant was more than the cost of housing that defendant for life. Some were suggesting that the cost alone should be enough to persuade people to abolish the death penalty. There were others who were already on the record as saying that the answer was to delay or reject my legislative package.

Republican senator Kirk Dillard was taking the lead on the legislation, but even he conceded that there was not enough time left in the legislative session to do anything until the fall session began. "It took the governor's commission nearly two years to put its recommendations together, and it took the governor's office a month to reduce the commission report to legislation form," Dillard said. "So, it is highly unlikely we will pass anything before we adjourn for the summer."

Pate Philip, Illinois Senate president, was particularly critical of the reduction in the eligibility factors. "You have about twenty opportunities for the death penalty," he said. "He's just erased about fifteen of them. I don't agree with the fifteen erased off."

Cook County state's attorney Richard Devine declared that he would be lobbying legislators, and that some of the proposals needed more study, such as videotaping of police lineups and the interrogations of suspects.

The introduction of the legislative package was almost simultaneous with three other developments in the death penalty world.

In Maryland, Democratic governor Parris Glendening suspended all executions and ordered a study be conducted on whether the death penalty in that state was racially discriminatory. Glendening was a lame duck like me—he was barred by statute from seeking a third term. He announced the moratorium and said he would not allow the execution of Wesley Baker to go forward.

"It is imperative that I, as well as our citizens, have complete confidence that the legal process involved in capital cases is fair and impartial," he said. Although Glendening still supported the death penalty, he said, "Reasonable questions have been raised in Maryland and across the country about the application of the death penalty."

Maryland, of course, was where Kirk Bloodsworth was the first person in the United States to be exonerated from death row by DNA testing.

Baker, who was sentenced to death for the murder of a white woman after he stole her purse in 1991 in a shopping mall, was among five men facing execution before the end of Glendening's term. He had previously signed off on two executions and commuted a third defendant's sentence from death to life in prison without parole. Maryland's death row population of thirteen was tiny compared to Illinois. Nine of them were black and most of the victims were white and nine of the thirteen were convicted in suburban Baltimore County, prompting Glendening to say, "Use of the death penalty ought not to be a lottery of geography."

Nine other states, including Virginia, Nevada, Arizona, Connecticut, and Delaware, were also conducting studies of the death penalty.

I was heartened to hear the news. I really had come to believe the problems with the death penalty system, particularly the arbitrariness of it, were an issue in every death penalty state, not just in Illinois.

But a more significant local development was the revelation that a group of defense lawyers had organized and were soliciting more lawyers to join their cause—submission of clemency applications for everyone on death row in Illinois, which now stood at 160 men and women.

The *Chicago Tribune* broke the news that the group was intent on filing petitions for all the condemned with the Illinois Prisoner Review Board, the state agency responsible for hearing testimony on such petitions and then forwarding recommendations to me, by the end of August so that I could consider them all before I left office in January.

The group, led by Northwestern's Larry Marshall and Rob Warden and assistant Illinois appellate defender Chick Hoffman, intended to address what they believed was a fundamental question that had been left hanging. The reforms going forward were critical, but a look backward was equally important to consider the impact of the system on people who were already under a sentence of death.

The potential for clemency hearings for all death row prisoners would tax the fourteen-member review board, and there were fears being voiced that more resources would be needed. In the first two rounds of hearings so far that year, the board had heard just over 250 cases and about the same number would be routine for the rest of the year. But tacking on more than 150 additional cases would almost certainly require more attorneys and more hearing days.

That wasn't my concern at the moment, however. I couldn't control who would or would not file petitions for clemency or control what the review board did or did not do. Commutations of death row prisoners was not unheard of, but it was rare.

Since the reinstatement of the death penalty, a total of forty-five men and women had received gubernatorial commutations nationally. Only two—Earl Washington and Donald Paradis—were actually exonerated. In 1994, Virginia governor Douglas Wilder, a Democrat, commuted Washington's death sentence for rape and murder to life in prison without parole. Washington was released in 2000 after he was exonerated by DNA testing in 2000. In 1996, Idaho governor Phil Batt, a Republican, citing the possibility of innocence, commuted the death sentence of Donald Paradis, who had been convicted of a 1981 murder. Subsequently, in April 2001, Paradis obtained a new trial based on a ruling that the prosecution had withheld evidence that supported his claim of innocence and the charges were dismissed.

The single largest act of commutation was in January 1991 in Ohio. Governor Richard Celeste, a Democrat who was an opponent of capital punishment, commuted the sentences of eight prisoners, including four women, who were on death row. He rejected a request from the state public defender to commute all 101 inmates on death row. Five of the eight defendants had diminished mental capacity or mental illness.

In 1986, before leaving office, New Mexico governor Toney Anaya, also a death penalty opponent, commuted the death sentences of all five death row inmates to life in prison.

Only one death row inmate's sentence had been commuted in Illinois since the death penalty was reinstated. In January 1996, my predecessor, Governor Jim Edgar, a Republican, commuted the death sentence of Guinevere Garcia, who had been convicted of murder, even though she did not request clemency. The *Tribune* noted that as a result, the law was amended to require that death row prisoners give written consent to apply for commutations, except in circumstances where they are mentally or physically prevented from doing so.

The specter of commutation hearings for the entirety of the Illinois death row population was stirring the emotions of abolitionists and proponents alike. But it was bound to be most felt by the two groups most directly affected—family members of those who were on death row and the families of their victims. Soon, the media would begin—understandably—interviewing victims' family members in great detail, stoking fires of emotion statewide.

Meanwhile, Cook County Chief Criminal Court judge Paul Biebel took a huge step toward pulling back the covers on the dozens of claims that Chicago Police lieutenant Jon Burge and men under his command had tortured suspects into giving confessions to murders. For years, torture claims had been advanced time and again, but demands for an in-depth investigation had fallen on deaf ears. Now, Biebel had appointed a special prosecutor to review the more than sixty cases. One in particular had been brought to my attention—that of Aaron Patterson, who was on death row for a double murder on Chicago's South Side that he said he falsely confessed to committing after he was tortured by detectives working for Burge. In August 2000, Patterson had been granted a hearing by the Illinois Supreme Court to air evidence on the torture claims. That hearing was still pending. I realized that I was going to have to confront the Burge claims long before Biebel's special prosecutor could get engaged and certainly before the judge hearing Patterson's evidence would make any kind of a ruling.

If I felt pressure starting to build, I refused to show it and in fact was more determined than ever to push ahead with the commission reforms. In June, I spoke via closed circuit television to a US Senate subcommittee chaired by Wisconsin Democratic senator Russ Feingold, a death penalty opponent who had introduced legislation calling for a suspension of the federal death penalty and formation of a national commission to study the death penalty system in all states with it.

Feingold said, "There's no question in my mind that there will be significant changes in the death penalty system in America. And when someone writes the history . . . the most important name will be George Ryan." That was flattering and it made me feel good, even if I thought it was an exaggeration.

Pushback on the recommendations of the commission was voiced at the hearing. Kent Scheidegger of the Criminal Justice Legal Foundation in California said that death penalty appeals should be limited to an average of four years. That proposal got a sharp rebuke from Larry Marshall who noted that exoneration cases can take many years before evidence of innocence is discovered and scores of innocent people would have been executed by that time. And Druanne White, a South Carolina prosecutor, contended that the proposed reduction in the aggravating factors—the crimes that qualified for a death sentence—would adversely affect the rights of victims.

Scott Turow, a member of my commission, also testified at the hearing. "Capital punishment is invoked in cases where emotions are most likely to hold sway and where rational deliberation is most problematic for everyone," he declared. "Because this is a system which in rare instances tempts bad faith, it is a system that I believe merits the enhanced safeguards that our commission has proposed."

In my remarks to the subcommittee, I quoted the conclusion of the commission that "No system, given human nature and frailties, could ever be devised or constructed that would work perfectly and guarantee absolutely that no innocent person is ever again sentenced to death.

"That is a powerful statement," I said. "It is one that I will ponder. In the meantime, I do know this—I said two years ago, and I say now, until I can be sure that everyone sentenced to death is truly guilty, until I can be sure with moral certainly that no innocent man or woman is facing a lethal injection, no one will meet that fate.

"We all want to punish the guilty. But in so doing, we must never punish the innocent," I said. "We must protect the innocent. It is fundamental to the American system of justice."

Just days after the hearing, the US Supreme Court ruled that executing the mentally impaired was unconstitutional, ending a long and hard-fought battle by advocates and lawyers representing death row inmates with diminished mental capacity. The Illinois legislature had passed a law that spared the mentally ill from the death penalty, but Governor James Thompson vetoed it. My commission had recommended abolishing the execution of the mentally impaired. It appeared that the US Supreme Court had taken that fight off the table in Illinois.

I thought the ruling was an excellent decision and I said so publicly. "I think it's long overdue," I said. "Why would you put a mentally [impaired] person like Anthony Porter—why would you put a guy like that on death row? Even if they committed the crime," I said. "I never understood that."

The *Chicago Tribune* estimated that at least ten current death row inmates in Illinois might be affected by the decision. The newspaper also reported that nationwide, perhaps as many as forty inmates whose mental capacities were under the commonly accepted benchmark of an IQ of seventy, had already been executed. For them, the ruling was too late. I felt that was just egregious.

Larry Marshall summed up my feelings perfectly. "It didn't just start to be cruel and unusual punishment and yet we have killed scores of people. This ruling speaks loudly about the death penalty and where the country and the courts are going."

Not long after, I finally met Anthony Porter in person. He brought his family with him. His mother, Clara, was handicapped and needed a wheelchair. When no one could find a wheelchair for her, someone brought a desk chair with wheels to the curb and they rolled her into the building.

When I was informed they were coming, but were being delayed while someone fetched the chair, I said, "There's got to be a wheelchair in this building. Get a wheelchair and bring it and put her in it and bring her upstairs."

So, the security guards hustled around and found a wheelchair and took it downstairs and put her in it and wheeled her upstairs with Porter and the rest of his family.

Anthony was uncomfortably buttoned up in a suit and tie. I imagined, though I did not ask, that it was probably the suit he was supposed to be buried in. Not unexpectedly, he was not an articulate man. His IQ had been measured at around fifty-one. But as best he could, he described the indignities and sufferings of being incarcerated for seventeen years. Most importantly, he really didn't understand why.

As we sat in my office sixteen floors above the bustle of traffic along Randolph Street, Porter described life on death row and how, in preparation for his death, the guards had asked him to order the traditional last meal and had measured him for the burial suit and for a coffin. He spoke calmly in a matter of fact way. To me, it felt cold and premeditated.

I realized that's just what it was. And I realized that Anthony Porter had become, for me, the face of death row. I also realized that I was very much in uncharted waters.

When they left, I told them to keep the wheelchair.

# 26

# ALL TALK, NO ACTION

The legislative package based on the commission's proposals received a lot of nice words of support, but there was no real action, just a lot of political theater. The legislation got caught up by two things. One, because I had already announced that I was not seeking reelection, I had little political power or leverage to move the package along. And two, the House and the Senate members were fresh off a primary election. No one wanted to rock the boat over the death penalty. People were afraid that they were going to be seen as soft on crime if they went along with the recommendations and made any major changes—or if they even looked like they were making major changes in the death penalty.

The House passed a limited part of the program and sent it over to the Senate. They didn't even come close to adopting the entire eighty-five recommendations, but I thought it was a start. The Democrats needed an issue for some of the African American legislators to bring home during their election campaigns and in some of their districts reforming or abolishing the death penalty played well.

The Senate, though, just basically killed the whole package. Control of the Senate, at that time, was in the hands of Pate Philip, leader of conservative Republicans. Pate was an ex-marine, and he treated everything as if it was a charge up the hill—straightforward. "Finesse" was not a word in his dictionary. "Blitz," however, was.

The commission bill never had a chance.

Both the House and Senate assigned the recommendations to subcommittees for hearings after the spring legislative session adjourned. The hearings were held in various parts of the state. In the General Assembly, putting a bill in a subcommittee for hearings simply means it isn't going anywhere—the equivalent of Siberia. The commission's proposals were no exception. They just withered and died.

The *Chicago Tribune* published a scathing editorial that said in part:

> Illinois has gotten credit for leading the nation in an examination of the capital punishment system, leading the search for flaws and fixes. Yet critical debates like this one are frustratingly rare. The silence is especially deafening in the state legislature. Senate and House committees heard testimony this summer on some of the commission recommendations, but most legislators exhibited as much interest as if they had been observing dandelions sprout. The proceedings, to them, appeared little more than grudging symbolism.
>
> One representative . . . dozed off during testimony. Most of his fellow panelists bounced in and out of the hearing room, or chatted among themselves.

I was spending a lot of time thinking about what the next step should be, but the more I thought about it, the more I really didn't know what to do. There was a case to be made to commute all the death sentences to at least life in prison based strictly on the horrible track record of the system. But since my remarks in Oregon in March, the public outcry to keep the death penalty had increased.

The failure of the General Assembly—the Senate, really—to act on the commission's reforms brought me to the point where I was thinking that to make sure we didn't execute an innocent person in Illinois, the state should commute every sentence to a life without parole.

In August, the Illinois Supreme Court provided some fuel for my position when it upheld the DuPage County death sentence of Mark Ballard, but expressed interest in Ballard's argument that the Illinois death penalty was unconstitutional. In 1997, Ballard killed his roommate, Patricia Noland, because she wouldn't give him money for drugs. According to the evidence in the case, Ballard lured Noland to a home where they once lived, and attempted to subdue her with chloroform. When that failed, he hit her in the head with a hammer about thirty times. When she still didn't die, Ballard hit her with an iron bar.

Ballard's lawyers had argued that with twenty different "aggravating factors," the legislature had created so many reasons that a person could get sentenced to death that the system resembled the unconstitutional state of things that it was in when the US Supreme Court struck it down in 1972.

Justices Moses Harrison II and Thomas Kilbride dissented, although for different reasons.

Justice Harrison said, "The proceedings which culminated in Ballard's convictions and sentence of death were fatally flawed because they did not comport with the new rules enacted by our court governing the conduct of cases in which the State is seeking the death penalty." He went on to say that the procedures contained in these rules were "indispensable for achieving an accurate determination of innocence or guilt and are applicable to all capital cases now coming before us. Because Ballard was tried, convicted, and sentenced without the benefit of the new rules, his convictions and death sentence should be vacated, and the cause should be remanded to the circuit court for a new trial."

Justice Kilbride said Ballard's conviction and sentence should be set aside,

> because the trial proceedings were not conducted in accordance with the new Supreme Court rules governing capital cases. The procedures in capital cases prior to this court's adoption of the new rules were unreliable and did not adequately protect a defendant's constitutional rights. Consequently, since the new rules were promulgated to address the deficiencies of constitutional dimension that regularly occurred under the old system, the rules must be applied retroactively to all capital cases currently pending on direct appeal.

Justice Mary Ann McMorrow basically invited challenges to the death penalty by writing a special concurring opinion on Ballard's argument relating to the aggravating factors. McMorrow said that "the Illinois death penalty statute appears on its face to be quite extensive. Indeed, the current number of aggravating factors is almost three times what it was when the statute was first enacted and is one of the highest in the country."

After McMorrow analyzed all the factors, she concluded,

> Thus, for a first-degree murder *not* to be death eligible in Illinois, the murder must be of a single individual, the victim must *not* be one of those listed among the aggravating factors (e.g., community policing volunteer, teacher), the murder must be unaccompanied by any of the

> fifteen felonies contained in the felony-murder aggravating factor, and the murder must be deliberated upon for less than three hours.

Justice McMorrow noted that considering those facts, one would be tempted to conclude that, in Illinois, as commission member Thomas Sullivan declared, "It is virtually impossible to find a murder case that is not potentially death-eligible."

On August 23, I used my amendatory veto power to strike down an antiterrorism bill and at the same time to try once again to force the legislature to enact changes recommended by the commission. At the same time, the bill basically didn't do anything that existing federal statutes covered. But I was angry that the legislature had done virtually nothing on the commission proposals and instead had passed this antiterrorism bill that actually *expanded* the death penalty in Illinois. So, I responded by vetoing the bill. At the same time, I said that I would accept the provision if the legislature would agree to also pass a list of nearly twenty of the eighty-five reforms recommended by the commission, including barring the execution of anyone who is mentally impaired and to record the interrogation of suspects.

My amendatory veto power allowed me to recommend changes in a bill and as a result of my action, when the legislature convened in Springfield for the veto session, they would have three possible choices.

They could override my veto, which required three-fifths majority in the House and the Senate. They could enact the original bill and then accept my additions—action which would require simple majorities. Or they could do neither, which would mean my veto would stand.

"Illinois' legislative response to the tragic events of September eleventh should not compromise our state government's integrity by succumbing to the urge to enact largely symbolic legislative changes," I said.

I was troubled by how easy it had been for the legislature to pass the death penalty expansion bill before any real attention was paid to carrying out the much-needed reforms. "Given our state's capital punishment track record, there can be little doubt that reform should take precedence over expanding death penalty eligibility in what most believe to be a flawed system," I said.

The existing death penalty statute had numerous provisions that covered just about every conceivable murder circumstance that would be committed by terrorism, I believed. And I wasn't going to let this go through unless the legislature made some compromises. I was convinced there was no possible way that those seeking to override my veto would be able to get the requisite votes in both the Senate and House.

Earlier in the month, I granted full pardons to former death row inmates Steven Smith and Carl Lawson, both of whom were among the thirteen exonerated from death row in Illinois. Both were now eligible to seek financial compensation—such as it was—from the state of Illinois.

I granted these pardons as lawyers for the death row inmates were scrambling to file the last of their clemency petitions by the August 29 deadline. The current death row population was about 160 and with just days to go, about 130 petitions had been filed. A couple dozen of them, it appeared, were resisting filing any petitions under the theory that if their sentences were commuted, they would not get the same attention from lawyers that capital cases get. Some said they would rather die on the gurney rather than die a natural death years later in prison. Attorney Jed Stone told the media that his client, Edward Moore, who was sentenced to death for murdering a woman in Grundy County, didn't want a commutation. "Ed's position is that he believes in the judicial system and that with life without parole, no one will take seriously his claim of innocence," Stone said.

But the clemency movement lawyers said that they would file petitions for everyone whether the defendants wanted to or not. The lawyers believed it was appropriate to make an argument for clemency because there were questions about the integrity of the criminal justice system. They believed that I should grant them commutations even if the defendants didn't want them.

At the same time, the Cook County state's attorney's office, where about half of the death row cases were prosecuted, was helping the families of victims to prepare for the clemency hearings, helping them file the required notices to be able to address the prisoner review board. John Gorman, a spokesman for Cook County state's attorney Richard Devine, told the media, "We have been reaching out to a couple hundred Cook County families . . . about their right to step up and speak," he said. "We're telling them that if they need help, we'd be happy to help them."

Of course, the media was all over me to comment about these developments. During an appearance in downstate Mount Vernon, I said that I had not yet decided whether to commute any death sentences. "I'm going to think about all these things and see how it all falls into place between now and when I leave."

What was unfolding really was unprecedented in scale and scope. The legal counsel for the Prisoner Review Board evoked criticism when he suggested that the board might not be able to accommodate all the requests due to a manpower shortage.

Bill Ryan, president of the Illinois Death Penalty Moratorium Project, was incensed. "That's ludicrous," he declared. "That almost makes me speechless. We're talking about people's lives. I think George Ryan knows how screwed up and how unjust the death penalty system is. I'm confident he's going to do the right thing."

Locke Bowman, one of the clemency lawyers, declared, "This is really an historic occasion for Governor Ryan to make a lasting impact on the reform of the death penalty system in Illinois."

I felt as if people were trying to speak to me through the media. The pressure was starting to build. I was trying not to fuel the flames of passion that were starting to become more intense.

As the calendar flipped to September, the Prisoner Review Board announced that it would hold hearings on the death row clemency petitions from October 15–18 in Springfield and Chicago. The final total was 171 petitions—one for each person on death row.

Each side—the advocates for the inmates and the family members of victims—would be given fifteen minutes. The time limit was immediately criticized by Cook County state's attorney Richard Devine as the "Reader's Digest form of justice."

I declined to overrule the review board's time limit, saying, "You spend an hour or two hours to tell their stories, but we've got to get their message consolidated."

The review board said it would make its recommendations by the end of the day on October 18, the last day of the hearings. I wondered what this was going to look like—the hearings and the subsequent recommendations.

On Wednesday, September 4, Justice Harrison cleaned out his desk on his last day as an Illinois Supreme Court justice. He had announced his retirement back in May. During an interview with the *St. Louis Post-Dispatch* he stood strong in his belief that the death penalty system was broken. "My personal belief is that there's no hope for morality in the state of Illinois as long as we have the death penalty," he said. "It's morally wrong."

He gave me an opening I did not expect when asked whether he thought I should commute all death sentences to life without parole.

"He has the power to do it and he should do it," Harrison declared.

# 27

# RAISING THE VOLUME

"I don't know how I could pick and choose."

With those words, said in response to a reporter's question, I unintentionally raised the volume in what was turning into a war of words over the clemency process.

I said I was strongly considering a blanket commutation to life in prison without parole for all of the death row prisoners. I said I had to determine whether it was going to be "for everybody or for anybody."

At that moment, I didn't think that I could pick and choose among the scores of cases and say, "You're going to die because the system was fair to you and you're not going to die because the system was unfair to you." How was I supposed to know who was guilty and who had been tried fairly? Whether it was bogus evidence or a jailhouse snitch or torture or DNA testing not being available—there were so many steps in every capital punishment case that had proven to be vulnerable to mistakes or misconduct by police or prosecutors.

I made the comments after being informed that Cook County state's attorney Richard Devine was claiming that the rights of the families of the victims were being trampled because of the fifteen-minute time limit for each inmate's clemency hearing.

"If that's the case," I said, "maybe we ought to have a blanket commutation," although I added that I had not yet made up my mind whether to do so. In a not-so-veiled comment directed to the legislature, I also said that my decision might be helped if the General Assembly would act on my recommended changes to the death penalty system.

Devine immediately fired back. "His suggestion to treat all of these cases in one blanket move and to say he can't pick and choose among these is irresponsible and an insult to the hundreds of victims' families who have lost a loved one due to violent crime," he declared.

As the clemency process came under fire, the media, which largely had initially embraced the idea of a blanket commutation, started to back away. The *Chicago Sun-Times* was first, and then a number of other newspapers expressed skepticism about commuting every sentence to life. In my view, they were trying to have things both ways. They still supported the moratorium and they agreed that the system was broken, but in the same breath they said that the system probably wasn't broken for this defendant or that defendant. One writer suggested that in order to make sure that public support for the reform of the death penalty remained strong, I should make sure some executions took place in the future. That, to me, was the height of idiocy.

There was an onslaught of public criticism from victims' families. I understood that what I was saying was probably hurtful. But I could not erase their pain and I had come to believe that even execution does not provide true closure.

The media was shifting away from the flaws in the system to the crimes and victims and the families. They gave voice to people who portrayed me as a heartless man who wanted to rob people of justice. For these people, there was no justice without death. The theme of story after story was that stopping an execution was the equivalent of letting someone out of prison or reversing a guilty verdict. That was the furthest thing from my mind. Yes, there were people on death row who were guilty of the crimes they committed, but I believed that keeping them in prison for the rest of their lives did not mean they were escaping justice. But with a seemingly endless supply of victims' families to interview and crimes to rehash, the message they all shared was crystal clear: no commutations.

*Chicago Sun-Times* columnist Mary Mitchell was scathing in her denunciation of a blanket commutation. "The governor's 'all or nothing' attitude is not merciful," she wrote. "It is callous. It is also dangerous. When people believe there is no justice for them and their family, they start taking the law into their own hands. Under Ryan's proposal even a Hannibal Lecter would be spared.

"Like the survivors, the wrongfully convicted don't want mercy. They want justice," she wrote. "Unfortunately, blanket clemency affirms the notion that we've given up. Justice is too much to ask."

Dawn Pueschel was very angry. Nineteen years earlier, in 1983, her brother, Dean, and her sister-in-law, Jo Ellen, had been beaten to death with baseball bats in their apartment on the North Side of Chicago. Their eleven-year-old son had been horribly beaten, but somehow managed to survive. Two brothers, Reginald and Jerry Mahaffey, were convicted and sentenced to death.

"We are the ones who have no rights as survivors," she told the *Sun-Times*. "Our loved ones were not able to say which persons killed them. No. The death penalty is not going to bring our loved ones back, but it is a closure. People forget about the families that have to survive. None of us should have to go through this, but Governor Ryan is pushing this so he can go out with a big bang. How can he do it?

"I am still going to court after nineteen years," she said. "There was never a single mistake made. I think it is a travesty of justice that they are going to commute these sentences and give these people life without parole. Well, life doesn't mean life."

Robert Weides, whose eighteen-year-old son Jeffrey, a bar manager who had been killed in a tavern shootout in April 2001, was still in pain. The gunman, Luther Casteel, had been sentenced to death for killing Jeffrey and a bar patron. "Taking the easy way out is no comfort to the thousands of victims of high crimes of deliberate murder," Weides said. He noted that Casteel had not filed a petition for clemency and that there was no doubt about Casteel's guilt. He said that my comment that trying to pick and choose would be like flipping a coin was preposterous. "It's called intelligence," Weides said. "Doesn't he have any?"

In a letter to the editor at the *Sun-Times*, Julie Hyman of Grayslake, a suburb north of Chicago, wrote, "Governor Ryan is deciding whether to commute the death sentences of 157 inmates in Illinois. The man who killed my father nine years ago is one of them. Jonathan Preston Haynes systematically selected my father, Martin R. Sullivan, MD, DDS, from a phone book before he brutally shot him to death in his office. My father was executed because of one man's belief.

"Now Governor Ryan believes the white supremacist murderer should be released from death row. . . . If Governor Ryan chooses to overturn all

157 death sentences, he will in this case grant leniency to a self-proclaimed Nazi who wishes to eradicate all but the white race."

As the petitions were filed, the names of some of those seeking relief from death sentences became public.

It was a litany of evil.

One of the more horrific was the case of Fedell Caffey and Jacqueline Williams, who were convicted of murdering twenty-eight-year-old Debra Evans, who was pregnant, and her two children, ages seven and ten, and then slicing Evans's unborn child from the womb. The disclosure that Williams and Caffey were seeking clemency triggered emotional letters to the editor.

"Governor Ryan, get the electric chair ready," wrote Stella Rocco. "Debra Evans was a friend of mine. It made me sick. It would be a shame if Jacqueline Williams would get away with this murder."

Ruth McDonald, Evans's aunt, wrote from Genoa City, Wisconsin, "Williams and Caffey should not spend the rest of their lives in jail," she said. "We are all victims of this crime if they are allowed to live. If any crime deserves the death penalty, this one does."

Gladys Young, whose husband, Chicago police officer Gregory Young, was murdered in 1997 during a robbery, reported that she attended a meeting convened for victims' families in Cook County. "We sat in a room and learned that our rights as family members of victims are about to be trampled upon by the governor of Illinois. We were told the governor, through his Prisoner Review Board, is going to limit our ability to speak out against petitions for clemency by the inmates who killed our relatives. This is wrong.

"I fear the governor is going to disregard the pain and suffering that the man who killed my husband inflicted upon my family," she said. "Blanket clemency . . . is an insult to me and every person whom these inmates affected."

Other inmates seeking clemency included Edward Spreitzer, a member of the "Ripper Crew," and a codefendant of Andrew Kokoraleis, whose execution I had allowed to go forward back in 1999.

Henry Brisbon was on the list as well. In 1973, he and three other men stopped a car on Interstate 57. The couple in the car, James Schmidt and Dorothy Cerney, were dragged out onto the shoulder of the road, forced to lie down, and then Brisbon shotgunned them to death. For that, Brisbon received a sentence of one thousand to three thousand years—the death penalty was not on the books at the time of the crime. But five years later, in 1978, Brisbon shanked an inmate to death at the Statesville Correctional Center and that got him a death sentence and a ticket to death row. Once quoted as saying that he would keep killing people no matter how many times he was convicted, Henry Brisbon was now seeking clemency.

The swell of outrage from the victims' families was still growing when, on Monday, September 16, Illinois attorney general Jim Ryan filed lawsuits, one in Sangamon County, where Springfield was located, and the other in the Illinois Supreme Court. The lawsuit in Sangamon County was an attempt to stop the clemency hearings, specifically claiming the fifteen-minute time limit was unfair to victims' families. The lawsuit in the Supreme Court sought to block clemency hearings for two dozen inmates who had not signed clemency petitions and nine other inmates whose death sentences previously had been put aside by the Illinois Supreme Court and were awaiting new sentencing hearings.

Ryan, who was running to take my place as governor, called a news conference.

"While we are trying to improve the accuracy and fairness of the system, we also have another job to do and that is to respect the dignity and the rights of crime victims," he declared.

Ken Tupy, legal counsel to the Prisoner Review Board, said the fifteen-minute limitation was only advisory—a guideline for the panel to follow. "There's no other way to hear so many petitions in a timely fashion," Tupy declared. "But it's not like the panel would cut off a victim in the middle of a statement."

He said the guideline had always been twenty minutes and was only shortened to fifteen to accommodate the scores of petitions received. He noted that the attorney general had never before objected to the guideline.

I saw the lawsuits as a bald-faced ploy for publicity by Ryan, who was trailing in the polls by a significant margin to Democratic candidate Rod Blagojevich.

My staff issued a statement saying that I welcomed the attorney general's "new-found concern for fairness and justice" and that I believed that my "entire review of the capital punishment system now and in the future is constitutional and, more importantly, the only right, moral, and just thing to do."

Northwestern's Larry Marshall was even more blunt, calling the lawsuits a "very cynical political ploy."

"It's not about that Mr. Ryan is attorney general," Marshall said. "It's about that Mr. Ryan wants to be governor."

Meanwhile, prosecutors filed responses to the clemency petitions—all ninety cases in Cook County and dozens filed by the attorney general on in cases in downstate counties. Most of them focused on legal issues and contended that the defendants had not received fair trials and that the flaws that had been identified in the thirteen exonerations were not present in these cases. Moreover, courts had ruled and upheld the convictions and sentences and claims by the defense of defective trials had been rejected.

The filings included written statements from victims' families, including exhortations to carry out the executions. Some included gruesome crime scene photos of murder victims. The appeal was raw and emotional. Filings from the attorney general's office contained the upside-down world claim that the thirteen exonerations were proof that the system actually worked correctly.

"These releases do not demonstrate a broken system, but rather a system that contains vigorous appellate and collateral avenues of relief," the filings said.

That flew in the face of the facts as I knew them and was patently ridiculous. I believed that the thirteen exonerees were alive only because serendipitous miracles had occurred that prevented the state from doing what it wanted to do—kill them.

The evidence had shown me that these exonerations came from such acts as DNA testing, witness recantations, and confessions from the real killers. In the case of Gary Gauger, his full exoneration was the result of a federal wiretap during an investigation of a motorcycle gang—an act that could not have been more removed from and unconnected to Gauger's case.

On October 10, Sangamon County circuit judge Donald Cadagin dismissed Attorney General Ryan's lawsuit. Ryan claimed a victory, saying that the Prisoner Review Board had agreed it would not set time limits for comments.

It was a hollow victory, I thought. The Prisoner Review Board had said from the outset that the fifteen-minute limit was strictly a guideline and that no one would be cut off. And in fact, Judge Cadagin ruled that Ryan had no standing to bring the case.

The following day, the Illinois Supreme Court rejected Ryan's other lawsuit.

The rulings cleared the way for the clemency hearings to begin the following week. No one really had any idea what this would look like. If the files and the news accounts from victim's families were any indication, it was going to be painful.

# 28

# RISING PRESSURE

The last half of 2002 was like dealing with Andrew Kokoraleis all over again. The pressure was on me and me alone to decide when the death penalty would next be used or if it would be used at all. I was right where I'd been when I declared the moratorium. I'd hoped that with a moratorium, a deep look into the issue would uncover that moral certainty or that "aha" moment to bring some closure to the issue. Instead, the debate continued down the same track: death penalty opponents telling me that a broken system tainted all death sentences and death penalty supporters and victims' families telling me that a few bad cases didn't taint all cases—that it would be easy to pick and choose who had been treated unfairly. I was sent lists of people considered guilty beyond a shadow of a doubt.

With the clemency hearings about to start, the media began airing reports from victims' family members speaking about the horrors inflicted on their loved ones. Some dreaded going to testify because it was ripping open old wounds. Others were eager, it seemed, to make it clear that they wanted these condemned men and women to die on the gurney. A smaller group—much smaller—said they could live with commutations.

Ordinarily, the Prisoner Review Board's review of a case could take weeks or months and typically was a review of case files. Then, the board would give me a confidential recommendation on what the prisoner's future should be. It would then be up to me to make the final call. I could accept the board's recommendation or reject it or set my own course.

Amid the clemency petitions were a small group of death row inmates that went a step further—they were looking for full pardons based on innocence. Potentially, I thought, some of these cases might be exonerated before the sentence was carried out. I told my deputy governor for criminal justice, Matt Bettenhausen, that I wanted a special level of scrutiny for these cases. Some of these cases particularly stood out. There was Aaron Patterson, who claimed to have been tortured by the Burge crew to falsely confess to a double murder. There was Madison Hobley, who had been sentenced to death for setting a fire that killed seven people in 1987, including his wife and infant son. Yet another was Leroy Orange who was convicted and sentenced to death for four murders in 1984. Although their lawyers had been filing appeals for years, they had yet to convince a judge that they were innocent.

In a media interview just prior to the commencement of the first hearings, Prisoner Review Board chairwoman Anne Taylor said, "I expect these cases are going to be challenging and interesting. And they'll be difficult to sort through."

She really didn't know what an understatement that was.

The rhetoric was on the rise before the first hearing began.

"The entire process is a profane burden and an insult. It's a terrible thing that is happening in the state of Illinois," declared Madison County state's attorney William Haine. "My time will be spent reminding the governor of his oath . . . to defend the Constitution of Illinois and of the United States."

The hearings were going to be televised live by cable news, and news agencies from around the world were readying to report on the proceedings as they unfolded. On the eve of the hearings, Cook County state's attorney Richard Devine called for a halt to the hearings—to cancel them all.

My spokesman, Dennis Culloton, responded on my behalf. "The governor has deep sympathy for the surviving family members and friends of these heinous crimes. However, the system of capital punishment in Illinois is badly broken and deeply flawed and each of the petitioners was convicted under that broken and flawed system. Executing the wrong inmate, as we have nearly done in Illinois thirteen times, would only compound the tragedy. A careful review of the cases now is the only prudent, just, and fair thing to do."

Handling this review was the fourteen-member Prisoner Review Board, consisting of former law enforcement officers, prison officials, and ex-state lawmakers. The board was evenly split between Democrats and Republicans. Each member was paid at least $70,000 a year. They were not viewed as bleeding heart liberals, not by any means. The board members were allowed to apply whatever standards they chose and vote for a reduction of a sentence for any reason—whether they suspected an inmate was wrongly convicted or simply because they felt sympathy. Or they could recommend that the sentences stand as imposed.

It is hard to describe the Prisoner Review Board hearings. But in their essence, they became a horribly painful reopening of wounds on both sides. The victim's families came forward, one after another, to provide heart-wrenching, tearful accounts of their losses. The testimony of family members of the defendants was just as sad—they, too, had lost loved ones. But overarching it all, the prosecutors presented in graphic detail the horrific acts that were perpetrated upon the victims. Defense attorneys portrayed the hearings as a significant step in the decades-long battle over the death penalty.

One prosecutor called the hearings "a profound insult to the administration of justice."

Some victims' families said execution was the only path to peace and resolution. At the same time, family members of inmates wept as they asked that death sentences be commuted to life without parole. It was, one Review Board member commented, an airing of the "unwarranted carnage exacted in their lives."

"I see the blood of my nephews on my hands every day, and it's not getting better," said Estella Jennings, who was the aunt of three victims of Sherrell Towns. She recalled how, in 1993, she cleaned blood from the floor of the trailer where the murders occurred.

Even Henry Brisbon had his defenders. His lawyer, Jean Maclean Snyder, said that there was no doubt he committed the double murder which resulted in the sentence of one thousand to three thousand years. "But he was not sentenced to death for that crime," she said, adding that the murder of a prison inmate which got him the death penalty "can't be used as a surrogate for that."

One of the Prison Review Board members, Arvin Boddie, was quoted by the media as saying during a break that he was "offended by the manner" in which the hearings were being conducted. "We're not taking the time that's necessary. . . . It's being done in a truncated manner and panels have little direction," he said. "I'm convinced it's not the best way to handle it for victims and not for inmates either."

Another board member, Susan Carol Finley, expressed irritation when the attorney for Jeffrey Rissley, who was convicted in the 1991 kidnapping, rape, and murder of a six-year-old girl, said Rissley deserved clemency in part because of mental illness. At least eighteen of the clemency hearings contained claims of mental illness or diminished mental capacity.

"I have trouble with all of these claims, that they're mentally ill," Finley said. "They're evil. That's what I'm looking at."

Separately, during a hearing on a different petition, Boddie declared, "This claim of mental retardation is a fraud or a sham, plain and simple." He warned the lawyer for Anthony Brown, who was condemned to death for the 1994 killing of star college basketball player Reginald Wilson and his girlfriend Felicia Lewis: "You have to remember you are under oath, you've got victims and people from the state of Illinois present. I'm to the point of getting sick and tired of hearing they didn't have the benefit of this or the benefit of that, or they were mentally retarded without any evidence to support it."

The raw emotion was aired every night on television and every morning in the newspapers. "This is like going to six wakes a day for 2 1/2 weeks," said board member Craig Findley.

The media began to turn on me and the process. A typical response came from the *State Journal-Register* in Springfield, which published an editorial with a headline calling the hearings a "cruel sham."

"One thing is for sure," the editorial said. "These rapid-fire clemency hearings are certainly not the best way to review such serious cases. They are also horribly cruel to the relatives of the victims, who attend these cursory hearings that are not long enough to achieve any real search for the truth, but plenty lengthy to dredge up nightmares of a horrific crime.

"This will give Ryan the legal authority to commute these sentences. But anyone listening to the prosecutors' and survivors' testimony ought to have trouble justifying a blanket commutation."

*Chicago Tribune* columnist Eric Zorn, who had written extensively about the wrongly convicted and who supported the moratorium, also weighed in. Noting that by the end of the first week of hearings, the

Prisoner Review Board had gone through about two-thirds of the petitions, he wrote,

> In the name of the decency he says motivates him on the issue of capital punishment, Governor George Ryan should call at least a temporary halt to the proceedings.
>
> He should postpone the resumption of hearings Monday, summon to the Capitol all of the members of his increasingly snappish review board, and spend a few days meeting with them behind closed doors to find out: Are the hearings doing any good?
>
> It all looks wise and deliberate on paper. But the process has proved excruciating for the families of the victims of the atrocious murders at the core of each case. They're not only reliving their most horrible moments during their testimony and news interviews, but they're also feeling additionally tortured by the looming uncertainty, they say, and by the sense that the burden is on them to display sufficient anguish to justify executions.

Zorn wondered whether this sample was good enough for me to get an idea whether I could pick and choose or whether I would just go ahead with a blanket commutation to stop the hemorrhaging.

"The hearings have been a public relations nightmare for foes of the death penalty, whose sound arguments and tales of justice gone awry have been drowned out by the steady roar of accounts of the sorts of murders—heinous, appalling, wanton—that give capital punishment its visceral appeal," Zorn wrote.

I was becoming the focal point of the attacks. A good example was the testimony of Wheeling police sergeant Bill Stutzman, whose fellow officer, Kenneth Dawson, was murdered on duty in 1985.

"I really wish that Governor Ryan was sitting here before us, so he could see the hurt in these families, hear the words that they're speaking," said Stutzman. He criticized me for not attending the hearings. "He has no intention of listening to these families. He's completely victimizing these families all over again."

I was getting so many calls from the media for a response that my office issued a statement saying I had "great sympathy" for victims' family members, and that I was watching some of the proceedings on closed-circuit television. We told the press I was not going to attend any hearings because I didn't want to give the impression that I favored any particular inmate.

My spokesman said I had not made up my mind.

"He isn't sure what to do. The only thing he knows is this: We had a system that is broken at a variety of levels. . . . We're sorry that the family members have to go through this again. But the family members would feel worse if we discovered after the fact that the wrong person had been executed for that crime."

In the midst of this, there was the appearance at the hearings of Abby Mann, Academy Award winner for his screenplay of *Judgment at Nuremberg*, a highly-acclaimed 1961 film about Nazi war criminals. He told the media he was finishing up a script for the Showtime network about the death penalty system in Illinois. His presence was a bit otherworldly.

"I'm about through with the script," Mann told the media. "Our justice system, my God, needs to be looked at," he said. "But to look at our justice system, it really is broken."

I was portrayed largely as the person responsible for this spectacle. The train of thought was that if I hadn't declared the moratorium and talked about the possibility of clemency for every death row inmate, then that team of lawyers wouldn't have filed so many petitions with the Review Board and the marathon hearings wouldn't have happened and the families wouldn't have to relive the crimes. It was tragic, but there wasn't a thing I could do about it.

Reporters became more accusatory in their questioning of me about the hearings, suggesting the hearings were my fault and could have been avoided. They questioned whether I had any sympathy for the victims' families and asked me why I didn't call the hearings off after it became obvious that each case would be described in gory detail and would tear open barely-healed psychological wounds. The media descriptions of the hearings were evocative, ranging from "theater of pain" to "grinding caravan of misery."

It didn't seem to matter that it wasn't in my power to disrupt the workings of the Prisoner Review Board or tell them how to handle the clemency petitions. Instead of asking the prosecutors why they were using every explicit detail, the media kept asking me how I could allow the prosecutors to use every explicit detail.

But then, on Tuesday of the second week of hearings, in what the media called an "about-face" and the result of a "public relations meltdown," I momentarily relented. During a ribbon-cutting ceremony in Springfield, asked once again about the question of a blanket commutation, I said, "At this point, I've pretty much ruled out blanket commutation based on the hearings and the information I've gathered so far."

But I cautioned, "Now that doesn't mean I won't do it. But I've pretty much decided that's probably not, as I said, an option I will exercise." I acknowledged, as I had many times, there were guilty people on death row who were rightly convicted. But as I also had said many times, I was bothered by the possibility of executing an innocent person.

"There isn't any question in my mind that there are guilty people that have been through these hearings that are asking for clemency," I said. "And we have to be able to try and sort out those people from the people that we think who have had some fault in the system that hasn't given them a fair trial or a fair hearing. That's been the attempt to do this all along, so we don't kill an innocent person."

The media were running around, asking people what they thought. Republican US House Speaker Dennis Hastert said, "I wish he'd certainly abandon this policy. I told him that and recommended that to him. Obviously, he didn't do it."

He added, "The issue of having blanket clemency hearings for everybody who has been condemned in this state, I think, is just obscene."

The hearings ended, mercifully, on Monday, October 28. Everyone was drained.

In the end, only one victim's family member stood up and argued for the innocence of the person convicted of the crime. Terry Hoyt testified in favor of the clemency petition filed on behalf of Montell Johnson, who was sentenced to death for the murder of Hoyt's twenty-three-year-old daughter, Dorianne Warnsley in 1994.

Johnson and Carl Stokes were accused of her murder. She had been shot, beaten with a hammer, and left to die by the side of a road near downstate Decatur. Stokes pleaded guilty, agreed to testify for the prosecution, and said Johnson was the killer, while Johnson said Stokes was the murderer.

Johnson was convicted and sentenced to death. Stokes got a fifteen-year prison sentence. It was during Johnson's trial, in which he defended himself without a lawyer, that Hoyt later said she began to believe Johnson's account. And so, she joined Johnson's mother to ask the Prisoner Review Board to spare Johnson's life.

This was exactly the kind of case that bothered me. There was no DNA evidence—in fact, there was no physical evidence linking either Stokes or Johnson to the murder. There were no witnesses who saw the crime. It was basically Stokes's word against Johnson's.

The following day, family members of some of the victims brought petitions to my office in Chicago. The petitions had been signed by more than three hundred family members of victims, demanding that I not issue a blanket commutation and also to make public the recommendations by the Prisoner Review Board.

Asked for a response, I said, "I'm going to do what I think is right, as I have through this whole process. I'm not going to be intimidated by petitions or state's attorneys or prosecutors or defenders or news people or anybody else. It isn't going to happen; that's my response and that's all I have to say about it."

# 29

# WRONG IS WRONG

Earlier in the year, when Matt Bettenhausen rolled a cart into my office in Chicago that contained a binder for every defendant on death row, I really did believe that I could separate the innocent from the guilty—the shaky cases from the rock solid. Now, with the hearings over, I had a little more than two months before the end of my term as governor to make up my mind on what I was going to do. I was still waiting for all the reports from the Prisoner Review Board and their recommendations, which were confidential. I started a series of review meetings with Bettenhausen and other members of the staff to look at all the cases, one by one.

To avoid any suggestion of trying to influence the review board, I had purposely stayed away from the Prisoner Review Board hearings. But as I began to review the cases, I began wondering if it would be prudent or worthwhile to hear personally from the families of victims. And so, I decided it was important for me to hear directly what they told the board and see the emotion on their faces.

"I think hearing from them in person will be, without question, part of my deliberative process," I said, announcing my intention during an address to the National Association of Criminal Defense Lawyers in Chicago. "No one wants to see the families of the victims go through any more pain."

The details were yet to be worked out. "I'm not sure just yet how we're going to work this out," I said. "If they want to bring all the victims into a room and hear me talk, I'll be glad to do it. I can't sit down with each one individually, there's no question about that."

The truth was that my staff had closely monitored the clemency hearings. Their reports, combined with the media accounts, presented a pretty clear picture. I was willing to meet with the victims' family members, but I wasn't sure that I could get much more from them than I already knew.

Still, I said, "I'll meet anybody—the prosecutors, the defense lawyers—anybody that will meet with me. Over the last three years, since I started this moratorium, I've spoken to just about everyone who's invited me to discuss our experience in Illinois."

Asked about blanket commutation, I said, "It probably is still an option, but one that I probably won't exercise after the hearings."

As my staff was beginning to work on a plan to make the meetings with victims' families happen, I received an open letter signed by more than 650 Illinois lawyers asking me to issue a blanket commutation. The signers included former prosecutors, defense lawyers, professors, and attorneys from some of the largest and most powerful law firms in Illinois.

Running nearly six pages, the letter said that a blanket commutation was the only sure way to avoid executing an innocent person. "A system, like the Illinois death penalty system, that cannot reliably distinguish the guilty from the innocent, surely cannot be entrusted to fairly and justly make the profoundly difficult decision whether a particular defendant is deserving of the ultimate punishment," the letter said.

The letter was organized by the Northwestern Center on Wrongful Convictions and the University of Chicago's MacArthur Justice Center. It was an attempt to convince me that the idea of a blanket commutation was not a radical position, but in fact was embraced by many leading members of the criminal justice community.

Then, in the legislature, the House voted 84 to 30 to defeat my proposed reforms that I had tacked onto the death penalty for terrorism bill that the General Assembly had passed and that I had vetoed. It looked more and more like I was heading for a showdown over my proposals to fix the death penalty system.

On November 15, I was the featured speaker at the Northwestern University School of Law. My staff had arranged for Paula Gray to be present but didn't tell her that the reason was that I was going to announce that I had issued her a pardon based on innocence. Paula Gray was a tragic figure in the prosecution of the Ford Heights Four—Dennis

Williams, Willie Rainge, Kenneth Adams, and Verneal Jimerson—for the 1978 murder of Lawrence Lionberg and the rape and murder of Carol Schmal. Just seventeen and mentally disabled, Gray had first claimed to police that she held up a cigarette lighter as the crimes were committed. But prior to trial, Gray recanted her testimony and then was charged with murder, rape, and perjury. She was convicted and sentenced to fifty years in prison. She had been released on parole after eight years.

Meanwhile, Williams, Rainge, Adams, and Jimerson were exonerated after an investigation by Northwestern University journalism students and DNA testing excluded them from the crime. They had been pardoned, but nothing had been done on Gray's behalf and I felt that she had been put through hell for more than two decades. It was time to do something.

As I addressed the audience, I said, "One of the few perks of this job is that occasionally you can bring some good news to people. This morning, I pardoned Paula Gray." The crowd exploded in applause and everyone rose to their feet seemingly as one. As Gray put her hand to her forehead as if steadying herself, Dennis Williams walked over and embraced her.

Gray's perjury conviction had been vacated a year earlier by Cook County Circuit Court judge William O'Neal, who said Gray had been initially forced to tell a version of the crime that the police believed had occurred. "The coercion of Ms. Gray to tell their concocted, inculpatory story and subsequent suppression of reliable evidence pointing to the guilt of others was both abhorrent and illegal," Judge O'Neal declared. Despite the ruling, and although her codefendants had been exonerated, the Cook County State's Attorney's Office was seeking to appeal Judge O'Neal's ruling.

"I don't understand it," I said. "I don't understand how anyone can be opposed to righting the wrong the system committed against Paula Gray."

I quoted from Judge O'Neal's ruling in announcing the pardon. "Wrong is wrong, be it illegal actions of the street thug or the conduct—as in this [Gray's] matter—by officers of the law and court."

As I left Northwestern, I was handed a letter from noted American playwright Arthur Miller, who wrote *The Crucible*, a play based on the Salem witch trials of 1692 and 1693 in the Massachusetts Bay Colony. Miller referenced a case in Connecticut involving a seventeen-year-old boy, Peter Reilly, who falsely confessed to murdering his mother.

"Having had some experience with a false confession by a seventeen-year-old boy, Peter Reilly, accused of murdering his mother, and later judged innocent, I appeal to you [to] do whatever you can to prevent the state from killing any of its citizens," Miller wrote. "As you no doubt know, since the emotions raised by the accusations of murder are so intense, the likelihood of error in sentencing is high. Such was the case with Peter Reilly and I presume with others as well."

On the Friday before Thanksgiving 2002, the Illinois Prisoner Review Board delivered their recommendations for the nearly 160 death row prisoners. I immediately began to review them over the weekend.

Meanwhile, we decided to schedule two meetings for the victims' families—one in Springfield at the mansion and one in Chicago.

Whatever my decision was going to be—blanket commutation or decisions on a case-by-case basis—I didn't want anyone to complain that they never had an opportunity to meet with me face to face and make their case and tell me how they felt. I strongly believed their thoughts and beliefs were very much a part of the decision process.

I felt the meetings would also give me an opportunity to explain why I declared the moratorium and established the Capital Punishment Commission—in essence, why I had concluded that the system needed to be reformed. We decided to keep these meetings private because we believed that people needed to express themselves without the spotlight of the media.

I met first with the victims' families. This was very difficult for everyone. I knew going in that I wasn't going to win any of them over when I explained to them what my thinking was. They carried pictures of their relatives with them to show me what had been taken from them. There were a lot of tears; a lot of anger. I saw it in their faces and I heard it in their words. They heard me out and allowed me to say that I really did feel the pain that they felt and understand their losses.

I also tried to explain to them that I didn't think that the anger and sorrow over the loss of their loved ones would go away if the murderer were executed. I was very honest with them. I told them I didn't believe that an eye for an eye was going to make them less angry or make everything better. I said that executions wouldn't bring their relatives back and that I seriously doubted that executions would help them forget.

They talked about closure and how executions would provide that. I found myself wondering whether that really was the purpose of capital punishment. Was it to soothe the families of the victims? And I also had to ask myself whether it actually did that. I cannot imagine losing a family member to murder. Nor can I imagine spending every waking day for twenty years with a single-minded focus to watch a killer die.

Although the meetings were private, some of the family members talked to the media afterward. The media seized on comments by some that I said a blanket commutation was off the table. I did say that a blanket commutation was not a likely occurrence. And I was speaking the truth at that moment.

It was not easy to listen for several hours and hear the exhortations of people to kill other people so they could get closure and, yes, revenge for the loss of their loved ones. It was hard to remain stoic and not be moved.

# 30

# MARCH FOR LIFE

In the aftermath of the clemency hearings, the *Chicago Tribune* published a particularly acerbic editorial that said, in part:

> The hurry-up clemency hearings that were supposed to highlight flaws in this state's capital punishment system instead have drenched Illinois citizens in vivid, painful reminders of why the death penalty exists. As a result, Governor George Ryan's threat to unilaterally commute all current death sentences has backfired in his face and undermined the crucial cause of capital punishment reform.

This prompted a joint response from the Center on Wrongful Convictions, the Illinois Coalition Against the Death Penalty, and Murder Victims Families for Reconciliation. On December 15, they held a "National Gathering of the Death Row Exonerated" at Northwestern University. This was supposed to have been held the following year to commemorate the fifth anniversary of the National Conference on Wrongful Convictions and the Death Penalty that Larry Marshall had first organized in the fall of 1998. But it was moved up and was a direct appeal to me, although I was not there.

This time, thirty-six men who had been exonerated from death row across the country walked onto a stage at Northwestern University's Law School. One by one, they introduced themselves and lit a candle. The flames were intended to represent the lives that would have been snuffed out had their executions taken place. This group of exonerated death row prisoners was even larger than the group Marshall brought together the first time he convened such a conference.

Marshall said, “Governor, we urge you to side on the side of life.”

Reverend Jesse Jackson was there as well. He was a long-time friend and a strong proponent of abolishing the death penalty across the country. He and I had always been able to work together on issues that were important to his community. I appreciated his promise to support me at a time when I was getting as much criticism as I was praise.

He spoke as if he were talking directly to me.

“You can make a decision that will change the course of a nation,” he said. “In truth, the nation’s soul is on trial.”

This was the beginning of perhaps the most intense lobbying effort by the antideath penalty movement to date.

The following day, at 4:40 a.m., a most unusual public demonstration began on the shoulder of Illinois State Highway 53. Exonerated death row inmate Gary Gauger pointed across the street to the Stateville Correctional Center, the institution which—until the execution of Andrew Kokoraleis—had housed the Illinois death chamber. It was where Gauger, had he not been exonerated, would have been put to death by lethal injection.

“Look at it,” Gauger declared, gesturing toward the prison with its circular towers that housed inmates. “That place really is Gothic, like something out of a *Batman* movie. Unreal.”

And then, as a handful of reporters watched, Gauger, accompanied by his wife, Sue, and Larry Marshall, stepped off on the first lap of what was to be a thirty-seven-mile relay of exonerated men. They were carrying a scroll to deliver to my office at the Thompson Center in downtown Chicago.

This appeal was called “Dead Men Walking.”

“We are the exonerated,” the scroll said. “We have each walked in the valley of the shadow of death. The courts and the public were certain that we were guilty and that we had forfeited our right to live. Only through miracles did the truth emerge. The truth proved we were victims of wrongful convictions.”

The men exchanged the scroll like a baton. Some held it aloft like an Olympic torch. Some were clad in sweatpants, others in suits and ties. There were vans following the men, carrying those who would drop in for their leg and picking up those who completed theirs.

About ten miles from downtown, men stopped leaving. As new men joined, the group grew in size. At the Cook County Criminal Courts building at 26th Street and California Boulevard, where many of these exonerated men had been housed and tried and convicted, they paused. It was later reported to me that Perry Cobb, who was exonerated with his codefendant Darby Tillis in 1987, pulled a harmonica out of his pocket and played "Amazing Grace." And they all sang. It was spontaneous. There was no media to impress. They later said the moment was cathartic and powerful.

Anthony Porter and David Protess led the last leg. The group, which included Maria Cunningham, whose husband Dick had been so tragically stabbed to death, as well as about a dozen exonerees and supporters, marched over the Chicago River and up to the Thompson building. There, a member of my staff accepted the scroll and promised to deliver it to me. He reiterated that blanket commutation was on the "back burner." He also added, however, that I had been "reviewing each of these cases for three years."

That night, I attended the Chicago premier of the play *The Exonerated*, a ninety-minute dramatization of the stories of several death row exonerees with actors, including Richard Dreyfuss, Jill Clayburgh, Mike Farrell, and Danny Glover portraying the exonerees. It was staged at the Chicago Center for the Performing Arts, which was at full capacity when Lura Lynn and I entered. The play, created by Jessica Blank and Erik Jensen, had been running Off-Broadway for about two years in New York City and this was the first performance elsewhere. Rob Warden had been instrumental in bringing the play to Chicago and some of the actors had volunteered to take part specifically because the performance essentially was for me. It was a one-night stand.

The audience included death row exonerees from around the country, including five of the six exonerees featured in the play, members of the Illinois legislature, as well as lawyers and advocates for abolishing the death penalty and for fixing the criminal justice system. Larry Marshall and Rob Warden were there, of course, as was Barry Scheck, who along with Peter Neufeld had cofounded the Innocence Project in New York City that was exonerating inmates through the use of DNA testing.

As Lura Lynn and I watched the play, about half, if not most of the audience, was watching me to try to discern some small piece of intelligence about what I was thinking. In a way, I was an audience of one on this night.

It was a powerful performance and provided an emotional and visceral dimension for me. At the conclusion, the actors joined to thank me for declaring the moratorium. The auditorium exploded in a standing ovation that left me trembling in my seat.

Never, in my thirty years in politics, had I never received a standing ovation such as that for a single decision.

I stepped up toward the front of the stage and shook hands with the actors, including Dreyfus, who was holding the letter that the inmates had carried from Stateville penitentiary to my office downtown. He handed it to me and said, "In an era when we have come to expect so little from our elected officials, you gave us more, much more."

Before I left, Robin Hobley, sister of death row inmate Madison Hobley, approached.

"Governor Ryan," she said. "When are you going to meet with family members of the people on death row? You met with the families of victims. We have things to say too."

I didn't hesitate.

"I will," I told her. "I will do it. We will set it up."

As I left the theater, I felt as I had been socked in the gut. And although I didn't say it, I felt that blanket commutation was back on the table.

Not long after, I spent the afternoon with the family members of the death row inmates at Old St. Mary's Catholic Church in Chicago. After having listened to the victims' families, now I heard about a different kind of pain.

Many of these families lived with the twin agony of knowing that, in some cases, their family member was responsible for causing another family great pain, and that society was calling for a second killing—of their family member. Those parents, brothers, sisters, and children were not to blame for the crimes that were committed, yet they faced the realization that the state wanted to execute their sons or brothers or fathers.

It was evident that some of these family members were even more tormented by their belief that their loved one was really a victim—someone who they knew was truly innocent of the crime that sent them to death row.

At this meeting I looked into the face of Claude Lee, the adoptive father of Eric Lee, who was convicted of killing a Kankakee police officer in 1996 and was sitting on death row. Eric Lee had no criminal record but did have a history of mental illness when Officer Anthony Samfay pulled him over for a traffic violation. Evidence would later show that in the months prior to this confrontation, Lee had been diagnosed as being "dangerous" and "in need of a structured environment," but had not received any further psychiatric care.

Lee shot Samfay several times and fled. He later forced a woman to give up her car keys by displaying a pistol. He was caught driving the woman's car about an hour later. He was found guilty and sentenced to death. It had been a traumatic time in Kankakee.

I knew Claude Lee. We went to high school together. At the time, his home, on Myrtle Street, was about a mile from my home. I had known the Lee family for many years.

Lee approached me and we shook hands and he got right to the point.

"Are you going to kill my son?" he asked.

How do you respond to a question like that?

I said I was thinking long and hard about what to do and that I would be thinking of him and his family and his son.

We shook hands again and he walked away.

I was familiar with the case. While there was little doubt that Eric was guilty of killing the officer, our review determined there was no question that Eric was, at the time of the crime, seriously mentally ill and had been for many years. The crime he committed was terrible. He killed a police officer.

But already I had found myself questioning whether I could send another man's son to death under a deeply flawed capital punishment system like the one in Illinois. This was a deeply troubled young man with a documented history of mental illness. Could I rely on the system of justice in Illinois to not make a horrible mistake with a young man who was mentally unstable? Should this man be executed by the state?

Meeting with family members of the condemned was just as difficult as the meetings I had with the victims' families. It was no less emotional and they were just as honest as the families in the other meetings had been. I took my time and tried to answer all their questions. For a while, I sat in a chair and bounced young children on my knee. I later found out that among them were the grandchildren of Henry Brisbon, the man some said was a poster child for the death penalty. They didn't ask me if I was going to kill their grandfather, but they might as well have.

In the end, all these families—the families of the victims and the families of the condemned—were in their own way asking me not to destroy their belief in justice.

I didn't see how I could please both sides.

# 31

# PICKING AND CHOOSING

In the back of my mind, reaching a decision on each case individually was never going to be a simple thing, even though I kept talking about it. I had tremendous doubts about how capital punishment was administered in Illinois. I didn't trust it—for anyone. Although I allowed Andrew Kokoraleis to die three years earlier, I never felt completely comfortable with that decision. There was—and I guess there always will be—a concern in the back of my mind because of the gravity and finality of an execution.

We continued to review the cases. I took those books and files with me everywhere I went. I read them at the office, at home, while shuttling between Chicago and Springfield on the state plane, in the van while driving from event to event. I even read some of them during lunch and dinner. It was a lot to take in, but I wanted to make sure I understood each case thoroughly.

It became clear through my review that the system used to put these approximately 160 people on death row was just broken. And when I worked backward in each case, I found broken aspects of the system in virtually every case. There were accusations of coerced confessions and police torture, inadequate defense lawyers, convictions of black defendants by all-white juries, and the repeated use of jailhouse snitches and informants as key witnesses. In a lot of the cases, the evidence of guilt appeared to be overwhelming, but I wondered if I could really trust the evidence and the witnesses and the record.

Two days after the exonerated death row inmates marched from Stateville Correctional Center to Chicago, US attorney Patrick Fitzgerald and Cook County state's attorney Richard Devine announced that four men convicted of a 1997 murder had been wrongly convicted.

Why? Because a police informant had given false testimony and because the police had improperly gotten a confession out of one of the men. Two of the men were immediately released from prison.

The convictions of Omar Aguirre, Edar Duarte Santos, Luis Ortiz, and Robert Gayol, were vacated. They had been convicted of the torture-murder of a fifty-six-year-old furniture dealer, Sindulfo Miranda, on the Northwest Side of Chicago in July 1997.

Aguirre had been implicated by a police informant, Miguel LaSalle, who falsely claimed that he had overheard the men plot the crime, then saw them with the victim around the time of the crime. LaSalle even claimed he spoke to Santos on a cell phone during the crime. Following Aguirre's arrest in November 1997, a lengthy police interrogation resulted in Aguirre falsely confessing and implicating Santos. Ortiz confessed and implicated Gayol but said he did so only after he was beaten by detectives. Santos confessed to punching the victim but denied taking part in the murder.

In 1999, Aguirre had been convicted by a Cook County Circuit Court jury and was sentenced to fifty-five years in prison. Santos, meanwhile, remained in the Cook County jail awaiting trial. Finally, in early 2002, Santos pleaded guilty in return for a sentence of only twelve years. Ortiz also pleaded guilty and was sentenced to twenty-five years in return for his testimony against Gayol, who was convicted at trial and sentenced to life in prison.

The truth came to light when the FBI and US Attorney's Office in Chicago developed evidence that the crime actually had been one of a series of drug-related kidnappings and torture committed by members of the Latin Kings street gang.

These convictions had, once upon a time, looked rock solid. There were confessions. There were guilty pleas. How could this happen? Although none of the four were sentenced to death and so no potential executions were in play, the facts of the case took my breath away.

In mid-November, the Illinois House of Representatives overrode my amendatory veto of the antiterrorism bill—and with that, my amendatory legislation, which contained many of the recommendations of my commission that fell to the wayside.

At the same time I was reviewing the cases of the men sitting on death row, I wanted to make sure that exonerated men who had already been released from prison had their records and, as much as possible, their reputations cleared. At the top of that list were Rolando Cruz, Gary Gauger, and Steven Linscott.

Cruz and Gauger had been sentenced to death and Linscott to forty years in prison. All had been exonerated of murder convictions. I granted them pardons based on innocence, announcing my decision in a speech at the University of Illinois College of Law in Champaign, Illinois. Together, the three cases represented prosecutions built on false confessions that defense lawyers claimed had been manufactured. Cruz was said to have provided details that only the killer would know by recounting a dream or vision that he allegedly had. Gauger's confession said that he didn't remember the crime because he blacked out. Linscott also was said to have revealed details of the crime that he said came to him in a dream.

"Three men, three statements described as visions or dreams that were used against them," I said. "The only vision they saw was of a justice system run amok—of their dreams being dashed and ruined by the criminal justice system. I wish them well. They have been through hell."

Significantly, in that speech, I said for the first very time that in the course of my review of the death penalty and the problems with the justice system, I had concluded that if I had the power to act alone, I would abolish capital punishment.

"There's one thing that I'm somewhat disturbed about, and that's that I think most people that are family members who feel it is their right to have death as the penalty," I said. "And I'm not sure why that is. . . . But they claim that the only way that they can get closure on the issue is to kill the person that killed their loved one . . . I'm not critical of it. I just think it's kind of a wrong situation."

I explained that along with the errors that were inherent in the system, and the unfairness that had been found everywhere, I just didn't buy into the "eye for an eye" argument from the victims' families. When I had met with the families of victims, there was no denying their pain at losing a loved one in a tragic way. Their emotion was powerful. But it was also clear that a lot of them felt they had a "right" to see their loved one's murderer die.

That bothered me. They told me that the only way they could get any closure was by seeing the murderer die.

I seriously doubted that I would find any closure over the death of a loved one by seeing the murderer die. An execution does not bring anyone back. I believed that the pain of losing someone is separate from a feeling of revenge. I didn't think getting revenge helped you get over a loss. I didn't think it made you feel better.

In the end, that argument was never going to overcome all the problems we had with the capital punishment system. Although my words sounded as if I were criticizing families who had been through so much pain, I had to speak my truth. I thought they were misleading themselves if they thought that seeing a murderer die was going to end their suffering.

That very same day, the Illinois Supreme Court upheld three more death sentences. The court affirmed the conviction and death sentence for Lenard Johnson, who had been convicted in 1991 of murdering an eleven-year-old boy and raping two girls, ages eleven and thirteen, in Montgomery County. Johnson had pled guilty but had been appealing saying his mental competence at the time he pled guilty was questionable.

Joseph Miller's 1994 conviction and death sentence for the murders of three women in Peoria County also was allowed to stand. Miller claimed that his trial attorneys failed to adequately represent him because he rejected the prosecution's offer of life in prison in exchange for a guilty plea thinking that he could get an even more lenient sentence if he went to trial—an impossibility.

The state high court also let stand the death sentence for Roosevelt Lucas, who had been convicted in the 1987 slaying of Robert Taylor, a superintendent at the Pontiac Correctional Center, who was fatally stabbed in the heart in his office. Lucas claimed his trial attorneys failed to call or fully prepare witnesses on his behalf during his original trial and that a prosecution witness committed perjury. The court held that the affidavits from the defense witnesses that Lucas said were not called basically repeated the evidence already presented at trial. In addition, the court said the alleged perjurer's testimony was outweighed by the testimony of two eyewitnesses who said they saw Lucas attack Taylor.

The machinery of death, despite the moratorium, was still humming in Illinois.

# 32

# A MATTER OF CONSCIENCE

Manny's Deli on Jefferson Street, just east of the Dan Ryan Expressway, is one of my favorite places to eat lunch in Chicago. There hasn't been a politician, including presidents, who has ever come through the city who didn't visit here and sample the corned beef sandwiches and the latkes. But beyond the food, one of the main reasons I always liked to eat there was because it's an old-fashioned deli.

In Manny's, no one puts on airs. When I went there, occasionally someone would yell, "Hi, Governor!" But for the most part, I could grab my tray and go through the cafeteria-style line like anyone else. I would pay for my food at the end of the line and then wade into the dining room and find the first open table and chairs. Nobody reserved a table for me; and the people sitting next to you—from all walks of life—would almost always just barely look up from their sandwiches. If they recognized you, you'd get a nod or a small comment, but they always went right back to their plates. Although I've eaten in some of the best restaurants in the world, Manny's will always be special.

There's one more reason Manny's is memorable. As the debate about whether I would empty death row continued around me, I decided to have lunch at Manny's. As I munched on my corned beef sandwich, my cell phone rang. My staff back at the office wanted to connect me to a caller—Nelson Mandela!

I tried to maintain my composure, but I was shocked. I was sitting in a delicatessen with all kinds of working stiffs in jeans and businesspeople in suits—and I'm on the phone with one of the best known, renowned, and respected men in the world.

And he called me.

I had met him in Johannesburg during my trip there to develop business opportunities for Illinois. But our meeting had been brief because he was in ill health. At the time, he praised me for having the courage to declare a moratorium on the death penalty. I appreciated that coming from him. He had spent a majority of his life in prison—unjustly—and he never preached revenge or violence. He was a man who truly defined "turn the other cheek."

His voice came through strong and clear.

"I urge you to issue a blanket commutation for everyone on death row," Mandela said. "Revenge of this kind—the death penalty—has never made the world a better place. Governor Ryan, the United States has always set the standard for the world as far as justice, except where the death penalty was concerned. You can set a new standard."

"Thank you," I said.

The conversation was over almost as quickly as it began. I was mightily impressed that he felt that it was important to reach out to me on this issue and share his thoughts.

As the time left in my term dwindled, Mandela's call was not the only one I received and not the only one from South Africa. Archbishop Desmond Tutu, a lifelong opponent of capital punishment, also called to tell me how important it was to take a bold step and grant a blanket commutation.

"Your decision is important because it will show that the United States is moving in the right direction to join the majority of the rest of the world," he declared. "It is impossible for any man to decide who should live and who should die, regardless of the crime that they committed. That power, Governor Ryan, rests solely with God."

Other world leaders, including those from Mexico, Poland, the Vatican, and the European Union, similarly urged me to commute all death sentences in Illinois.

Those calls, especially Mandela's, had an impact. Mandela and Archbishop Tutu had devoted their lives to righting the wrongs they saw around them. Mandela changed the direction of his country without a civil war. Desmond Tutu won a Nobel Peace Prize. It was humbling that they would think enough about what I was doing and what I was going through to want to call me and give me their thoughts.

Just before Christmas, Larry Marshall asked me to dinner. I agreed, not only because of all the time and effort he had put into educating me and pushing for reform and for a blanket commutation, but because I genuinely liked him. I trusted him. I believed his heart and mind were in the right place. I just wasn't sure I was going to do what he wanted me to.

We met at Riva's Restaurant on Chicago's Navy Pier, a place well-known among politicians and public officials. I figured Larry was going to use this opportunity to make his "final argument" to me on why I should issue a blanket commutation. And I was right.

He had a list of reasons why I should go ahead and commute everyone. I had heard them all before. But his last point was different. He recounted the story from the Old Testament's Book of Esther.

From 486 to 465 BC, Ahasuerus was the king of Persia, Larry began. From all the women in his kingdom, he chose Esther, an orphan of Jewish descent, to be his queen. She was instructed by her cousin, Mordecai, to keep her Jewish heritage a secret.

Sometime later, Mordecai, whose Jewish origin was well-known, offended one of Ahasuerus's high officials, who sought and obtained Ahasuerus's permission to have all the Jews in Persia killed. Mordecai concluded that the only hope for his people was to beseech Esther to approach the king, reveal she was a Jew, and persuade him to rescind his decision.

Doing that held great peril for Esther because she would be exposing herself to the decree against the Jews and because the king was known to frequently execute those who approached him without having been summoned. It was understandable, then, that Esther expressed great trepidation in response to Mordecai's pleas.

Mordecai then made one final appeal to Queen Esther. He told her that she was in a truly unique position to change history and save countless lives. And he challenged her to consider the following question: "Who knows whether it was for this very moment that you have come to power?"

"Queen Esther," Larry continued, "rose to the occasion. She approached the king and persuaded him to do all in his power to save innocent lives. You, Governor, are standing in an Esther moment. You, and only you are in a position right now to spare the lives of those who do not deserve to be killed, and to thereby change history. And, I hope I am not being presumptuous when I ask, 'Who knows whether it was for this very moment that you have come to power?'"

It was a story that was unfamiliar to me. But its power and relevance to the moment in which I found myself was undeniable.

On Monday, December 30, a letter was delivered to my office containing the signatures of 428 law professors from across the country—more than twenty pages of names and law schools—urging me to consider a blanket commutation.

"The clemency power traditionally has been used not only to correct injustices in individual cases, but also as a response to problems in the systemic application of the law," the letter said. "It can promote healing after issues of great divisiveness have been resolved."

The letter followed similar ones in November and December from 650 Illinois lawyers and twenty-one retired Illinois judges, including Richard J. Fitzgerald, the former chief judge of the Cook County Criminal Court.

This appeal was organized by Anthony G. Amsterdam, a professor at New York University, one of the most—if not *the most*—distinguished law professor in the United States. Among his many achievements was his argument in the US Supreme Court that resulted in the 1972 ruling that declared the death penalty unconstitutional.

The letter said it was proper for me, as governor, "to assess clemency petitions and to grant commutations and pardons when the circumstances so justify, even if that means a general grant of clemency to remedy systemic problems."

Amsterdam told the media that the sheer number of law professors was a clear indication that a blanket commutation was appropriate. "To get 428 signatures on detailed legal analysis is incredible," he told the *Chicago Tribune*. "You can't get ten people in a law school to agree to the length of a metal yardstick."

When the media asked about my reaction to the letter, my spokesman Dennis Culloton said that my position was unchanged. "We've been reviewing each case individually," he said, repeating that blanket commutation was "on the back burner."

On New Year's Eve, Reverend Jesse Jackson visited with inmates on death row at Pontiac Correctional Center. When he emerged, he called for me to issue a blanket commutation. That plea was echoed a few days later by death row exonerees Anthony Porter, Gary Gauger, and Perry Cobb who also called for outright pardons for inmates who had claimed they were tortured by detectives working under Jon Burge, the disgraced Chicago police lieutenant who oversaw the torture of scores of defendants.

At about the same time, the news broke that Francis Boyle, a professor of international law at the University of Illinois Law School in Champaign, Illinois, and a death penalty opponent, intended to nominate me for the Nobel Peace Prize. Boyle said he was moved to make the nomination after hearing me speak about my journey. "His speech clearly came from the depths of his soul," Boyle said.

Boyle said that I deserved recognition for my "crusade against what is clearly a racist and class-based death penalty system here in Illinois." It would be the first of six such nominations for the peace prize.

My last days in office were incredibly busy. Not only were we packing up our offices in Chicago and Springfield, but also Lura Lynn and I were packing up our belongings at the Governor's Mansion in Springfield. We were going to return home to Kankakee with boxes of books, papers, artwork, and an assortment of awards that had been conferred on me during my term.

As the packing continued, so did the discussions on each and every death row case. Many times, we worked into the early morning hours, buried in the binders, categorizing facts, and assessing the allegations that made quite a few of the convictions suspicious. And within my staff, there was a growing voice advising me against a mass commutation. They believed in the guilt in some defendants—based on evidence that under the law at the time made them eligible for the death penalty.

But the more I looked at those cases, the more I realized that I couldn't decide that one would live while another would die. Even though we were trying to classify each of the cases and find patterns in the errors that were prevalent in capital cases, I couldn't really be sure that there weren't errors in every case. There were just too many possibilities to consider.

And so, I began to lean more and more toward a blanket commutation—that it was the only way to make sure that an innocent person wasn't put to death. And then, I decided that was the only way to go. I was also deeply concerned because the General Assembly had done virtually nothing on the recommendations of my commission. Nothing. The legislation had been sabotaged, undercut, blocked, and basically left shipwrecked.

I had hoped the legislature would act, but in fact it had not.

In the end, my decision was a matter of conscience. A big part of my discomfort with the death penalty went beyond the documented problems with the administration of the law. There was also a personal aspect to it. As a religious person, it offended me. I have always prayed every day—every morning. I still do. And I have to say that the personal pleas from the clergy who contacted me, not only at the end of my term but at the beginning of it when I was weighing the Kokoraleis decision, played a part in my decision.

There was a mantra in what I heard from ministers and pastors and priests: God gives us life through our parents and life and death is not for us to decide. God provides us with the means and the knowledge to protect life and to prolong it. But ending the life of another person is not part of that package.

I knew in my heart that this is what I believed.

As governor, I had been thrust into a position where I had to decide on life or death. And I realized I couldn't do it. And I say that now, even though I did allow an execution to take place. I realized that it had been impossible for me to walk away from that decision, even after all of those years.

I was bothered by it then. And I always will be.

When I looked into my heart and my mind, I saw I did not have it in me to condemn another human being to death. And my conscience was only strengthened by the fact that the evidence building against the capital punishment system as a whole led any reasonable person to conclude that the system did not serve justice, but violated justice.

And so, now that I had reached my decision, what was left was deciding when to do it and where.

There definitely was a promise I intended to keep. I had promised all the victims' family members that I would not surprise them. And so, letters were prepared to be delivered to the doors of each and every family member by a member of the Illinois State Police. The letters explained that my decision was a difficult one, but that I felt it was the only way to prevent the execution of an innocent person. I signed off by saying, "May God bless you."

I had decided that if I were going to err, I was going to err on the side of life.

My term as governor was set to end at noon on Monday, January 13, 2003. At that time, I would be sitting on the stage behind the newly-elected governor, Democrat Rod Blagojevich, when he took the oath of office and assumed the duties of governor.

I decided that during my last week in office I would bring the death penalty debate that had dominated my term to a close. I would give a series of speeches at law schools in Chicago and describe my thinking and announce my final decisions then. The debate over capital punishment in Illinois was still supercharged with emotion—on both sides—and I decided that I wanted to speak to audiences that were sympathetic to my decisions.

During our review of the cases, I had flagged the files of the eleven men who had been put on death row by Burge. Each of them had described being suffocated, shocked by a cattle prod, or by a hand-cranked generator that sent electricity to alligator clips that had been attached to their genitals and other parts of their body as they were being interrogated and being beaten until they did what the officers wanted them to do—sign confessions.

Some of these cases, I thought, demanded more of a response that just a commutation of the death penalty that had been imposed on them. I concluded that for four of these men anything less than a pardon for the crimes that put them on death row was an injustice.

So, on Friday, January 10, 2003, during a speech at the DePaul University School of Law, I announced the pardons of Aaron Patterson, Madison Hobley, Leroy Orange, and Stanley Howard.

"Today, I shall be a friend to Madison Hobley, Stanley Howard, Aaron Patterson, and Leroy Orange," I said. "Today, I am pardoning them of crimes for which they were wrongfully prosecuted and sentenced to die."

Patterson, of course, had been on my mind for many months, after I learned the details of his case—that he had used a paper clip to scratch a desperate plea for help into a metal bench in an interrogation room: "Police threaten me with violence. . . . Slapped and suffocated me with plastic. . . . Signed false statement to murders." Patterson had been threatened with a gun during his interrogation. He was convicted and sentenced to death for a double murder on Chicago's South Side in 1986 based on his confession and false testimony from witnesses. There was no forensic or physical evidence connecting him to the crime.

Hobley was convicted and sentenced to death after Chicago police detectives working under Burge asserted that Hobley confessed to setting a fire that killed his wife, son, and five other people in 1987 on the South

Side of Chicago. Hobley claimed that the officers tortured him and when he refused to give a confession, the detectives just concocted one.

Stanley Howard had been sentenced to death in 1987 for a 1984 murder during an armed robbery on the South Side of Chicago. He had been convicted largely on the basis of his confession that was extracted by Burge's men who had beaten him.

Leroy Orange had been convicted and sentenced to death for four murders in 1984 on Chicago's South Side. His half-brother, Leonard Kidd, also was arrested, and during an interrogation by Burge detectives, gave a confession that implicated Orange. Before Orange's trial, Kidd recanted, said his statement was the result of police torture, and actually testified at Orange's trial that he committed the murders alone and without Orange's knowledge. Orange was convicted basically on his confession, which he said came after he had been beaten, suffocated, and given electric shocks by Burge's detectives.

Their torture claims had been corroborated over and over again.

"The system has failed for all four men," I said. "And it has failed the people of this state."

I added, "In some way I can see how rogue cops, twenty years ago, could run wild. I can see how, in a different time, they perhaps were able to manipulate the system. What I can't understand is why the courts can't find a way to act in the interest of justice."

My speech was televised and was marked by frequent standing ovations. The *Chicago Tribune* reported that just before I began speaking, a hush fell over the Pontiac Correctional Center where many of the death row inmates were housed. One inmate told the newspaper later that even the guards and staff were watching. And when I announced the pardons, the inmates erupted in cheers.

I thought that this kind of decision sent a message that I had kept my word to study each case individually and judge each one on its merits. And in fact, I had studied each case. And based on the merits in these four cases, I decided that pardons were not only justified, but were necessary.

Of course, Cook County state's attorney Richard Devine, whose office prosecuted the majority of the death row inmates, was—as he had been—vocal in his opposition. He accused me of jumping into bed with the defense attorneys. "All of these cases would have been best left for consideration by the courts, which have the experience, the training, and the wisdom to decide innocence or guilt," Devine declared. "By his actions today, the governor has breached faith with the memory of the dead victims, their families, and the people he was elected to serve."

I have thick skin. I knew this sort of reaction was coming. And I understood it. The Richard Devines of the world have a constituency and a job to do. I just didn't quite see it the same way prosecutors largely did.

For me, a question remained.

"What does it take?" I asked, regarding the failure of the legislature to enact reforms. "Now we can say the number of wrongfully convicted men is not thirteen, but seventeen. And I would ask, 'Will that be enough?'"

# 33

# COMMUTATION

We chose Northwestern University Law School to announce that I was going to empty death row because its Center on Wrongful Convictions, as well as the university's journalism students, had done so much to uncover injustice.

The lecture room in Lincoln Hall where I gave my speech was overflowing with students, professors, exonerees, family members of some of the death row inmates, and people who had worked hard for years to expose the death penalty system in Illinois for what it was and to either enact changes in the system or to abolish it altogether. And, of course, the media. My speech was being televised live.

Illinois state police were stashed in a nearby classroom—surreptitiously ushered in and remaining out of sight—just in case there was a problem. Before I could even enter the room, Aaron Patterson showed up and was pitching a fit because a friend of his who also was on death row, whom Patterson believed to be innocent, had not been pardoned at the same time Patterson was. He was threatening to disrupt my presentation. Matt Bettenhausen helped calm Patterson—who likely had not slept since his release more than twenty-four years earlier—and mollify him at least for the day.

Behind me were Larry Marshall and Bettenhausen, both of whom had done so much for me in different, but critical ways. I looked out at the faces of Dave Protess, journalism students, and private investigator Paul Ciolino—all of whom had literally turned the justice system upside down—not because they wanted to destroy the justice system but because they believed in it and wanted to see it work properly. Some members of my Capital Punishment Commission were present, including Thomas Sullivan, the former US attorney who had provided great leadership.

I had spent thirty-five years in government. One of the few disappointments of my legislative career and as a statewide elected official was that the General Assembly failed to work with me to reform the capital punishment system. I was about the lamest lame duck that had ever walked the face of the Earth.

That didn't matter. What I was about to say came with a conviction of conscience.

> Four years ago, I was sworn in as the 39th governor of Illinois. That was just four short years ago; that's when I was a firm believer in the American system of justice and the death penalty. I believed that the ultimate penalty for the taking of a life was administrated in a just and fair manner. Today, three days before I end my term as governor, I stand before you to explain my frustrations and deep concerns about both the administration and the penalty of death. It is fitting that we are gathered here today at Northwestern University with the students, teachers, lawyers, and investigators who first shed light on the sorrowful condition of Illinois's death penalty system.
>
> Professors Larry Marshall, Dave Protess, and their students along with investigator Paul Ciolino have gone above the call. They freed the falsely accused Ford Heights Four, they saved Anthony Porter's life, they fought for Rolando Cruz and Alex Hernandez. They devoted time and effort on behalf of Aaron Patterson, a young man who lost fifteen years of his youth sitting among the condemned, and LeRoy Orange, who lost seventeen of the best years of his life on death row. It is also proper that we are together with dedicated people like Andrea Lyon who has labored on the front lines trying capital cases for many years and who is now devoting her passion to creating an innocence center at De Paul University. You saved Madison Hobley's life.
>
> Together you spared the lives and secured the freedom of seventeen men who were wrongfully convicted and rotting in the condemned units of our state prisons. What you have achieved is of the highest calling. Thank you.
>
> Yes, it is right that I am here with you, where, in a manner of speaking, my journey from staunch supporter of capital punishment to reformer all began. But I must tell you—since the beginning of our journey, my thoughts and feelings about the death penalty have

changed many, many times. I realize that over the course of my reviews, I had said that I would not do blanket commutation. I have also said it was an option that was there, and I would consider all options.

During my time in public office I have always reserved my right to change my mind if I believed it to be in the best public interest, whether it be about taxes, abortions, or the death penalty. But I must confess that the debate with myself has been the toughest concerning the death penalty. I suppose the reason the death penalty has been the toughest is because it is so final. It is the only public policy that determines who lives and who dies.

In addition, it is the only issue that attracts most of the legal minds across the country. I have received more advice on this issue than any other policy issue I have dealt with in my thirty-five years of public service. I have kept an open mind on both sides of the issues of commutation for life or death. I have read, listened to, and discussed the issue with the families of the victims as well as the families of the condemned. I know that any decision I make will not be accepted by one side or the other. I know that my decision will be just that—my decision; based on all the facts I could gather over the past three years.

I may never be comfortable with my final decision, but I will know in my heart, that I did my very best to do the right thing.

Having said that I want to share a story with you: I grew up in Kankakee, which even today is still a small midwestern town, a place where people tend to know each other. Steve Small was a neighbor. I watched him grow up. He would babysit my young children, which was not for the faint of heart since Lura Lynn and I had six children, five of them under the age of three. He was a bright young man who helped run the family business. He got married and he and his wife had three children of their own. Lura Lynn was especially close to him and his family. We took comfort in knowing he was there for us and we for him. One September [at] midnight he received a call at his home. There had been a break-in at the nearby house he was renovating. But as he left his house, he was seized at gunpoint by kidnappers. His captors buried him alive in a shallow hole. He suffocated to death before police could find him. His killer led investigators to where Steve's body was buried. The killer, Danny Edward, was also from my hometown. He now sits on death row. I also know his family. I share this story with you so that you know I do not come to this as a neophyte without having experienced a small bit of the bitter pill the survivors of murder must swallow.

My responsibilities and obligations are more than my neighbors and my family. I represent all the people of Illinois, like it or not. The decision I make about our criminal justice system is felt not only here, but the world over. The other day, I received a call from former South African president Nelson Mandela who reminded me that the United States sets the example for justice and fairness for the rest of the world. Today, the United States is not in league with most of our major allies: Europe, Canada, Mexico, most of South and Central America. These countries rejected the death penalty. We are partners in death with several third world countries. Even Russia has called a moratorium.

The death penalty has been abolished in twelve states. In none of these states has the homicide rate increased. In Illinois last year we had about one thousand murders; only two percent of that one thousand were sentenced to death. Where is the fairness and equality in that? The death penalty in Illinois is not imposed fairly or uniformly because of the absence of standards for the 102 Illinois state attorneys, who must decide whether to request the death sentence. Should geography be a factor in determining who gets the death sentence? I don't think so, but in Illinois it makes a difference. You are five times more likely to get a death sentence for first-degree murder in the rural area of Illinois than you are in Cook County. Where is the justice and fairness in that? Where is the proportionality?

The Most Reverend Desmond Tutu wrote to me this week stating that "to take a life when a life has been lost is revenge, it is not justice. He says justice allows for mercy, clemency and compassion. These virtues are not weakness."

[I quoted former California governor Pat Brown, who wrote nearly fifty years earlier] "In fact, the most glaring weakness is that no matter how efficient and fair the death penalty may seem in theory, in actual practice it is primarily inflicted upon the weak, the poor, the ignorant and against racial minorities."

I never intended to be an activist on this issue. I watched in surprise as freed death row inmate Anthony Porter was released from jail. A free man, he ran into the arms of Northwestern University professor Dave Protess who poured his heart and soul into proving Porter's innocence with his journalism students. He was forty-eight hours away from being wheeled into the execution chamber where the state would kill him. It would all be so antiseptic and most of us would not have even paused, except that Anthony Porter was innocent of the double murder for which he had been condemned to die. After Mr. Porter's case there was the report by *Chicago Tribune* reporters Steve Mills and

Ken Armstrong documenting the systemic failures of our capital punishment system. Half of the nearly three hundred capital cases in Illinois had been reversed for a new trial or resentencing. Nearly half!

Thirty-three of the death row inmates were represented at trial by an attorney who had later been disbarred or at some point suspended from practicing law. Of the more than 160 death row inmates, thirty-five were African American defendants who had been convicted or condemned to die by all-white juries. More than two-thirds of the inmates on death row were African American. Forty-six inmates were convicted on the basis of testimony from jailhouse informants. I can recall looking at these cases and the information from the Mills-Armstrong series and asking my staff, "How does that happen? How in God's name does that happen? I'm not a lawyer, so somebody explain it to me." But no one could. Not to this day.

Then over the next few months, there were three more exonerated men, freed because their sentence hinged on a jailhouse informant or new DNA technology proved beyond a shadow of doubt their innocence. We then had the dubious distinction of exonerating more men than we had executed. Thirteen men found innocent, twelve executed. As I reported yesterday, there is not a doubt in my mind that the number of innocent men freed from our death row stands at seventeen with the pardons of Aaron Patterson, Madison Hobley, Stanley Howard, and Leroy Orange. That is an absolute embarrassment. Seventeen exonerated death row inmates are nothing short of a catastrophic failure.

But the thirteen, now seventeen men, is just the beginning of our sad arithmetic in prosecuting murder cases. During the time we have had capital punishment in Illinois, there were at least thirty-three other people wrongly convicted on murder charges and exonerated. Since we reinstated the death penalty there are also ninety-three people—ninety-three—where our criminal justice system imposed the most severe sanction and later rescinded the sentence or even released them from custody because they were innocent. How many more cases of wrongful conviction have to occur before we can all agree that the system is broken?

Throughout this process, I have heard many different points of view expressed. I have had the opportunity to review all of the cases involving the inmates on death row. I have conducted private group meetings, one in Springfield and one in Chicago, with the surviving family members of homicide victims. Everyone in the room who wanted to speak had the opportunity to do so. Some wanted to express their grief, others wanted to express their anger. I took it all in. My commission and my staff had been reviewing each and every case for three years.

But I redoubled my effort to review each case personally in order to respond to the concerns of prosecutors and victims' families. This individual review also naturally resulted in a collective examination of our entire death penalty system.

I also had a meeting with a group of people who are less often heard from, and who are not as popular with the media. The family members of death row inmates have a special challenge to face. I spent an afternoon with those family members at a Catholic church here in Chicago. At that meeting, I heard a different kind of pain expressed. Many of these families live with the twin pain of knowing not only that, in some cases, their family member may have been responsible for inflicting a terrible trauma on another family, but also the pain of knowing that society has called for another killing. These parents, siblings, and children are not to blame for the crime committed, yet these innocent stand to have their loved ones killed by the state. As Mr. Mandela told me, they are also branded and scarred for life because of the awful crime committed by their family member. Others were even more tormented by the fact that their loved one was another victim, that they were truly innocent of the crime for which they were sentenced to die.

It was at this meeting that I looked into the face of Claude Lee, the father of Eric Lee, who was convicted of killing Kankakee police officer Anthony Samfay a few years ago. It was a traumatic moment, once again, for my hometown. A brave officer, part of that thin blue line that protects each of us, was struck down by wanton violence. If you will kill a police officer, you have absolutely no respect for the laws of man or God. I've known the Lee family for a number of years. There does not appear to be much question that Eric was guilty of killing the officer.

However, I can say now after our review, there is also not much question that Eric is seriously ill, with a history of treatment for mental illness going back a number of years. The crime he committed was a terrible one—killing a police officer. Society demands that the highest penalty be paid. But I had to ask myself: Could I send another man's son to death under the deeply flawed system of capital punishment we have in Illinois? A troubled young man, with a history of mental illness? Could I rely on the system of justice we have in Illinois not to make another horrible mistake? Could I rely on a fair sentencing?

In the United States the overwhelming majority of those executed are psychotic, alcoholic, drug-addicted, or mentally unstable. They frequently are raised in an impoverished and abusive environment. Seldom are people with money or prestige convicted of capital offenses, even more seldom are they executed. To quote Governor Brown again, he said, "Society has both the right and the moral duty to protect itself against its enemies. This natural and prehistoric axiom has never successfully been refuted. If by ordered death, society is really protected and our homes and institutions guarded, then even the most extreme of all penalties can be justified. Beyond its honor and incredibility, it has neither protected the innocent nor deterred the killers. Publicly sanctioned killing has cheapened human life and dignity without the redeeming grace which comes from justice metered out swiftly, evenly, humanely."

At stake throughout the clemency process, was whether some, all, or none of these inmates on death row would have their sentences commuted from death to life without the possibility of parole. One of the things discussed with family members was life without parole was seen as a life filled with perks and benefits. Some inmates on death row don't want a sentence of life without parole. Danny Edwards wrote me and told me not to do him any favors because he didn't want to face a prospect of a life in prison without parole. They will be confined in a cell that is about five-feet-by-twelve feet, usually double-bunked.

Our prisons have no air-conditioning, except at our supermax facility where inmates are kept in their cell twenty-three hours a day. In summer months, temperatures in these prisons exceed one hundred degrees. It is a stark and dreary existence. They can think about their crimes. Life without parole has even, at times, been described by prosecutors as a fate worse than death.

Earlier this year, the US Supreme Court held that it is unconstitutional and cruel and unusual punishment to execute the mentally retarded. It is now the law of the land. How many people have we already executed who were mentally retarded and are now dead and buried?

Although we now know that they have been killed by the state unconstitutionally and illegally.

Is that fair?

Is that right?

This court decision was last spring. The General Assembly failed to pass any measure defining what constitutes mental retardation. We are a rudderless ship because they failed to act. This is even after the Illinois Supreme Court also told lawmakers that it is their job and it must be done.

I started with this issue concerned about innocence. But once I studied, once I pondered what had become of our justice system, I came to care above all about fairness. Fairness is fundamental to the American system of justice and our way of life. The facts I have seen in reviewing each and every one of these cases raised questions not only about the innocence of people on death row, but about the fairness of the death penalty system as a whole.

If the system was making so many errors in determining whether someone was guilty in the first place, how fairly and accurately was it determining which guilty defendants deserved to live and which deserved to die?

What effect was race having?

What effect was poverty having?

And in almost every one of the exonerated seventeen, we not only have breakdowns in the system with police, prosecutors, and judges, we have terrible cases of shabby defense lawyers. There is just no way to sugar coat it. There are defense attorneys that did not consult with their clients, did not investigate the case, and were completely unqualified to handle complex death penalty cases. They often didn't put much effort into fighting a death sentence. If your life is on the line, your lawyer ought to be fighting for you.

As I have said before, there is more than enough blame to go around.

I had more questions.

In Illinois, I have learned, we have 102 decision makers. Each of them are politically elected, each beholden to the demands of their community and, in some cases, to the media or especially vocal victims' families. In cases that have the attention of the media and the public, are decisions to seek the death penalty more likely to occur? What standards are these prosecutors using? Some people have assailed my power to commute sentences, a power that literally hundreds of legal scholars from across the country have defended.

But prosecutors in Illinois have the ultimate commutation power, a power that is exercised every day. They decide who will be subject to the death penalty, who will get a plea deal, or even who may get a complete pass on prosecution. By what objective standards do they make these decisions? We do not know. They are not public.

There were more than one thousand murders last year in Illinois. There is no doubt that all murders are horrific and cruel. Yet, less than two percent of those murder defendants will receive the death penalty. That means more than ninety-eight percent of victims' families do not get, and will not receive, whatever satisfaction can be derived from the execution of the murderer.

Moreover, if you look at the cases, as I have done—both individually and collectively—a killing with the same circumstances might get forty years in one county and death in another county. I have also seen where codefendants who are equally or even more culpable get sentenced to a term of years, while another less culpable defendant ends up on death row.

In my case-by-case review, I found three people that fell into this category: Mario Flores, Montell Johnson, and William Franklin. Today, I have commuted their sentences to a term of forty years to bring their sentences into line with their codefendants and to reflect the other extraordinary circumstances of these cases. [Applause]

Supreme Court justice Potter Stewart has said that the imposition of the death penalty on defendants in this country is as freakish and arbitrary as who gets hit by a bolt of lightning. For years the criminal justice system defended and upheld the imposition of the death penalty for the seventeen exonerated inmates from Illinois death row. Yet when the real killers are charged, prosecutors have often sought sentences of less than death. In the Ford Heights Four case, Verneal Jimerson and Dennis Williams fought the death sentences imposed upon them for eighteen years before they were exonerated. Later, Cook County prosecutors sought life in prison for two of the real killers and a sentence of eighty years for a third. What made the murder for which the Ford Heights Four were sentenced to die less heinous and worthy of the death penalty twenty years later with a new set of defendants?

We have come very close to having our state Supreme Court rule our death penalty statute—the one that I helped enact in 1977—unconstitutional. Former State Supreme Court justice Seymour Simon wrote to me that it was only happenstance that our statute was not struck down by the state's high court. When he joined the bench in 1980, three other justices had already said Illinois' death penalty was unconstitutional. But they got cold feet when a case came along to revisit the question. One judge wrote that he wanted to wait and see if the Supreme Court of the United States would rule on the constitutionality of the new Illinois law. Another said precedent required him to follow the old state Supreme Court ruling with which he disagreed.

Even a pharmacist knows that doesn't make sense. We wouldn't have a death penalty today and we all wouldn't be struggling with this issue, if those votes had been different. How arbitrary. Several years after we enacted our death penalty statute, Girvies Davis was executed. Justice Simon writes that he was executed because of this unconstitutional aspect of the Illinois law—the wide latitude that each Illinois state's attorney has to determine what cases qualify for the death penalty. One state's attorney waived his request for the death sentence when Davis's first sentencing was sent back to the trial court for a new sentencing hearing. The prosecutor was going to seek a life sentence. But in the interim, a new state's attorney took office and changed directions. He once again sought and secured a death sentence. Davis was executed.

How fair is that?

After the flaws in our system were exposed, the Supreme Court of Illinois took it upon itself to begin to reform its rules and improve the trial of capital cases. It changed the rule to require that state's attorneys give advance notice to defendants that they plan to seek the death penalty to require notice before trial instead of after conviction. The Supreme Court also enacted new discovery rules designed to prevent trials by ambush and to allow for better investigation of cases from the beginning.

But shouldn't that mean if you were tried or sentenced before the rules changed, you ought to get a new trial or sentencing with the new safeguards of the rules? This issue has divided our Supreme Court, some saying yes, a majority saying no. These justices have a lifetime of experience with the criminal justice system and it concerns me that these great minds so strenuously differ on an issue of such importance, especially where life or death hangs in the balance.

What are we to make of the studies that showed that more than fifty percent of Illinois jurors could not understand the confusing and obscure sentencing instructions that were being used? What effect did that problem have on the trustworthiness of death sentences?

A review of the cases shows that often even the lawyers and judges are confused about the instructions—let alone the jurors sitting in judgment. Cases still come before the Supreme Court with arguments about whether the jury instructions were proper. I spent a good deal of time reviewing these death row cases. My staff, many of whom are lawyers, spent busy days and many sleepless nights answering my questions, providing me with information, giving me advice.

It became clear to me that whatever decision I made, I would be criticized. It also became clear to me that it was impossible to make reliable choices about whether our capital punishment system had really done its job. As I came closer to my decision, I knew that I was going to have to face the question of whether I believed so completely in the choice I wanted to make that I could face the prospect of even commuting the death sentence of Daniel Edwards, the man who had killed a close family friend of mine. I discussed it with my wife, Lura Lynn, who has stood by me all these years. She was angry and disappointed at my decision like many of the families of other victims will be.

I was struck by the anger of the families of murder victims. To a family they talked about closure. They pleaded with me to allow the state to kill an inmate in its name to provide the families with closure. But is that the purpose of capital punishment? Is it to soothe the families? And is that truly what the families experience?

I cannot imagine losing a family member to murder. Nor can I imagine spending every waking day for twenty years with a single-minded focus to execute the killer. The system of death in Illinois is so unsure that it is not unusual for cases to take twenty years before they are resolved. And thank God. If it had moved any faster, then Anthony Porter, the Ford Heights Four, Ronald Jones, Madison Hobley, and the other innocent men we've exonerated might be dead and buried.

But it is cruel and unusual punishment for family members to go through this pain, this legal limbo for twenty years. Perhaps it would be less cruel if we sentenced the killers to TAMMS to life and used our resources to better serve victims. My heart ached when I heard one grandmother who lost children in an arson fire. She said she could not afford proper grave markers for her grandchildren who died. Why can't the state help families provide a proper burial?

Another crime victim came to our family meetings. He believes an inmate sent to death row for another crime also shot and paralyzed him. The inmate, he says, gets free health care while the victim is struggling to pay his substantial medical bills and, as a result, he has forgone getting proper medical care to alleviate the physical pain he endures. What kind of victim services are we providing? Are all of our resources geared toward providing this notion of closure by execution instead of tending to the physical and social service needs of victim families?

And what kind of values are we instilling in these wounded families and in the young people? As Gandhi said—an eye for an eye only leaves the whole world blind.

[I quoted President Abraham Lincoln who frequently spoke of binding up wounds as he sought to preserve the Union.]

"We are not enemies, but friends," Lincoln said. "We must not be enemies. Though passion may have strained, it must not break our bonds of affection."

[I said I had to consider not only the horrible nature of the crimes that put men on death row in the first place, but the terrible suffering of the surviving family members of the victims, the despair of the family members of the inmates and at the same time watched in frustration as members of the Illinois General Assembly failed to pass even one substantive death penalty reform.]

Not one. They couldn't even agree on *ONE*.

How much more evidence is needed before the General Assembly will take its responsibility in this area seriously? The fact is that the failure of the General Assembly to act is merely a symptom of the larger problem. Many people express the desire to have capital punishment. Few, however, seem prepared to address the tough questions that arise when the system fails. It is easier and more comfortable for politicians to be tough on crime and support the death penalty. It wins votes. But when it comes to admitting that we have a problem, most run for cover.

Prosecutors across our state continue to deny that our death penalty system is broken or they say if there is a problem, it is really a small one and we can fix it somehow. It is difficult to see how the system can be fixed when not a single one of the reforms proposed by my Capital Punishment Commission has been adopted. Even the reforms the prosecutors agree with haven't been adopted.

So, when will the system be fixed? How much more risk can we afford? Will we actually have to execute an innocent person before the tragedy that is our capital punishment system in Illinois is really understood?

[I noted that several months ago, a federal judge ruled the federal death penalty was unconstitutional and noted that with the number of recent exonerations based on DNA and new scientific technology, there was little doubt that innocent people had been executed in the past.]

As I prepare to leave office, I had to ask myself whether I could really live with the prospect of knowing that I had the opportunity to act, but that I failed to do so because I might be criticized. Could I take the chance that our capital punishment system might be reformed, that wrongful convictions might not occur, that enterprising journalism students might free more men from death row? A system that's so fragile that it depends on young journalism students is seriously flawed.

[I quoted President Lincoln again.] "There is no honorable way to kill, no gentle way to destroy. There is nothing good in war. Except its ending."

He was talking about the bloody war between the states. It was a war fought to end the sorriest chapter in American history—the institution of slavery.

While we are not in a civil war now, we are facing what is shaping up to be one of the great civil rights struggles of our time. Stephen Bright of the Southern Center for Human Rights has taken the position that the death penalty is being sought with increasing frequency in some states against the poor and minorities. Our own study showed that juries were more likely to sentence to death if the victim were white than if the victim were black—three-and-a-half times more likely to be exact. We are not alone. Just this month Maryland released a study of their death penalty system and racial disparities exist there too.

This week, Mamie Till died. Her son Emmett was lynched in Mississippi in the 1950s. She was a strong advocate for civil rights and reconciliation. In fact, just three weeks ago, she was the keynote speaker at the Murder Victims' Families for Reconciliation Event in Chicago. This group, many of whom I've met, opposes the death penalty even though their family members have been lost to senseless killing. Mamie's strength and grace not only ignited the civil rights movement—including inspiring Rosa Parks to refuse to go to the back of the bus—but inspired murder victims' families until her dying day.

Is our system fair to all? Is justice blind?

These are important human rights issues. Another issue that came up in my individual, case-by-case review was the issue of international law. The Vienna Convention protects US citizens abroad and foreign nationals in the United States. It provides that if you're arrested, you should be afforded the opportunity to contact your consulate. There are five men on death row who were denied that internationally-recognized human right. Mexico's president Vicente Fox contacted me to express his deep concern for the Vienna Convention violations. If we do not uphold international law here, we cannot expect our citizens to be protected outside the United States.

My commission recommended the Supreme Court conduct a proportionality review of our system in Illinois. While our appellate courts perform a case-by-case review of the appellate record, they have not done such a big picture study. Instead, we tinker with a case-by-case review as each appeal lands on their docket.

In 1994, near the end of his distinguished career on the Supreme Court of the United States, Justice Harry Blackmun wrote an influential dissent in the body of law on capital punishment. Twenty years earlier he was part of the court that issued the landmark Furman decision. The court decided that the death penalty statutes in use throughout the country were fraught with severe flaws that rendered them unconstitutional.

Quite frankly, they were the same problems we see here in Illinois. To many, it looked like the Furman decision meant the end of the death penalty in the United States. This was not the case. Many states responded to Furman by developing and enacting new and improved death penalty statutes. In 1976, four years after it had decided Furman, Justice Blackmun joined the majority of the United States Supreme Court in deciding to give the states a chance with these new and improved death penalty statutes. There was great optimism in the air. This was the climate in 1977 when the Illinois legislature was faced with the momentous decision of whether to reinstate the death penalty in Illinois.

I was a member of the General Assembly at that time and when I pushed the green button in favor of reinstating the death penalty in this great state, I did so with the belief that whatever problems had plagued the capital punishment system in the past were now being cured. I am sure that most of my colleagues who voted with me that day shared that view.

But twenty years later, after affirming hundreds of death penalty decisions, Justice Blackmun came to the realization, in the twilight of his distinguished career, that the death penalty remains fraught with arbitrariness, discrimination, caprice, and mistake. He expressed frustration with a twenty-year struggle to develop procedural and substantive safeguards.

In a now famous dissent, he wrote in 1994: "From this day forward, I no longer shall tinker with the machinery of death."

[I paused and took a breath.]

One of the few disappointments of my legislative and executive career is that the General Assembly failed to work with me to reform our deeply flawed system. I don't know why legislators could not heed the rising voices of reform. I don't know how many more systemic flaws we needed to uncover before they would be spurred to action.

Three times I proposed reforming the system with a package that would restrict the use of jailhouse snitches, create a statewide panel to determine death eligible cases, and reduce the number of crimes eligible for death. These reforms would not have created a perfect system, but they would have dramatically reduced the chance for error in the administration of the ultimate penalty.

[I noted that as governor, I have the constitutional power to act in the interest of justice and fairness.] Our state constitution provides broad power to the governor to issue reprieves, pardons, and commutations. Our Supreme Court has reminded inmates petitioning them that the last resort for relief is the governor. At times the executive clemency power has perhaps been a crutch for courts to avoid making the kind of major change that I believe our system needs.

Our systemic case-by-case review has found more cases of innocent men wrongfully sentenced to death row. Because our three-year study has found only more questions about the fairness of the sentencing; because of the spectacular failure to reform the system; because we have seen justice delayed for countless death row inmates with potentially meritorious claims; because the Illinois death penalty system is arbitrary and capricious—and therefore immoral—I no longer shall tinker with the machinery of death.

I cannot say it more eloquently than Justice Blackmun. The legislature couldn't reform it. Lawmakers won't repeal it. But I will not stand for it. I must act. Our capital system is haunted by the demon of error, error in determining guilt, and error in determining who among the guilty deserves to die.

Because of all of these reasons today I am commuting the sentences of all death row inmates. This is a blanket commutation.

[Thunderous applause]

I realize it will draw ridicule, scorn, and anger from many who oppose this decision. They will say I am usurping the decisions of judges and juries and state legislators. But as I have said, the people of our state have vested in me to act in the interest of justice.

Even if the exercise of my power becomes my burden, I will bear it. Our constitution compels it.

I sought this office, and even in my final days of holding it, I cannot shrink from the obligations to justice and fairness that it demands. There have been many nights where my staff and I have been deprived of sleep in order to conduct our exhaustive review of the

> system. But I can tell you this: I will sleep well knowing I made the right decision. As I said when I declared the moratorium, it is time for a rational discussion on the death penalty.
>
> While our experience in Illinois has indeed sparked a debate, we have fallen short of a rational discussion. Yet if I did not take this action, I feared that there would be no comprehensive and thorough inquiry into the guilt of the individuals on death row or of the fairness of the sentences applied.
>
> To say it plainly one more time—the Illinois capital punishment system is broken. It has taken innocent men to a hair's breadth escape from their unjust execution. Legislatures past have refused to fix it. Our new legislature and our new governor must act to rid our state of the shame of threatening the innocent with execution and the guilty with unfairness. In the days ahead, I will pray that we can open our hearts and provide something for victims' families other than the hope of revenge.
>
> Lincoln once said: "I have always found that mercy bears richer fruits than strict justice." I can only hope that will be so. God bless you. And God bless the people of Illinois.

And then, it was over. I had done what no other governor had ever done—declared a moratorium on the death penalty. And then I had signed off on the largest death row commutation in the nation's history. There had been 171 men and women on death row. I pardoned four, commuted three to terms of forty years with a chance of parole, and the remaining 164 were commuted to life in prison without parole. It was my last speech as governor of Illinois.

Once again, the golden lights of the Colosseum were alit.

# 34

# REFORM AT LAST

Death row in Illinois began repopulating just two months later. In late February, a jury in downstate Coles County convicted twenty-six-year-old Anthony Mertz of murdering twenty-one-year-old Shannon McNamara, who was found dead in her apartment in Charleston, Illinois, the home of Eastern Illinois University, which both had previously attended.

There was no imminent danger of being executed, however. First, there were years of appeals to go, but just as significant, my successor as governor, Rod Blagojevich, had said that he would not consider lifting the moratorium until death penalty reforms were enacted by the General Assembly.

Two months later, in April 2003, in a development that the *Chicago Tribune* called "little short of amazing" considering the fierce opposition just months earlier before I emptied death row, the legislature finally passed death penalty reform legislation—not all of it, but perhaps some of the most important recommendations.

Perhaps the most significant and also controversial—videotaping of not only confessions but the interrogations leading up to the confessions in homicide cases—sailed through the Senate without a vote in opposition. A bill also passed that banned execution of the mentally impaired and also defined how such a determination would be made. The Illinois Supreme Court was given authority to overturn death sentences as a manifest injustice rather than requiring some legal inadequacy or shortfall to set such sentences aside. Greater access to DNA testing was authorized. The number of "aggravating factors," those that qualified crimes for the death penalty, was reduced, narrowing the pool of cases where prosecutors could seek the death penalty. Jailhouse informant testimony would be eligible for pretrial scrutiny. In addition, pilot programs were established to begin the process of using sequential lineups, a procedure in which witnesses are shown photographs of possible suspects one at a time instead of in a group. Group photographic arrays had been shown to result in mistaken witness identifications when witnesses made a comparative judgment and picked the person who most looked like the suspect they believed they saw.

The legislation still had to be approved by Governor Blagojevich, but all indications pointed to that happening not too far down the road. The videotaping bill, championed by Democratic state senator Barack Obama, would make Illinois the first state in the nation to require such taping by law. Two other states, Minnesota and Alaska, required the taping of interrogations as a result of court rulings.

Shortly after the legislation passed through both the Senate and the House, Blagojevich said that he was not going to end the moratorium "anytime soon."

He told the *Chicago Tribune* editorial board,

> The decision for me on an issue like lifting the moratorium won't be driven by what happens in the state Senate or the House. It will be driven by whether or not the system in Illinois has been reformed in such a way where we can have no doubt that we're [not] going to make any mistakes. And it begs the question of whether we can ever get to a point in Illinois that we can feel comfortable with that.

He indicated that he thought the reforms did not go far enough yet—that there needed to be more provisions to fund defense for indigent defendants. He wouldn't commit to what it might take to result in a suspension of the moratorium.

"I'm not going to promise that we're not going to lift it. I don't know," he said. "But it's certainly not imminent and I have not seen anything to suggest that we can feel confident that the system is foolproof."

In July, Blagojevich signed the legislation, a package of six bills, that included the videotaping measure as well the other reforms passed by the General Assembly. Also included were provisions aimed at stopping racial profiling by police making traffic stops as well as requiring the expunging of arrest records of defendants later determined to be innocent.

Obama, who by then was a Democratic candidate for president, said the videotaping of interrogations was "landmark legislation." He added, "With this law in place, it's going to be much harder to convict an innocent person based on a false conviction. Conversely, it can be a very powerful tool to convict the guilty."

The reaction to my decision to empty death row was about what you would expect. Families of victims and prosecutors were deeply upset and were vocal about saying so. Death penalty opponents praised the action and hoped it would—as it apparently did—spur the legislature to get off its hands and do something to reform the system.

The Illinois attorney general's office filed a lawsuit challenging the commutations, in particular the commutations of about two dozen death row inmates who had refused to sign clemency petitions as well as a handful of cases involving inmates whose death sentences had been set aside by the courts and were waiting resentencing hearings.

In January 2004, the Illinois Supreme Court ruled that all the commutations were valid. "This is a difficult question with little to guide us, but we believe that the grant of authority given the governor under [the Illinois Constitution] is sufficiently broad to allow Governor Ryan to do what he did," wrote Justice Bob Thomas, one of the most conservative justices on the court.

Larry Marshall, one of the lawyers who argued in favor of the legality of the commutations, summed it up perfectly.

"The fact the Supreme Court spoke not just unanimously and resoundingly, but spoke through the voice of its most conservative justice is a very strong testament to the message that the court wanted to send here, which is that agree or not agree as a matter of policy with what the governor did, there is no legal or constitutional question about his authority and the legitimacy of what he did," Marshall declared.

That same month, the last death penalty reform from the original package finally was passed. The legislation outlined a disciplinary process for police accused of testifying falsely on the witness stand. At a bill signing ceremony, my old friend, Democratic senator Emil Jones—the man I played pool with so many years ago when I was just a freshman legislator—was there.

"The system was so flawed it could cause a guilty person to go free and an innocent person to be incarcerated," Jones said. "This piece of legislation will go a long, long way to assuring that we in Illinois have a fair and just criminal justice system."

I couldn't have said it better. But then, I had been saying it for years.

The moratorium was never lifted. Eight years later and more than a decade after I imposed the moratorium, the death penalty finally died in Illinois. In March 2011, Governor Pat Quinn signed a bill that made Illinois the sixteenth state to abolish the death penalty.

"I have concluded that our system of imposing the death penalty is inherently flawed," Quinn declared. "Since our experience has shown that there is no way to design a perfect death penalty system, free from the numerous flaws that can lead to wrongful convictions or discriminatory treatment, I have concluded that the proper course of action is to abolish it."

If I had been asked when I left office whether Illinois would ever abolish the death penalty, I likely would have said, "Probably not in my lifetime."

In my first year as governor in 1999, ninety-eight people were executed in the United States. It was, and still remains, the highest number of executions in a single year since the reinstatement of the death penalty.

The number of executions began dropping gradually after that. In 2002, my last year in office, sixty-six people were executed. In 2016, twenty people were executed, the lowest number since 1991 when fourteen people were executed.

The number of death sentences imposed nationally dropped during that same time. In 1998, 295 people were sentenced to death in the United States. In 2019, only thirty-four death sentences were imposed.

At the same time, the number of states with the death penalty has dropped. When I imposed the moratorium in 2000, the death penalty was in place in thirty-eight states. As of this writing, the total is down to twenty-eight. In addition to Illinois, nine other states have abolished the death penalty: New York, New Jersey, New Mexico, Connecticut, Maryland, Delaware, Washington, New Hampshire, and Colorado. In addition, three states have moratoriums in place: Oregon (2011), Pennsylvania (2015), and California (2019).

Ten death penalty states haven't executed anyone in at least ten years, and some have gone more than one-quarter of a century without an execution.

Wyoming and Kansas last executed someone in 1992. Oregon's last execution was in 1997. Pennsylvania last executed anyone in 1999. The last executions in California, North Carolina, Nevada, and Montana were in 2006. Kentucky's last execution was in 2008 and Indiana's last execution was in 2009. In 2020, Utah and Louisiana will pass the ten-year mark without an execution.

One could argue that after setting aside these twelve states where there have been no executions in at least a decade, the number of "active" death penalty states is really sixteen, not twenty-eight. In 2019, US attorney general William Barr said that the executions of condemned federal prisoners would resume, although it was unclear how soon any of the sixty-two defendants on the federal death row would be executed. The last federal execution was in 2003.

At the close of 2019, the Death Penalty Information Center reported that for the fifth consecutive year, less than thirty executions were carried out and fewer than fifty death sentences were imposed. In fact, in 2019, twenty-two executions were carried out and just thirty-four death sentences were imposed. Perhaps just as significant, the death row population in the United States dropped for the eighteenth consecutive year. In 2000, the year I declared the Illinois moratorium, the death row population in the United States was about 3,700. By the end of 2019, the total stood at less than 2,700, a drop of about 28 percent.

There are those who say that my declaration of the moratorium rekindled the antideath penalty movement in the United States. There is no doubt that the death penalty system has declined in the years since then as a result of many factors, including zealous advocacy by defense lawyers, intrepid reporting by journalists, and courageous action by politicians and policy makers. I will leave it to the historians to assess the impact of my actions.

Nonetheless, I am proud to have played a part in preventing the possible executions of innocent people and proud to have played a role in reforming the criminal justice system.

It was not a path I expected.

But it was a path I am glad I took.

# EPILOGUE

On November 8, 1994, the same day I was reelected to a second term as Illinois secretary of state, a mud flap taillight assembly fell off a semi-trailer on an interstate highway near Milwaukee, Wisconsin. The one hundred-pound piece of metal pierced the gas tank of a minivan containing the Reverend Duane Willis, his wife, Janet, and six of their nine children. The gas tank exploded, and all the children perished. Willis and his wife survived.

This enormous tragedy, a horrible accident, ultimately led to a federal investigation of workers in Illinois driver's license facilities. The driver of the truck from which the taillight assembly fell off was identified as Ricardo Guzman, a Mexican immigrant. Although Guzman was never convicted of a crime, state workers at the driver's license facility in McCook, Illinois, where he obtained his trucker's license, were convicted of accepting bribes—including from Guzman—to approve licenses for nonqualified applicants—such as Guzman.

The federal investigation, which was called Operation Safe Road, eventually resulted in charges against seventy-nine people, including me.

In December 2003, about eleven months after I left the governor's office, a federal grand jury indicted me on charges of racketeering, mail fraud, and making false statements. The investigation of driver's license facilities was expanded to other aspects of the secretary of state's office. I was accused of receiving cash and gifts in return for allowing associates to profit from contracts and other business with the state.

I went to trial in US District Court in Chicago in September 2005. I contested the charges, but after a long trial, that included the replacement of two jurors who had failed to disclose their criminal backgrounds, I was convicted. The jury returned its verdict in April 2006, concluding that I had—according to the prosecution's theory—deprived Illinois citizens of their right to my honest services as a public official.

In September 2006, I was sentenced to six and a half years in prison. I read a statement to Judge Rebecca Pallmeyer before she imposed the sentence.

"When they elected me as the governor of this state, they expected better, and I let them down. For that, I apologize," I said. "I should have been more vigilant. I should have been more watchful. I should have been a lot of things, I guess. But I obviously failed," I said.

My lawyers appealed the conviction and in August 2007, the US Court of Appeals for the Seventh Circuit upheld the jury's verdict in a split decision. Judge Michael Kanne dissented, focusing on improper jury deliberations. He noted, "My colleagues in the majority concede that the trial of this case may not have been 'picture-perfect'—a whopping understatement by any measure."

My lawyers requested that the entire appeals court rehear the appeal as a group—a rehearing known as en banc—but the motion was denied. However, Judge Kanne was joined by two other judges, Ann Williams and Richard Posner, to declare that "a cascade of errors" had turned my trial, which lasted from September 2005 until April 2006, into "a travesty."

Had I been granted a new trial as my lawyers contended I should have been, who knows what the verdict would have been the second time around? Some might say I would be reconvicted. Others would say differently. Both are speculation. If I learned anything during my study of the death penalty, it is that you can never tell what juries will do.

I entered Oxford Federal Correction Institution on November 7, 2007. Not long after, I was transferred to the federal prison in Terra Haute, Indiana, where I served my sentence in the minimum-security camp that is part of the prison structure.

In 2010, the US Supreme Court, in its decision, *Skilling v. United States*, held that the honest services law was restricted to the payment of bribes. Albert Alschuler filed a postconviction petition on my behalf noting that during the trial, of the eighty-three prosecution witnesses, none of them testified that I took anything from anybody to perform my official acts. That petition, however, was denied and a later appeal to the Seventh Circuit also was rejected. That decision later prompted Alschuler to write a scathing memoir for the *Valparaiso University Law Review* detailing how Appeals Court judge Frank Easterbrook engaged in numerous falsehoods. In the article titled, "How Frank Easterbrook Kept George Ryan in Prison," Alschuler, a law professor at Northwestern Pritzker Law School and a highly-regarded legal scholar, said that I was "almost certainly punished for conduct that is not a crime."

I am not here to debate what happened. It happened. I served my sentence and on January 30, 2013, I was released to home confinement in Kankakee. I officially completed my sentence on July 3, 2013.

I lost the love of my life, Lura Lynn, on June 24, 2011. I had been allowed to visit her bedside for two hours in January 2011. It was extraordinarily difficult. She recognized me, but struggled to be able to speak. Efforts by my lawyers to be released so I could spend the waning days of her life with her were rejected by the Federal Bureau of Prisons. Three months later, on September 24, my older brother, Tom, died. I remained in prison for both funerals.

Since my release on July 3, 2013, I have resumed my life. I know all too well that when many people hear my name, they think first of my trial, the conviction, and the prison term. Yes, I went to prison. It happened, I got through it and I have moved on.

In February 2020, I turned eighty-six. I have slowed down a little over the years, but I'm not quite ready to give up on trying to make a difference in society. I have had a lot of time since 2003 to think about whether I've made a difference in this world.

I came to see the abolition of the death penalty as perhaps the greatest opportunity before me to leave the world a better place than what it is now. That belief—that feeling—has not subsided in me. If anything, after five years as a prisoner of the criminal prosecution system, I have an intimately better understanding of the fundamental reforms that are needed and the consequences of leaving things as they are.

While some people in Illinois saw my opposition to the death penalty as my attempt to divert attention away from my legal troubles, there were even more people who realized that my work to clean up the death penalty system and the federal investigation were two completely separate things.

They always were.

And they still are.

While I was reviewing the death row cases while considering whether to grant some commutations or a blanket commutation, Danny Edwards, the man convicted of killing my Kankakee neighbor, Steve Small, wrote me a letter. He said that he didn't want his sentence commuted. He wanted to stay in the system and take his chances on death row. Would I please not commute his sentence?

I didn't do that, of course. I commuted his sentence along with all the others on death row. The Small family was hurt and upset. I understood that because I was the man who commuted the sentence of the man who killed Steve.

I am sorry. I did what I thought I had to do and what was right at the time. That doesn't mean that I wasn't saddened and hurt about what happened to Steve Small. In the end, I did what I felt had to be done for the system.

As tough as it was to do, I know it was the right thing to do.

And I would do it again.

# INDEX

# ABOUT THE AUTHORS

**George H. Ryan Sr.**, was the 39th governor of the State of Illinois. Born in 1934, the son of a pharmacist in Maquoketa, Iowa, Ryan was first elected to state office in 1972 as an Illinois state representative. He served two terms as minority leader of the House of Representatives and one term as Speaker of the House. He served as Illinois lieutenant governor from 1983–1991, as Illinois secretary of state from 1991–1999, and then was governor from 1999–2003. Ryan was the first governor in US history to suspend the death penalty, declaring a moratorium in 2000. In 2003, as he left office, Ryan emptied death row in Illinois by issuing a blanket commutation order. He was indicted in 2003 and convicted of federal corruption charges relating to conduct while he was Illinois secretary of state. He served nearly six years in prison and was released in 2013. Age eight-six, Ryan lives in Kankakee, Illinois, and still travels extensively to speak about the death penalty and the criminal justice system, as well as to support humanitarian efforts in Cuba.

**Maurice Possley** is a Pulitzer Prize-winning journalist and author of three nonfiction books. Ryan cited the reportage of Possley and his colleagues at the *Chicago Tribune* when he declared the moratorium and emptied death row. Possley is currently the senior researcher for the National Registry of Exonerations, a national database of more than 2,500 wrongful convictions maintained by the University of Michigan Law School, Michigan State University College of Law, and University of California Irvine Newkirk Center for Science & Society.